JOB READY SQL

Job Ready SQL

Kimberly A. Weiss

Haythem Balti

Wiley

Acknowledgments

Although Kim and Haythem are the main authors of this book, *Job Ready SQL* would not have been possible without the hard work of the content development and instruction teams at Wiley Edge.

About the Authors

Kimberly A. Weiss is a senior instructional designer at the mthree Global Academy and a veteran course developer, specializing in computer science courses since 2002. She was an assistant professor in computer science for more than 10 years before deciding to focus exclusively on course design. She has worked with multiple universities and in corporate training settings to develop interactive instructional content appropriate for the target learners and course goals.

Haythem Balti is the dean of education solutions at the Wiley Edge Academy and product owner of the Job Ready book collection. Haythem created courses used by thousands of Wiley Edge and Software Guild graduates. He earned his doctorate in computer engineering and computer science from the University of Louisville.

About the Technical Writer

Bradley Jones is the owner of Lots of Software, LLC. He has programmed in a variety of languages and tools ranging from C to Unity on platforms ranging from Windows to mobile and including the Web as well as a little bit of virtual reality for fun. In addition to programming, he has authored books on C, C++, C#, Windows, the Web, and many more technical topics and a few nontechnical topics. Bradley is recognized in the industry as a community influencer as well as being recognized as a Microsoft MVP, a CODiE Judge, an international technology speaker, a bestselling technical author, and more.

About the Technical Editor

As a solutions architect, **Valerie Parham-Thompson** focuses on distributed SQL database design, deployment architecture, and ecosystem integration. Prior to her current role, she was a principal consultant for a multinational database consultancy, helping to scale and optimize large, highly available data storage on a variety of open-source database systems. Her previous experiences supporting production systems and running a web development agency allow her to field questions from users across the organization.

Contents at a Glance

Contents

Lesson 7: Database Management Using DDL 123

Lesson 11:
Adding JOIN Queries   223

Lesson 12:
Sorting and Limiting
Query Results   253

Lesson 13: Grouping and Aggregates 271

Lesson 14: Pulling It All Together: Adding Data to the Vinyl Record Shop Database 291

Introduction

Modern computer applications rely heavily on databases, even when the program in question isn't designed to help users manage data. Computer games rely on databases to keep track of characters, character attributes, items that each character can use during gameplay, and even locations within the game. A learning management system (LMS) uses databases to keep track of learners, instructors, content, grades, attendance, and communication between users.

A database can contain data that is **structured** or **unstructured**. Modern database software programs hosting databases can usually handle both structured and unstructured data, but it is still good to understand the difference.

In a database with structured data, which we will call a structured database, the data is organized in a specific pattern. This makes it easy to control what data is available and where to find specific pieces of data. In a structured database, the developer can limit what kinds of data are stored in the database to improve **data integrity** and reduce the amount of redundant data. This comes as a trade-off in that creating new data and accessing stored data are relatively slow compared to creating and accessing data in an unstructured database. Structured databases are best for datasets that contain predictable types of data, such as bank accounts, personnel records, and inventories.

Relational databases are highly structured in that they organize data into one or more **tables** or **relations**, where each table represents a logical group of data. In day-to-day professional work, we usually say **table**. **Relation** is the formal, academic term, which you may run into if you read about databases in other contexts. *Relation* is also the basis for the term *relational database*. At a more abstract level, the term **entity** is also used to refer to a table, especially during the design phase of a database and before the database is built on a server.

Job Ready SQL provides readers with an understanding of relational databases and Structured Query Language (SQL). SQL is a domain-specific language designed for managing data held in a relational database management system.

A SQL Course Within a Book

This book contains a full-fledged SQL course that is used by the Wiley Edge Global Academy and the Software Guild to train our alumni in SQL and other topics, such as data analysis and data science.

Features to Make You Job Ready

As you read through this book, enter the code listings and play with the code. If you also take a hands-on approach to doing the exercises, you will be better able to take what you learned to the next level.

Most important, this book (as well the Job Ready series) goes beyond what many books provide by including lessons that help you pull together everything you are learning in a way that is more like what you would find in the professional world. This includes building a more comprehensive example than what you get in the standard short listings provided in most books. If you work through the "Pulling It All Together" lessons, then you will be better prepared for many of those jobs that require SQL.

WHAT DOES THIS BOOK COVER?

As mentioned, this book is a complete SQL programming course. It is broken into several parts, each containing a number of lessons.

Part 1: Introduction to Database Concepts The first part of this book focuses on introducing database concepts including structured and unstructured data, as well as relational database concepts.

Part 2: Applying SQL The second part focuses on getting you set up to use MySQL. This includes help for installing MySQL and setting up the tools you will need to work through this book. Additionally, this section dives into the basics of MySQL including query design and development and the basics of database management.

Part 3: Data Management and Manipulation The third part focuses on going beyond the basics of MySQL and focuses on learning about concepts you'll need to design and develop complex databases and advanced querying of the data stored on MySQL. This includes CRUD operations, joins, select queries, sorting, and aggregation. Finally, this section also includes lessons on how to leverage Python to query SQL data.

READER SUPPORT FOR THIS BOOK

There are several ways to get the help you need for this book.

Companion Download Files

As you work through the examples in this book, you should type in all the code manually. This will help you learn and better understand what the code does.

However, in some lessons, download files are referenced. You can download the files from www.wiley.com/go/jobreadysql.

How to Contact the Publisher

If you believe you have found a mistake in this book, please bring it to our attention. At John Wiley & Sons, we understand how important it is to provide our customers with accurate content, but even with our best efforts an error may occur.

To submit your possible errata, please email it to our Customer Service Team at wileysupport@wiley.com with the subject line "Possible Book Errata Submission."

PART I

Introduction to Database Concepts

Lesson 1

Exploring Relational Databases and SQL

SQL is used to access data. Before jumping into SQL and how it is used, it is important to step back and consider how information that you will access has been stored. In this chapter, you'll dive into the topic of data and databases to set the foundation for then accessing the information. You will get a high-level look at databases in general and at relational databases specifically.

Learning Objectives

By the end of this lesson, you will be able to:

- Describe what a relational database is, how it works, and how it differs from a database management system (DBMS)
- Define database tables, relations, columns, attributes, rows, records, tuples, and data types
- Identify the ACID properties
- Know about entity integrity and uniqueness using keys
- Discuss database backup strategies

SAVING DATA

To be useful, software systems must *remember*. If your character started at the beginning (level 0) every time you fired up a video game, or your online banking app reset your balance to $0 when you logged off, or your phone forgot your contacts when it rebooted, you wouldn't use them. To remember, applications must save data in a way that allows ready access to that data when needed.

There are a few options for saving data.

- Write text or bytes directly into a file
- Store data in a relational database
- Store data in a nonrelational database

The first option of writing directly into a file can be cumbersome. In this case, the file typically is expected to be local (on the same computer as the program that is accessing the file). This means there is a high risk of losing data if something happens to that computer.

In a software environment, databases (relational or not) are preferable to files because they can store data separately from the application itself, often on a completely separate server. While this might slow down access to the data to a small degree, the fact that they are separate means that multiple applications can access the same database and that changes to the data in the database are immediately accessible to any application that uses that data.

Nonrelational databases are becoming more common today, but relational databases are standard across many industries as a way of storing data in a predictable and reliable way that allows applications to easily retrieve that data as needed.

WHAT IS A DATABASE?

In real life, most people work with databases every day, often without realizing it. Most computer applications depend on some kind of data access to work correctly. Any advanced system with a goal of identifying objects and performing specific actions on those objects (such as an employee list, an inventory, or a course roster) depends on a database. A **database** is a structured representation of data that can be read from and written to, and a database is often stored separately from any application that uses the data.

Database Uses

Modern computer applications rely heavily on databases, even when the program in question isn't designed to help users manage data. Computer games rely on databases to keep track of characters, character attributes, items that each character can use during gameplay, and even locations within the game. A learning management system (LMS) uses databases to keep track of learners, instructors, content, grades, attendance, and communication between users.

As a concrete example, consider a modern smartphone. The phone itself has a database that stores connection information, OS version, model number, serial number, and similar data about the device itself.

A smartphone also has a variety of applications on it, many of which have their own databases. Common examples include a contact list, a calendar, email apps, photo galleries, social networking apps, and shopping apps. While these apps store data for internal use, the user can grant permission for some apps to access data stored in other apps. For example, a calendar app may be connected to the contact app's database so that the user can easily add appointments with specific people to their calendar, while Facebook can access photos stored on the phone so that the user can share the photos with friends.

In none of these cases, though, does the user have direct access to the database itself. Instead, the application's front end (the part the user interacts with) includes tools that allow the user to create and retrieve data, update existing data, and even delete data that the user no longer needs. The software developer must incorporate the database into the application in a way that allows the application to access and manage the data.

Data vs. Information

When talking about databases, data and information are invariably mentioned. The terms *data* and *information* are often used interchangeably in casual speech, but from a software perspective, there is a very clear difference between the two. Specifically:

- The term **data** refers to individual, raw facts. In many cases, individual pieces of data are meaningless on their own.
- When we process data, the result is **information**. Unlike the raw data, information is useful and normally corresponds to the end user's specific needs.

As an example, consider a piece of data like *smith*. On its own, this is meaningless. While you might first think it is someone's last name, there isn't enough information here to tell you exactly whose name it is. It could also be an occupation rather than a name.

In a specific context, however, this piece of data can be combined with other data to give you useful information. As part of a course roster, for example, it could be combined with a first name to reference a specific student. In a job application or online profile, it could reference the person's work experience, with a completely different name.

Structured vs. Unstructured

A database can contain data that is **structured** or **unstructured**. Modern database software programs hosting databases can usually handle both structured and unstructured data, but it is still good to understand the difference.

In a database with structured data, which we will call a *structured database*, the data is organized in a specific pattern. This makes it easy to control what data is available and where to find specific pieces of data. In a structured database, the developer can limit what kinds of data are stored in the database to improve **data integrity** and reduce the amount of redundant data. This comes as a trade-off in that creating new data and accessing stored data are relatively slow compared to creating and accessing data in an unstructured database. Structured databases are best for datasets that contain predictable types of data, such as bank accounts, personnel records, and inventories.

> **NOTE** *Data integrity* refers to the reliability and accuracy of the data. A *dataset* is a collection of related information that is composed of separate elements but can be manipulated as a group.

A database with unstructured data typically does contain some amount of structure, but without the strict controls inherent to a structured database. Unstructured databases are typically a little faster than structured databases, but they are also prone to duplicate or redundant data. Unstructured databases are often found in applications that have unpredictable or irregular kinds of data, such as social media posts, online product reviews, and similar user-generated content.

> NOTE In this lesson, we will look only at structured databases, specifically **relational databases**.

Database vs. DBMS

As mentioned earlier, a database is a representation of data that can be read from and written to and is often stored separately from any application that uses the data. The fact that the database is separate from an application means that it can be made available to multiple applications, such as allowing access to a contact database from a calendar app or posting photos from an image database using a social media app. While any application that uses a specific database must know how to access the data, the data itself is simply a pool that any authorized app can pull from.

A **database management system (DBMS)** is a software system that manages databases. The DBMS executes commands, provides security, enables network access, and provides admin tools for database administrators (DBAs) to work with database files.

A subset of DBMSs includes relational database management systems (RDBMSs) that are designed specifically to work with relational databases. There are many options for RDBMSs, including MySQL, PostgreSQL, Microsoft SQL Server, Oracle Database, and DB2. The choice of DBMS determines some factors of how the data itself is organized, but in large part, all RDBMSs do the same thing.

While a specific RDBMS will be used in this book, keep in mind that all RDBMSs do essentially the same things in the same way. If you understand how one RDMBS works, you can easily transfer that knowledge to a different RDBMS.

RELATIONAL DATABASE CONCEPTS

Relational databases are highly structured in that they organize data into one or more **tables** or **relations**, where each table represents a logical group of data. In day-to-day professional work, we usually say *table*. *Relation* is the formal, academic term, which you may run into if you read about databases in other contexts. Relation is also the basis for the term **relational database**. At a more abstract level, the term **entity** is also used to refer to a table, especially during the design phase of a database and before the database is built on a server.

> **NOTE** The relational database model was first proposed by Edgar F. Codd in 1970, with the main goal of reducing duplicate data in a database and thereby making it easier to retrieve and manage specific data.

A table can be imagined as a two-dimensional grid of cells.

- A **row** in a table is a horizontal group of cells, one cell high. It holds facts about one discrete thing represented by the table. That thing could be anything such as a person, a credit card transaction, or a professional sports mascot.

- A **column** in the table is a vertical strip of cells, one cell wide. Every cell in the column holds the same type of data, but each cell is a fact about a different thing. For example, if the table includes data about people, then the table could include separate columns for name, phone number, and address.

- A **cell** represents the intersection of a row and a column. Each cell contains a single piece of data.

The following is a concrete example:

Name	Abbr	Capital	Established	Population
Alabama	AL	Montgomery	Dec 14, 1819	4,874,747
Alaska	AK	Juneau	Jan 3, 1959	739,795
Arizona	AZ	Phoenix	Feb 14, 1912	7,016,270
Arkansas	AR	Little Rock	Jun 15, 1836	3,004,279
California	CA	Sacramento	Sep 9, 1850	39,536,653

Column ⇩

Name	Abbr	Capital	Established	Population
Alabama	AL	Montgomery	Dec 14, 1819	4,874,747
Alaska	AK	Juneau	Jan 3, 1959	739,795
Arizona	AZ	Phoenix	Feb 14, 1912	7,016,270	⇐ Row
Arkansas	AR	Little Rock	Jun 15, 1836	3,004,279
California	CA	Sacramento	Sep 9, 1850	39,536,653

In the data in this table, each **row** represents one state. Rows are also known as **records** or **tuples**. The term **record** is common, while **tuple** is an academic term. A **database**

record is a single row in a table in the database, and each row in a table is considered a separate object from the other rows in the same table.

Each **column** represents a fact about a state: its name, abbreviation, capital, date established, and current population. There's a subtle nuance here. The term *column* refers to a strip of vertical cells, but it also refers to a definition: an overall name (*Abbr, Capital, Population*) and restrictions on the size, shape, and type of data allowed as values in the column. In fact, when a developer says *column*, they're usually talking about the definition, rather than the cells themselves. To reduce confusion, we may call the value of a record's column a **field**. Academically, column definitions are also called **attributes**.

> **NOTE** The size, shape, and type of data allowed in a column will be discussed in more detail in Part 2, "Applying SQL." As an example, a Population field might be defined as one that can hold a whole number (the type) that is between one and four billion (the size and shape).

ACID COMPLIANCE

Relational databases provide rich and powerful ways to model our data, and it doesn't stop there. A relational database's data structures and algorithms also provide behavior guarantees. They can't guarantee an action will always work, but they can guarantee the state of a database after an action succeeds or fails. They also guarantee predictable behavior when multiple users are interacting with a database. There are many types of guarantees.

The ACID properties are four of the most important guarantees. ACID is an acronym for the following:

- Atomicity
- Consistency
- Isolation
- Durability

Before jumping into ACID, you need to understand database transactions. A relational database allows the following actions:

- Read existing data
- Insert new data
- Update existing data
- Delete existing data
- Add or alter schema (tables and relationships)

A **transaction** is a set of one or more actions that represents a single, logical unit of work. Say you want to reserve three rooms at a hotel, and those room reservations are stored in at least three rows in a database. In most circumstances, you don't want to book *any* rooms if one or more room reservations fail—it's all or nothing. That makes your three-room reservation a transaction. It's a single unit of work that should succeed or fail as a unit.

If you purchase a concert ticket for an in-demand concert, the software system must first find an available ticket and then put it on hold until you can provide payment. That's a transaction. If it wasn't, the system might find an available ticket only to have another person purchase it before you. Without a transaction, the ticket could be purchased twice, or the system might waste time presenting tickets that are no longer for sale. Imagine selling tickets to a show that's predicted to sell out in 10 minutes without software that can handle transactions.

ACID Properties

As mentioned, ACID is an acronym for atomicity, consistency, isolation, and durability. The ACID properties are not required. You can run a database without them; however, for some situations, running without ACID is risky. In situations involving things, such as banking, medical records, and real-time decision-making, bad things can and will happen to your application if you ignore ACID.

Additionally, you never know what will happen when using a software. The network can fail, the operating system can crash, or another user can alter data that you're using. Given enough time, something *will* fail.

ACID-compliant databases are designed to withstand unexpected failures without corrupting your data. Let's look at each of the elements of ACID.

Atomicity

A transaction is atomic if it follows the "all-or-nothing" rule. If one action in the transaction fails, then the entire transaction fails. An atomic transaction never partially succeeds.

Imagine a scenario where you write a new row of data to a table with 10 columns. On the eighth column write, a power failure occurs, and your server immediately shuts down. If the database supports atomicity, it will notice the unfinished transaction and restore the data to its pre-transaction state when it comes back online.

Consistency

A transaction is consistent if it can move the database from only one valid state to another valid state. This means that the data processed during the operation is in a consistent state when the transaction starts and when the transaction ends as well. For example, when we transfer money from one account to another, consistency means that the sum of both accounts before the transfer and after it will be the same. If Account A has $200 and Account B has $100, the sum of both accounts would be $300. If $100 is transferred from Account A to Account B, then Account A would have $100, and Account B would have $200. The sum of both accounts is still $300. Consistency has been maintained.

A consistent database also enforces constraints on the types and sizes of data that are allowed. For example, the balance of an account is expected to be a numeric value. A birth-date is expected to be a date value. The database will maintain consistency by ensuring that the type of the data and size of the data are maintained.

Consistency also enforces primary and foreign key relationships. A primary key is a unique value assigned to each row of a table. For example, in a table containing bank account information, the account number would likely be unique and thus could be a pri-mary key. In regard to consistency, the system will never allow a duplicate primary key in a table to occur, and it will require that each record have a primary key value.

A foreign key is a value within the row of a table that is used to connect or is related to another table. For example, a store can have a table of customers, and each customer can have multiple orders. An order ID can be stored in the customer row that can then connect to a table of orders, as shown in Figure 1.1.

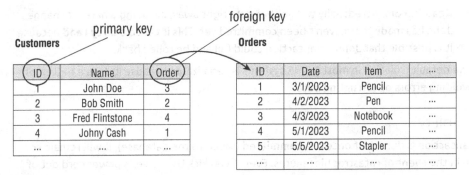

Figure 1.1 Customer orders

For foreign keys, most DBMS systems by default will not allow you to **orphan** a row, where the value used as a foreign key does not correspond to a value in the primary key of the related table. Using our example of customers and orders, there could be a Customer and Order relationship where a Customer can have one or more Orders. If you were to try to delete only a Customer row without first deleting its Orders, then the Orders associated with that Customer would have a foreign key pointing to a record that no longer existed.

> **NOTE** A properly configured relational schema will prevent this from happening by either rejecting the delete transaction outright or automatically deleting all the orders associated with the customer being deleted first. (This automation is called a **cascade delete**, and because it can lead to the deletion of millions of records without warning, it is usually not the preferred solution to resolving orphan keys.)

Isolation

A transaction is isolated if its effects are not visible to other transactions until it is complete. This is often referred to as *concurrency control*. A large database application may have hundreds or thousands of users making changes to it at the same time, so if transactions are not isolated, this could cause inconsistent data.

Imagine two users, John and Sally, accessing the database at once. John is updating data in the orders table. At the same time, Sally is reading data from the orders table, including records being edited by John. A DBMS has various levels of isolation it could apply. As a beginner, you need to know only two levels.

- **Serializable:** Sally will not receive her data until John's changes are committed. When John begins a transaction to change data, the data is **locked** until his transaction is complete.

- **Read Uncommitted:** Sally will get her data right away, including whatever changes John has made that haven't been committed yet. This is called a **dirty read** because it is possible that John's transaction could fail and be rolled back.

The default isolation in most DBMS systems is serializable because it does a better job of avoiding errors or corrupting data.

Durability

A transaction is durable if once it is **committed** (saved to the database), it will remain so, even in the event of catastrophic failures. Even if you kick the server's power cord out of the wall after a transaction, it will stay committed.

This means a transaction is not fully committed until it is written to permanent storage, such as a storage drive.

Databases and Log Files

In most ACID databases, a **transaction log** (sometimes referred to as a *journal* or *audit trail*) is a history of executed actions. The upshot of this is that even if there are crashes or hardware fails, the log file has a durable list of each change made to the database.

The log file is physically separate from the actual database data. This is important to ensure a database remains consistent. For example, when you insert a new row into a table, a few things happen.

1. The DBMS validates the incoming command.
2. A record is added to the log file specifying what changes are about to be made.
3. The DBMS attempts to make the changes to the actual data in the table or tables.
4. If successful, the log record is marked as committed.

If a failure occurs between steps 2 and 4, like a server reboot, the DBMS will scan the log file for uncommitted transactions when it comes back online. If it finds them, it will examine the actions performed and undo them, effectively restoring the database to its former, consistent state.

ENTITY INTEGRITY

One of the keystones of relational database design is **entity integrity**, which guarantees that each record in a table is unique within that table. All RDBMSs enforce entity integrity automatically, but the database creator has to appropriately define a primary key within each table for this to work. As data is added to a table, the RDBMS will check two properties to ensure that the new record is unique.

- That no other existing record in the table has the same primary key value as the new entry
- That there is a value entered for each field of the primary key

If a new record fails to meet both criteria, then the RDBMS will reject the record and prevent it from being added to the table.

Remember from our definitions for a relational database that a **record** is the collection of values for a single item in a table and that each record is independent of other records in a table. In this case, the term **unique** has its original definition of "one of a kind," so under the guidelines of referential integrity, the set of values in each row must be different from the set of values in all other rows of the table. This uniqueness serves two specific purposes.

- Reducing (but not necessarily eliminating) duplicate data
- Allowing the database to easily find specific records within a table

Ensuring Uniqueness

The relational design approach to meeting the requirements of entity integrity is to include one or more fields in each table whose sole purpose is to identify each individual record. In some cases, we can use an existing field to be the primary key. For example, we could use the entry date as a primary key in a table that tracks newspaper issues, on the grounds that each newspaper in the database issues only one paper per day. This is a called a **natural key** because it happens to be a piece of data we want to track anyway, so we don't need to create a separate field just to ensure uniqueness. Other examples of potential natural keys include a phone number or email address to identify people in a Contacts table. We typically want both of those values in such a dataset, and if each person has their own unique phone number or email address, either could work as a natural key.

A much more common approach is to use a **surrogate key**, a field (or collection of fields) that is created specifically to identify each record in a database, but which has no other purpose or meaning in the table. Because we are surrounded by databases, we are used to using surrogate keys for this purpose. For example, if you contact your bank, chances are good that they will want to use your account number to identify your account, rather than simply your name; your account number is unique, but your name probably isn't. In fact, we regularly use surrogate keys to identify things, such as Social Security numbers, bank account numbers, vehicle identification numbers, and product barcodes. Even when the key value includes some kind of meaning (such as where the person lived when they applied for a Social Security number or the product manufacturer code in a UPC), these values are only loosely connected to the object they identify, and the assignment itself is mostly arbitrary.

On their own, surrogate keys are completely meaningless, but they can serve the very useful purpose of uniquely identifying each object in a table. In a Contact table, a field named ContactID could be defined. Each person could then be assigned a different ContactID value as they are added to the table. While this doesn't prevent us from adding the same person to the contact list more than one time (and assigning a different ContactID value to each instance), it does allow the database to easily distinguish between John Johnson and his son John Johnson, Jr.

The term **candidate key** is used to refer to a field that is inherently unique to each record but that may not act as the primary key of the table. For example, in an employee table, it is highly likely that each employee's Social Security number will be included, and each employee has a unique value for that field. However, for security reasons, it will not be selected as the primary key, and the database designer will select either a different candidate key or a surrogate key to act as the primary key for that table.

Finding Records

The most important role of a primary key is to allow the database to find specific records in a database quickly and accurately. In a relational database, to reduce redundancy and improve efficiency, data is typically stored across many different tables, where each table focuses on one kind of data. In a product inventory database, for example, there will likely be separate tables for products, vendors, warehouse locations, and even categories. As a result, when all the details about a specific item must be retrieved, the database will have to search across tables to find the required information about that item.

For many databases, primary keys are **indexed** by default. Indexes are normally applied to columns (or groups of columns), and they are stored as a separate object from the rest of the table the index applies to. Each index acts as a pointer to records stored in tables in the database, and the RDMBS applies a default sort to the indexes, regardless of the order in which the records were added to the relevant table. These sorted primary keys include a connection (an index) back to the full records associated with each key. The fact that the indexes are both unique and sorted means that the database does not have to search through more records than necessary to find the required key values. Once the requested value is found in the index, the database knows it can stop looking for more instances of that value. Because the primary key is connected to the rest of the data in the associated record, the database can simply pull data from that record and safely ignore all other records in the table.

This is actually similar in concept to an index in a book. A book's index normally appears at the end of the book, where it is easy to locate. In addition, the terms in the index are sorted in alphabetic order, so the reader can easily find the term they are looking for. The index also tells the reader where to find the term in the book so that the reader can go straight to the correct location in the book.

This use of primary keys does have weaknesses, however. The biggest weakness is that the primary key index structure must be reindexed each time a new record is added or an existing record is deleted, which can slow down update processes within the database. In essence, this is similar to having to rewrite the index for a book when a chapter is deleted or added to the book. It is also not possible to change the value of a primary key, meaning that if a value is assigned incorrectly, you cannot change the value later to correct it. However, even with the weaknesses inherent to primary keys, they are an integral component in a relational database. While they can guarantee uniqueness only at the record level, they do allow the database to distinguish and find individual records in a table.

Other options for primary keys will be considered as we work through designing a database later in this book. For now, understand that the role of a primary key is to ensure that each record in a table is unique within that table.

BACKUP STRATEGIES

A lot of time and effort is put into the backup and recovery of database systems. In some businesses, losing access to the database can cost thousands of dollars per minute as orders can no longer be taken or customer data could be lost or compromised.

For this reason, it is important that the database administrator has backup and recovery options for both data and log files. Because logs contain all transaction information, they provide point-in-time restoration information. Full data backups tend to be very large and are done only periodically. Log backups tend to be much smaller.

As an example, nightly data backup might be performed nightly, while a log backup could occur every 10 minutes. If the data backup occurs at midnight and the server fails at 2:55 p.m., the last data backup would be restored, followed by restoring all the logged transactions until 2:50 p.m. We would lose changes only between 2:50 p.m. and 2:55 p.m. While this 5-minute loss is not great, it is better than the alternative if there were no log backups at all.

To further reduce losses, we could use multiple database servers and execute transactions on each. If one server fails, another can take its place. As you approach a true lossless solution, the cost of servers and software increases exponentially. An experienced database administrator has the job of matching budget to loss tolerance for a business.

SUMMARY

This lesson presented an overview of databases and relational database concepts, as well as information on ACID and the use of keys. This information is foundational for learning and working with Structured Query Language. Many of the terms presented in this lesson are used frequently when talking about data and databases, so it's good to learn what they mean early in the game. Most will also be revisited in subsequent chapters when they are directly applied to SQL. This includes the following:

- **Table/relation (academic)/entity (abstract):** A logical grouping of data in a relational database. A table defines valid facts and contains facts about one type of thing.
- **Row/record/tuple (academic):** A single, logical item in a table, comprised of one or more values or fields.
- **Column/field/attribute (academic):** Names a fact to be tracked in a table and restricts the size and type of the fact's data.

ACID was also covered in the lesson. When reliable data is essential, using an ACID-compliant database is a requirement. Only databases that are atomic, consistent, isolated, and durable are going to handle all the errors and failures that can occur while protecting the quality of the data.

Keys were also mentioned as they are a core part of organizing data in a way that can help you create uniqueness as well as help your records to be accessed quickly. As you begin to organize your data into a database that can be accessed with SQL starting in the next chapter, you'll see how primary and foreign keys are used.

Finally, no business should be without a backup and recovery plan that suits their budget and risk tolerance.

EXERCISES

The following exercises are provided to allow you to experiment with concepts presented in this lesson:

Exercise 1.1: Customers and Orders

Exercise 1.2: Libraries and the Books Within

Exercise 1.3: Your Scenario

> **NOTE** The exercises are for your benefit and help you apply what you learn in the lessons. Please note that these are to be done on your own, and thus solutions are not provided.

Exercise 1.1: Customers and Orders

In Figure 1.1, tables were shown for Customers and Orders. Create a list of at least three additional fields that could be added to each of the tables.

Exercise 1.2: Libraries and the Books Within

Assume that you will be creating a program that accesses a database containing information on libraries as well as information on the books each library contains. Do the following:

1. List the tables you could include.
2. Create the list of fields you might include within each row of each table you identified.
3. Create three rows of sample data for each of your tables.
4. Identify the fields in your tables (if any) that would be primary keys.
5. Identify the fields in your tables (if any) that would be foreign keys.

Exercise 1.3: Your Scenario

Come up with your own scenario for using a database. This can be a banking example that tracks accounts, a media database, a restaurant menu, or a store inventory system. Do the following for your scenario:

1. List the tables you could include.
2. Create the list of fields you might include within each row of each table you identified.
3. Create three rows of sample data for each of your tables.
4. Identify the fields in your tables (if any) that would be primary keys.
5. Identify the fields in your tables (if any) that would be foreign keys.

Lesson 2
Applying Normalization

Chapter 1 mentioned that to reduce redundancy and improve efficiency in a relational database, data is typically stored across many different tables, where each table focuses on one kind of data. In this lesson, you will learn the standard process for organizing your data.

Learning Objectives

By the end of this lesson, you will be able to:

- Understand the purpose of database normalization
- Describe and apply the first through third normalization forms
- Know when to apply denormalization to your tables

WHAT IS NORMALIZATION?

Relational database design has the goal of organizing data in a way that reduces redundant (or duplicate) data while also streamlining ways in which we can access that data.

The relational database model was proposed by E. F. Codd in his article "A Relational Model of Data for Large Shared Data Banks" in the June 1970 issue of *Communications of the ACM* (Association for Computing Machinery). Being an academic proposal, it is a bit dry, but the point of this paper was to propose a database model based on relations (tables), accessible via a universal language, and having a defined set of rules for splitting a dataset into relations. In discussing normal form, he notes that relations with simple domains lend themselves to storage in a simple, two-dimensional array, while other relations are more complex and require correspondingly more complex structures to represent them.

> **NOTE** You can find Codd's article at www.seas.upenn.edu/~zives/03f/cis550/codd.pdf.

Normalization is the process of breaking down these complex relationships into simpler structures. A properly normalized design improves performance and reduces the complexity of relationships by minimizing data duplication (redundancy). Codd showed that is possible for all data domains to be reduced to simple table relationships. A database where all relations are reduced in this manner, following the process of normalization, is said to be **normalized**.

Data Redundancy Is a Problem

Data redundancy is the act of storing the same piece of data multiple times in the database. Table 2.1 presents an example of client account information.

Table 2.1 Client Account Information

First-Name	Last-Name	Account-Num	Account-Type	Street	City	State	Zip
Eduino	Bayly	512663484	Checking	07755 Marquette Park	Spring	Texas	77386
Missie	Cavee	374078993	Savings	557 Roxbury Street	Peoria	Illinois	61656
Missie	Cavee	647794666	Checking	557 Roxbury Street	Peoria	Illinois	61656
Geordie	Eirwin	450433555	Savings	8 Cottonwood Terrace	Zephyrhills	Florida	33543
Davy	Louis	317202667	Credit Card	38 Commercial Hill	Columbus	Ohio	43204
Dorri	McNair	192333561	Checking	8208 Stuart Center	Fort Lauderdale	Florida	33355
Dorri	McNair	166808336	Savings	8208 Stuart Center	Fort Lauderdale	Florida	33355
Dorri	McNair	666343073	Investment	8208 Stuart Center	Fort Lauderdale	Florida	33355

First-Name	Last-Name	Account-Num	Account-Type	Street	City	State	Zip
Michael	McNair	439224678	Credit Card	8208 Stuart Center	Fort Lauderdale	Florida	33355
Annmarie	Rubenov	396112179	Credit Card	4 Loftsgordon Place	Jackson	Mississippi	39210

Looking at Table 2.1, you can see how the same address information is duplicated across many rows. Aside from the inefficacy of storing many copies of the same data (disk space), having the data duplicated like this can lead to data anomalies (incorrect data). Suppose Dorri McNair moves to a different state. Because this client appears in three separate rows, you would have to be sure to update the address correctly in all three rows. Possible resulting anomalies include the following:

- Updating only one or two rows and leaving the others unchanged.
- Mistyping the address in one row (such as *Stewart* instead of *Stuart*).
- If Dorri McNair chooses to open another account, the address associated with the new account would have to match the existing address.

As a result of each these cases, Dorri McNair could end up with at least two different addresses in the system, which means they may not receive mailed documents correctly or the ZIP code wouldn't match the account for validation. This type of error is called an **update anomaly**.

Another potential problem is deleting an address that is still in use. For example, if Michael McNair chooses to close their credit card account and the associated address is removed from the system, that could potentially delete the address associated with Dorri McNair, creating a **delete anomaly**.

Ideally, you should be able to go to one place and edit a single row to change a client's address for any rows associated with that client. If a client chooses to close an account, that will not affect other accounts that the client has with the bank.

Storage Reduction

In addition to data anomalies that can arise from redundant data, the storage requirements of a large database can be reduced significantly by following a principle that any given piece of data (such as an address) should be stored in a single location in the database. While this is a guideline more than a rule, reducing the size of the database affects not only the physical storage space that the database requires, but it also speeds up retrieval of data in the database.

Functional Dependencies

A **functional dependency**, as the name implies, is a dependency relationship. That is, "column A depends on column B" or "columns A, B, and E depend on columns C and D." In a well-designed table, all columns will depend on at least one column in the table. If there are columns that are independent of the others, they are candidates to be moved to a separate table.

Understanding how some data is dependent on other data is key to designing good database structures. As an example, in a table listing employee information with a Social Security number and a name, the name could be said to be **functionally dependent** on the Social Security number. This means if the Social Security number is known, then an employee's name can be found.

The converse situation is not true, however. Multiple employees can have the same name, so Social Security number is not functionally dependent on the name. You would need to be cautious to ensure that the table design did not have the Social Security number depending upon the name.

Another example of this situation is with ZIP codes in the United States. At a glance, it appears that state is a dependency of ZIP code because in nearly all cases, you can predict the state based on the ZIP code. However, there are a handful of ZIP codes that cross state lines. This means that ZIP code to state is not a dependency. Thus, it is critical in database design to fully understand the data and how it relates (or doesn't) to other data in the dataset.

NORMALIZING DATA

In general, the goal of normalization is to identify the **entities** (or tables) required by the database to minimize redundant information, while still retaining information about how data stored in separate tables is related across tables. Taking the list of bank clients in Table 2.1 as an example, client-specific information (name and address) should probably be stored separately from the account information so that client information can be updated without affecting account information. This means that the data shown earlier should be divided into (at least) two separate entities: client and account.

The process of normalizing data includes a series of steps that help identify the entities that can be used to organize the data. There are several levels of normalization, but the exact number and names of each form depends on the referenced source. For most purposes, only three normal forms are needed.

- First normal form (1NF)
- Second normal form (2NF)
- Third normal form (3NF)

If the data is in 3NF, it will typically meet all normalization requirements except the most stringent. This is typically the goal you should aim for.

In the next few pages, the process of **normalizing** a dataset will be presented. This process typically means looking at the data structure and applying each level of normalization before moving to the next level. So you'll start with 1NF, move to 2NF, and then apply 3NF.

For this exercise, the simple contact list shown in Table 2.2 will be used. This table is technically known as a **heap**, which is an unstructured collection of data.

Table 2.2 A Simple Contact List

FirstName	LastName	PhoneNumber	PhoneType
Bob	Smith	555-241-9371	Home
Jane	Doe	555-241-7235	Mobile
Barbara	Jamison	555-403-1639	Mobile
Joel	Anthony	555-403-8820	Home

FIRST NORMAL FORM

The first step toward normalization is to achieve First Normal Form, which can be referred to as 1NF. To achieve 1NF, the table must satisfy the following conditions:

- There is no top-to-bottom ordering to the rows.
- There is no left-to-right ordering to the columns.
- Every row can be uniquely identified.
- Every row/column intersection (field) contains only one value.

These conditions are worth a closer look.

Top-to-Bottom or Left-to-Right Ordering

The two conditions of no top-to-bottom or left-to-right ordering specify that the data in a table can be accessed in any order. In other words, you are not required to look at the first row to make sense of the second row. The same must be true of the columns. The data in Table 2.2 does not violate this condition.

Every Row Can Be Uniquely Identified

You should be able to identify each row by a unique value. The contact list heap table lacks a unique key. It is possible to have two contacts both named Bob Smith, with no way to distinguish between them. This is a violation of the third condition.

The violation of the third condition (unique identification of rows) can be solved easily by assigning a primary key to this table. There is no field that can be used as a natural key (or the third condition wouldn't be violated), so a surrogate key, ContactID, can be used so that a different number can be assigned to each contact. Table 2.3 presents the modified contacts table with the key added.

Table 2.3 Modified Contacts Table with a Key

ContactID	FirstName	LastName	PhoneNumber	PhoneType
001	Bob	Smith	555-241-9371	Home
002	Jane	Doe	555-241-7235	Mobile
003	Barbara	Jamison	555-403-1639	Mobile
004	Joel	Anthony	555-403-8820	Home
005	Bob	Smith	555-243-9372	Home

The new key allows for the two Bob Smith records to be distinguished based on their ID. One has an ID of 001 and the other 005.

Every Field Contains Only One Value

The fourth condition is that every field should contain only one value. This condition is intended to prevent multiple values from being stored in one field, such as comma-delimited data. For example, say you wanted to store multiple phone numbers per contact, like their mobile and home phones. You could just comma-separate the values like this:

FirstName	LastName	PhoneNumber	PhoneType
Bob	Smith	555-241-9371, 555-241-2035	Home, Mobile

This structure violates the fourth condition that every field contains only one value. This rule exists because adding multiple values to a single field causes multiple problems, the most important of which is that you cannot tell for certain which phone number corresponds to Home and which one corresponds to Mobile. Yes, you can guess based on the order in which they are presented, but that's not a guarantee. It would be much better if there were a one-to-one correlation between PhoneNumber and PhoneType, just as there is between FirstName and LastName.

This can be prevented by limiting the length of the field or simply by enforcing this rule in the application code (using a language such as C# or Java), but neither of those options will meet the need of associating multiple phone numbers with the same person.

The best option to resolve an issue of a field having multiple values is to create a new table for that data. In this case, PhoneNumber can be removed from the Contact table completely, and a new table can be created that includes the ContactIDs and PhoneNumbers for each contact. Including ContactID allows you to identify which phone number belongs to which contact, while also allowing you to include as many phone numbers as you want for each contact.

Doing this would give us two separate tables. The first table, shown in Table 2.4, would be for contacts with ContactID as the primary key. The second table, shown in Table 2.5, would be for telephone numbers, with TelephoneID as the primary key and ContactID as a foreign key.

Table 2.4 Contact Table

ContactID	FirstName	LastName
001	Bob	Smith
002	Jane	Doe
003	Barbara	Jamison
004	Joel	Anthony
005	Bob	Smith

Table 2.5 Telephone Table

TelephoneID	TelephoneNumber	PhoneType	ContactID
101	555-241-9371	Home	001
102	555-241-7235	Mobile	002
103	555-403-1639	Mobile	003
104	555-403-8820	Home	004
105	555-243-9372	Home	001

Summary of First Normal Form

For a table to meet the requirements of 1NF, each record must be unique, and no field should include multiple values. In most (but not all) cases, you can simply add a surrogate key to the table to satisfy the uniqueness criterion. For fields that have multiple values, however, it is usually best to create a separate table for those values and use a foreign key to connect the tables.

SECOND NORMAL FORM

In academic terms, a table is in second normal form (2NF) if and only if it is in 1NF and every non-primary-key column is functionally dependent on the entire primary key but not functionally dependent on any proper subset of the primary key. In plain English, you must already be in 1NF, and then all the columns except the primary key need to be strictly dependent on all fields included in the primary key.

Wait! How can there be more than one field in a primary key if any given table can have at most one primary key?

Technically, the definition of a primary key is that it is "a field or **a set of fields** that uniquely identifies each record in a table." While a surrogate key can always be created to act as a single-field primary key for any table, there are times when using existing keys makes more sense.

Look at an example like a retail order database. Table 2.6 contains a heap table for customer orders that includes the customer data and data related to products they've ordered.

Table 2.6 Customer Orders with Ordered Products

First-Name	Last-Name	Phone-Number	Phone-Type	OrderDate	Products-Ordered	Prices
Bob	Smith	555-241-9371	Home	Jan 5, 2021	Tablet, 32" TV	$300, $200
Jane	Doe	555-241-7235	Mobile	Jan 6, 2021	32" TV, Laptop	$180, $720
Barbara	Jamison	555-403-1639	Mobile	Jan 7, 2021	Laptop	$800
Joel	Anthony	555-403-8820	Home	Jan 7, 2021	Blu-Ray Player, Speakers	$200, $300
Jane	Doe	555-241-7235	Mobile	Jan 8, 2021	Speakers	$270

Right off the bat, it can be seen that this table does not yet satisfy 1NF, which also means it can't be in 2NF. Specifically:

- There is no primary key field, so each record cannot be guaranteed to be unique.

- Some customers have multiple orders, which creates redundant values for name and phone across multiple rows.
- Some orders have multiple items for Products-Ordered and Prices.

The table needs to be reworked to fit 1NF and then 2NF. As mentioned, start with 1NF.

Normalize to 1NF

When faced with a situation like Table 2.6, it's best to start by putting the data into tables that satisfy 1NF.

While a new field could simply be created as the primary key here, we know that at least two of these records have the same customer, so a surrogate key would simply "bake in" the redundant information about duplicate people. A better approach is to first identify how to split the original table into separate tables to reduce redundancy. Then the primary key of each table can be identified.

Start with a Product table that identifies each product being sold. Table 2.7 presents a basic product table based on the data from Table 2.6.

Table 2.7 A Basic Product Table

ProductName	ProductPrice
Tablet	$300
32" TV	$200
Laptop	$800
Blu-Ray Player	$200
Speakers	$300

Each product appears exactly once in this table, even though the same product may appear multiple times in the original table. To satisfy 1NF, this table can be a given primary key, as shown in Table 2.8.

Table 2.8 Basic Product Table with a Primary Key

ProductID	ProductName	ProductPrice
501	Tablet	$300
502	32" TV	$200
503	Laptop	$850
504	Blu-Ray Player	$200
505	Speakers	$300

A Customer table can also be created with its own primary key. Assume there is a business rule that allows only one phone number per person, so everything can be put in the same customer table as shown in Table 2.9.

Table 2.9 Customer Table

CustomerID	FirstName	LastName	PhoneNumber	PhoneType
001	Bob	Smith	555-241-9371	Home
002	Jane	Doe	555-241-7235	Mobile
003	Barbara	Jamison	555-403-1639	Mobile
004	Joel	Anthony	555-403-8820	Home

Each of these tables is now in 1NF, because each has a primary key to ensure uniqueness across records and because no field includes more than one value.

Composite Keys

All that's left is the order-specific information, including the date the order was placed and exactly which products were included in each order. Things get a little complicated at this point.

We cannot use either the product table or the customer table to store order information, because the same product can be included in multiple orders and a customer can place multiple orders. If we tried to use either table, either we would end up adding multiple values to the same field or we would end up with duplicate values across rows. A new table needs to be created just for Orders. This table includes the CustomerID to identify who placed the order, as well as the ProductID for the products they ordered, along with the OrderDate. An OrderID field will be included as well, because the table will need a primary key. Table 2.10 presents the new Order table.

Table 2.10 Order Table

OrderID	CustomerID	OrderDate	ProductID
401	001	Jan 5, 2021	501
401	001	Jan 5, 2021	502
402	002	Jan 6, 2021	502
402	002	Jan 6, 2021	503
403	003	Jan 7, 2021	503
404	004	Jan 7, 2021	504
404	004	Jan 7, 2021	505
405	002	Jan 8, 2021	505

The Order table is more streamlined, but it has obvious problems. Note that OrderID is repeated for each product in the same order. This violates the rule that primary key values must be unique across rows in the same table. One way to resolve this is to consider each item purchased to be a separate order, but imagine how many receipts you would get at a grocery store if each item had to be purchased separately!

This is where functional dependency, mentioned earlier in this lesson, really kicks in. First, note that for each OrderID, the CustomerID and OrderDate are the same, but the ProductID is different. This means that in this table, CustomerID and OrderDate are functionally dependent on OrderID, so we should put them together in the same table, as shown in Table 2.11.

Table 2.11 OrderID Functional Dependencies

OrderID	CustomerID	OrderDate
401	001	Jan 5, 2021
402	002	Jan 6, 2021
403	003	Jan 7, 2021
404	004	Jan 7, 2021
405	002	Jan 8, 2021

By creating the new entity shown in Table 2.11, the redundant data can be removed. But how do we know what products are on which orders?

A new table named OrderProduct can be created that includes OrderID and ProductID. Table 2.12 includes this OrderProduct table.

Table 2.12 OrderProduct Table

OrderID	ProductID
401	501
401	502
402	502
402	503
403	503
404	504
404	505
405	505

The OrderID field in this table effectively indicates who ordered what on which date, but a primary key needs to be determined. OrderID can't be used because it repeats for each item on the same order. Similarly, any given product could be on multiple orders, so it can't be the primary key either. However, the combination of OrderID + ProductID is unique in each record: no order will include the same item more than one time, and in fact, you want to prevent it from happening.

In this situation, it makes sense to combine OrderID and ProductID into a single primary key. When multiple fields are included in a primary key, it is called a **composite key**. Composite keys actually happen much more often in database design than you might expect. In this case, a composite key gives us the following advantages:

- It allows us to repeat OrderID as many times as necessary for each product included in the order.
- It allows us to repeat ProductID as many times as necessary for each time the product is ordered.
- It prevents us from accidentally adding the same product more than once to the same order.

Now let's extend the concept of functional dependency a bit to see how that works for 2NF. In the original table shown again in Table 2.13, notice that the product prices depend on who ordered the product, rather than on the product itself.

Table 2.13 Customer Orders with Ordered Products

First-Name	Last-Name	Phone-Number	Phone-Type	OrderDate	ProductsOrdered	Prices
Bob	Smith	555-241-9371	Home	Jan 5, 2021	Tablet, 32" TV	$300, $200
Jane	Doe	555-241-7235	Mobile	Jan 6, 2021	32" TV, Laptop	$180, $720
Barbara	Jamison	555-403-1639	Mobile	Jan 7, 2021	Laptop	$800
Joel	Anthony	555-403-8820	Home	Jan 7, 2021	Blu-Ray Player, Speakers	$200, $300
Jane	Doe	555-241-7235	Mobile	Jan 8, 2021	Speakers	$270

If you look closely at the information in the table, you will see that, specifically, Jane Doe appears to get a 10 percent lower price than what other customers pay. While the base price of each product should be dependent on the product itself (and therefore, in the Product table), a way is also needed to add in the actual price the customer pays at the time of the order. In this case, the price depends on both the product *and* the order.

As it happens, there is a table that uses the product and the order as the primary key: the OrderProduct table. Because the price paid depends on *both* values in the primary key,

Table 2.14 OrderProduct Table with a Nonkey Field Added for Price Paid

OrderID	ProductID	PricePaid
401	501	$300
401	502	$200
402	502	$180
402	503	$720
403	503	$800
404	504	$200
404	505	$300
405	505	$720

it makes perfect sense to add that into the table as a nonkey field, as shown in Table 2.14.

In a working database, a Quantity field would also be included to indicate how many of each product the customer ordered, and that would be functionally dependent on both the order and the product, so it would go into the OrderProduct table as well.

Summary of Second Normal Form

After applying second normal form, the original heap table is split into four individual tables, shown in Tables 2.15 through Table 2.18.

Table 2.15 Customer

CustomerID	FirstName	LastName	PhoneNumber	PhoneType
001	Bob	Smith	555-241-9371	Home
002	Jane	Doe	555-241-7235	Mobile
003	Barbara	Jamison	555-403-1639	Mobile
004	Joel	Anthony	555-403-8820	Home

Table 2.16 Product

ProductName	ProductPrice
Tablet	$300
32" TV	$200
Laptop	$800
Blu-Ray Player	$200
Speakers	$300

Table 2.17 Order

OrderID	CustomerID	OrderDate
401	001	Jan 5, 2021
402	002	Jan 6, 2021
403	003	Jan 7, 2021
404	004	Jan 7, 2021
405	002	Jan 8, 2021

Table 2.18 OrderProduct

OrderID	ProductID	PricePaid
401	501	$300
401	502	$200
402	502	$180
402	503	$720
403	503	$800
404	504	$200
404	505	$300
405	505	$720

Each of these tables meets the requirements of 1NF because each table has a primary key and a single value in each cell. Because 2NF applies only to tables that have a composite key, the first three tables (Customer, Product, and Order) are also automatically in 2NF.

The third table has a composite key that uses OrderID + ProductID. It meets the criteria for 2NF because the PricePaid field is functionally dependent on both the order and the product.

THIRD NORMAL FORM

For a table to be in third normal form (3NF), it must meet the following criteria:

- It is in 2NF (and by extension, in 1NF).
- No nonkey field depends on another nonkey field.

In essence, the goal of 3NF is to make sure that all data in a given table is relevant to the object (or *entity*) described by the table. Boiled down, this means that only data immediately relevant to a customer should be in a Customer table and only data immediately relevant to a product should be in a Product table.

While this seems logical, many novice database architects are afraid of having too many tables in a database. As a result, they try to reduce the required number of tables by consolidating fields into tables where they may not belong. An example of this is the Contact table from earlier, which is shown again in Table 2.19.

Table 2.19 Contact Table

FirstName	LastName	PhoneNumber	PhoneType
Bob	Smith	555-241-9371	Home
Jane	Doe	555-241-7235	Mobile
Barbara	Jamison	555-403-1639	Mobile
Joel	Anthony	555-403-8820	Home

This heap table was split into two normalized tables earlier in this lesson to allow the database to include multiple phone numbers for the same person and still meet the requirements of 1NF. Table 2.20 and Table 2.21 show the Contact and Telephone tables again.

Table 2.20 Contact Table

ContactID	FirstName	LastName
001	Bob	Smith
002	Jane	Doe
003	Barbara	Jamison
004	Joel	Anthony
005	Bob	Smith

Table 2.21 Telephone Table

TelephoneID	TelephoneNumber	PhoneType	ContactID
101	555-241-9371	Home	001
102	555-241-7235	Mobile	002
103	555-403-1639	Mobile	003
104	555-403-8820	Home	004
105	555-243-9372	Home	001

Both tables are in 2NF, but for 3NF, each field must describe the entity described by the table. The Contact table is good because people have first and last names, so both fields are appropriate for a table that describes people.

The Telephone table has a problem, though. The PhoneType depends on the phone number, which is not a key field. There is also a certain amount of redundancy here because both Home and Mobile are repeated throughout the table. If at some point, we wanted to change the existing terms to Landline and Cell, we would have to search through every record in this table to replace the current values.

As with both 1NF and 2NF, the best way to fix a problem with 3NF is to move the offending field (or fields) to another table. So, to resolve the offense in the Telephone table, a PhoneType table can be created as shown in Table 2.22.

Table 2.22 PhoneType Table

PhoneTypeID	PhoneType
301	Home
302	Mobile

The Telephone table can then be updated to use PhoneTypeID instead of PhoneType, as shown in Table 2.23.

Table 2.23 Updated Telephone Table

TelephoneID	TelephoneNumber	PhoneTypeID	ContactID
101	555-241-9371	301	001
102	555-241-7235	302	002
103	555-403-1639	302	003
104	555-403-8820	301	004
105	555-243-9372	301	001

While adding tables seems like it makes the database more complicated, there are a couple of advantages for our phone scenario.

- The PhoneType value has to be changed in only one place.
- Additional phone types can easily be created that are automatically standardized in the database. For example, you might choose to add Fax or Work as new phone types. You would simply add these new types to the PhoneType table with their own PhoneTypeID values that could then be used when adding new phone numbers to the Telephone table.

DENORMALIZATION

Normalizing a database is an art that takes lots of practice, and even with set rules, different database architects can come up with different designs for the same dataset. The goal of database design is to create a database that is as efficient as possible, and efficiency means that sometimes you don't really need all the tables that are identified as you apply the normal forms to a database. In fact, there are two more forms, fourth normal form (4NF) and fifth normal form (5NF), that many advanced database architects will apply in the initial round of normalization. As a general rule, however, if all the tables in a database meet the requirements for 3NF, then 4NF and 5NF aren't likely to change many things.

Once you get to 3NF, you should look at the actual efficiency of the database rather than the theoretical efficiency that 3NF gives us. Theoretically, 3NF gives us all of the following:

- Each piece of data lives in exactly one place in the database. This makes updates to existing values easier with less chance of update anomalies (such as having two different addresses in different places for the same customer) over time.
- It is easier to protect data that you don't want users to change. A person is much more likely to change their telephone number than their name, and you can give more access to the Telephone table while reducing access to the Contact table.
- It reduces the amount of repetitive data, which can save storage space.

However, additional complexities are also introduced, including the following:

- More tables mean more key fields. Key fields are indexed, so they might be loaded into memory when the database is opened. While memory is faster than hard drives, there is also less of it. Once memory is full, the RDBMS will resort to hard drive storage for any overflow, negating the advantages of indexed fields.
- It takes longer to retrieve data stored in multiple tables.
- It takes longer to add data when a new logical record (like a new contact) has to go into multiple tables.

When optimizing for extreme performance, there are times that you are less concerned with data protection and choose to move back toward 1NF. This is called **denormalization**.

As an example, in a simple Contact list like the one in this lesson, the phone type is likely to always be identified as part of the phone number, even when the person has only one phone number to choose from. This is because landline phones and mobile phones have different functions and restrictions. For example, you can send a text to a mobile phone but not to a landline, while a landline is much more likely to be shared by other people and a mobile number is typically assigned to a specific person. If phone type information is always wanted when a phone number is accessed, then it will take extra time to pull it out of a separate table than if the phone number and phone type were in the same table. As a result, you may choose to denormalize the structure a little bit by putting PhoneType back into the Phone table.

Because a well-normalized database tends to be slower, it is common for business intelligence and data warehousing systems to have both a normalized version of the database (especially for active data) and a denormalized version. These systems are used to process massive amounts of data, and having to do dozens of table joins and calculations over huge result sets can be a very slow process. The accepted solution to this problem is to periodically poll your database for changes, move the changed data into a denormalized structure, and do any known calculations (sales by day, month, quarter, year, etc.) in advance. Then when a user requests the reports, they can use this pre-optimized data to provide a quick response.

A large enterprise will often have databases that are normalized with good data protection for transaction processing and working with their applications. Then they also will have another set of denormalized databases (referred to as *data warehouses*) that are optimized for aggregating and reporting data.

As an example, an insurance company is likely to use a normalized database to keep track of clients and claims. Because a client wants to know the current status of any claim, the live database is connected to the application that the client can use to submit and monitor claims. However, the organization itself may want to look at specific aspects of the data to see what types of claims were made during a specific period of time or to try to correlate claim types to specific geographic areas. For this type of data analysis, the DBA will maintain a single, unnormalized dataset containing all fields that the data analyst might require, updated monthly or quarterly. The data analyst can then pull data from the unnormalized dataset much more quickly than if they pulled the data directly from the normalized tables.

> **NOTE** Table joins were mentioned in this section. A table join is used to connect two tables. You'll learn more about joining tables throughout the rest of this book with a deep dive in Lesson 11, "Adding JOIN Queries."

SUMMARY

Designing databases is a creative endeavor that is a mixture of art and science. Even with set guidelines for normalization, it's possible to have different designs for the same database, in part because of how the data is used and in other part because of how the designer thought through the systems during the design process. Moving a design from 1NF to 3NF has a great impact on the data integrity of your system, but at the cost of complexity and potentially performance.

The way you design a database for a dozen users is typically much less formal than the way you would design a database for a million users. Regardless of the situation you find yourself in, an awareness of good normalization techniques and an understanding of the application's data and needs is vital to building correct database designs. In the long run, it is most important to have a well-designed database from the outset. Taking time to normalize to 3NF is good to that end. After identifying a 3NF structure for the database, it may be appropriate to denormalize it a little, but you should do so only with justification.

Mastering this skill set takes a lot of practice. The next time you are out and about and see software "in the wild," take a moment to think about how you would structure its data. How would you design a system for a grocery store? What about a gas station? A small landscaping company doing quotes and billing? A bus scheduling system for a city? Spending time thinking about these scenarios will make you a better database architect.

EXERCISES

The following exercises are provided to allow you to experiment with concepts presented in this lesson:

Exercise 2.1: Employees

Exercise 2.2: Libraries and the Books Within

Exercise 2.3: Hotels

Exercise 2.4: Students and Courses

Exercise 2.5: On the Menu

Exercise 2.1: Employees

Table 2.24 contains a list of fields for an employee database and sample data for two employees. Use normalization to place these fields into a database.

Table 2.24 Employee Database

Fields	Sample Employee 1	Sample Employee 2
Name	John Doe	Julie Parks
Hire Date	September 1, 2023	August 12, 2020
Start Date	September 14, 2023	September 1, 2020
End Date	n/a	December 31, 2022
Employee ID	111333	012348
Hours	40	40
Hourly Wage	23.95	17.95
Phone number	415-555-1234 (mobile), 415-555-2345 (desk)	415-555-4567 (mobile), 415-555-5678 (desk), 415-555-6789 (home)
Department	Accounting	Maintenance
Supervisor	Sarah Johnson	Fred Moore
Office Number	A301	G302
Location	San Francisco, CA	Seattle, WA
Subordinates	Betsy Williams, Charlie Conrad, Doug Demiter, Elinore Engoles, Fred Filmore	n/a

Exercise 2.2: Libraries and the Books Within

In Exercise 1.1 in the Chapter 1, you created tables and fields for a library system. Review the tables you created to make sure they are complete. Consider the following situations:

- There can be multiple libraries.
- Each library can contain one or more copies of any book.
- Any book can be in one or more library but might not be in any library.

- Books can have authors, which should also be tracked, but only if they are listed on a book that is in the library database.
- Authors can be associated to one or more books.
- One book can have one or more authors.
- The information tracked for books should include the authors, the title, and a 13-digit ISBN.
- An ISBN can be associated to only one book, and a book can have only one ISBN.

After confirming you are tracking all the needed fields, normalize the fields in your tables. Is any denormalization necessary?

Exercise 2.3: Hotels

Design a database for a hotel. Your database must include the following:

- Room information, including how many beds and what size the beds are and available amenities, such as microwave, refrigerator, or coffee pot
- Guest information, including name, address, phone number, and email address
- Reservations, including start date, end date, who has reserved the room, and the number of guests

After identifying the fields for your database to be used in tables, apply normalization to create a final database design.

Exercise 2.4: Students and Courses

Table 2.25 contains fields for a database that lists students and the courses they are taking along with the fees. Normalize this table.

Table 2.25 Students and Course List

FirstName	Last-Name	Major	Semester	Class	Fees	Professor
Susie	Summers	Pre-med, Nursing	Fall, 2022	Biology 101	$150	Johnson
Susie	Summers	Pre-med, Nursing	Fall, 2022	Calculus 103	$120	Samuels
Peter	Parker	Physics, Anthropology	Fall, 2022	Biology 101	$150	Johnson
Peter	Parker	Physics, Anthropology	Fall, 2022	Physics 101	$220	Fredrick
Susie	Summers	Pre-med, Nursing	Spring, 2023	Biology 201	$120	Johnson

Exercise 2.5: On the Menu

Design a database for a restaurant menu. It must support the following activities:

- Generate a list of all items on the menu, including the name, a description of the dish, and its price.
- Group items on the menu by categories, including values such as appetizers, main dishes, salads, desserts, and beverages.
- Create a customer order, including a quantity and price for each item ordered, as well as the date and time the order was entered.
- Identify the employee who took the order.

As a stretch to the basics listed, include customer data required for delivery orders, including delivery address and contact information.

Once you've identified and created your base database information, use the steps in this chapter to apply normalization.

Lesson 3

Creating Entity-Relationship Diagrams

O nce you've gone through the steps of normalizing a database and determined what tables, fields, and

relationships the database should have, it is helpful to create a

visual representation of the database structure. This can be done

using an entity-relationship diagram (ERD).

Learning Objectives

By the end of this lesson, learners will be able to:

- Create an ERD that includes the tables, fields, and relationships identified at the end of the database normalization process
- Include appropriate metadata about the database components in the ERD, including primary and foreign keys, data types, and nullability of individual fields

USING ERDs

When discussing an abstract form of a database, the term **entity** is typically used to reference each object (such as people, things, places, and events) that will be managed in the database. An **entity-relationship diagram** (ERD) can be used to represent the entities and the relationships between the entities. Because each final version of an entity will be a table in the completed database, the terms *entity* and *table* are often used to mean virtually the same thing, where *entity* is an abstract representation of the same thing described by a *table* in a database.

The normalization steps described in the Chapter 2 help you to identify what tables and fields a database will have and how the tables themselves are related to each other. At the end of that process, however, you should create an ERD, a visual representation of the database structure that gives you the following advantages:

- It helps identify places where the proposed structure may not work. While normalization should help you identify exactly how the tables are related to each other, you may discover while building the ERD either that one or more tables aren't related to any of the other tables or that some of the relationships don't make sense when you try to map them to the normalized tables. Identifying these problems in the design phase will help avoid problems that might otherwise appear in the SQL scripts used to define the database.

- It allows the team to see the database's structure, which helps each team member quickly identify what fields are in which tables and how the tables are related.

- It gives you a single, condensed representation of the structure, which helps you write SQL statements more quickly, especially when the SQL statement references two or more tables.

Essentially, at the end of the normalization process, you have a description of the tables and fields you need to include in the database, kind of like the description of a house for sale on a realtor's web page. The description tells you what rooms are in the house and gives you a general idea of how the house is laid out (how many floors, whether there is a basement or a garage, and so on), but having a floor plan of the house lets you see exactly how the rooms are connected to each other and how much space each room has. An ERD is the equivalent of a floor plan or blueprint of the database.

As an example, in this lesson a ContactList database will be used that includes the following tables:

- **Contact:** Stores the names of people in the contact list

- **Phone:** Stores the phone numbers associated with the contacts, allowing us to associate multiple phone numbers with each individual
- **PhoneType:** Stores information about the types of phone number the database to distinguish among home numbers, work numbers, cell phone numbers, and so on.

For the Contact List database, there are a number of business rules that could be applied. For the example in this lesson, it is expected that a contact will have a phone number. Additionally, there may be phone types that are not used, such as a fax number.

> **NOTE** The tables for the ContactList database will be used within the examples shown throughout this lesson. You will start by focusing on the Contact table but then build out the other tables as well.

Available Tools

Because one of the main purposes of an ERD is to ensure that the database structure is correct, you should make sure that whatever tool you use will allow you to make changes to the structure at any point. One of the easiest tools to use, at least for the first couple of drafts, is pencil and paper. Starting with pencil and paper allows you to sketch out the design easily, as well as update the sketches as you find problems with the structure or ways to make it more efficient.

Once you have a draft sketch of the ERD, you can use a computer-based tool to create a digital version that you can save with the database documentation and share with team members. Most tools designed to create flowcharts and wireframes can also create ERDs, so chances are good that you already have something on your computer that you can use for this purpose. Suggestions include the following:

- **Draw.io:** A Chrome-based tool that is completely free to use and that allows you to save files to the cloud (Google Drive or OneDrive, primarily) or to your computer. Draw.io, which is shown in Figure 3.1, has a set of database-specific shapes that streamline the design process, and there is a desktop application if you prefer to install the application locally. You can find Draw.io at `app.diagrams.net`.
- **ERDPlus:** Another free, web-based tool designed specifically for ERDs and similar database structures. ERDPlus, which is shown in Figure 3.2, can be found at `erdplus.com`.

You may already have a design program that you use for wireframes and site maps, and if that tool also supports ERDs, feel free to use it. The focus here should be on building accurate ERDs, not on the tools you use to build them.

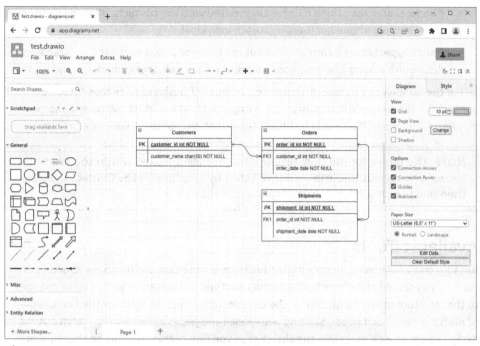

Figure 3.1 Draw.io

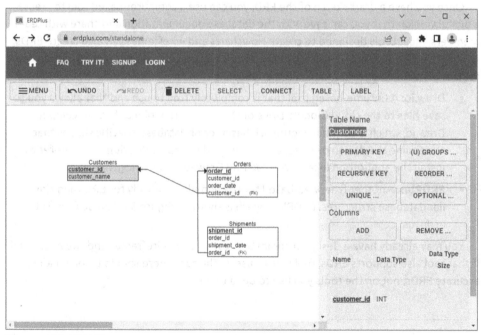

Figure 3.2 ERDPlus

ERD COMPONENTS

A well-designed ERD includes all the following information:

- The tables (entities) required by the database, including the name of each table
- A list of fields contained in each table
- Metadata about each field, including the name of the field, its data type, and whether it is nullable
- Identification of all primary and foreign key fields
- How each table is related to each other

A more detailed ERD might also contain information about indexes, how the keys are named, and details about the cardinality of each relationship, but for now, we'll focus on the basics.

> **NOTE** An ERD never includes data—just a description of the kind of data that the table will hold. That said, it is often useful to have access to sample data sets to help you identify what fields the ERD should include and what the appropriate data type is for each field.

At the time you are building an ERD, you will also want to define naming conventions that will be used with your objects. You'll want to ensure these naming conventions are used across all objects. There is a lot of flexibility in naming things in a database, and establishing a naming convention helps avoid coding problems down the road.

Note that SQL is not typically case-sensitive on its own; however, the programming languages you will use with SQL (such as C# or Java) probably are. As such, you should be consistent in using case when naming. The examples used in this lesson apply CamelCase, where each word is capitalized but not separated. CamelCase is only one naming option in the real world.

Another part of the naming convention is the use of singular versus plural nouns, especially for table names. In this example, we will use singular nouns in table names.

Creating Tables

A table is represented by a rectangle, normally divided into three sections horizontally. An ERD typically includes the name of the table in the topmost section (like a title), the primary key field(s) in the next section down, and the remaining fields in the bottommost section.

As an example, when a contact list is a normalized data set, a table that represents the contacts themselves is identified. This table can be named *Contact*. A surrogate key—a value that is created specifically to identify individual records in a table—is needed, so you need to include *ContactID* as the table's primary key. In addition, there are fields for other kinds of information associated with each contact, such as their name and their address. A basic ERD representation of this table looks like Figure 3.3.

Contact
ContactID
FirstName
LastName
Address

Figure 3.3 The ERD Contact table

Adding Fields

A basic list of fields is included in the table, but a well-designed ERD includes more information about each field beyond the name. For example, you need to know which fields are nullable and what data type each field will use.

The concept of *null* is covered in more detail elsewhere in this book, but the essential concept is that a field can be **required** or **nullable**. This is a business rule that determines whether a field must have a value or if it can be left empty.

To include this information, each required (non-nullable) field will be formatted in bold, and the data type will be added to the right of the field name. Take a look at the Contact table from Figure 3.3, and consider the choices for the fields in the ERD.

ContactID: The ContactID is a surrogate key that is required. For this example, the data type for the field can be set to an integer (INT).

FirstName and LastName: Both of the name fields are required, and both are strings. Because these fields are not a fixed length, VARCHAR is used as the data type. For this example, a limit of 25 characters can be set for the first name and a limit for 50 characters for the last name.

Address: Phone number information will be added in database, so address information isn't necessarily needed as part of the contact information. That means it is an optional field. Like FirstName and LastName, the Address field will contain strings of varying lengths, so VARCHAR can be used. For this example, a maximum length of 100 characters can be used.

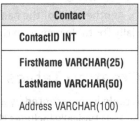

Contact
ContactID INT
FirstName VARCHAR(25)
LastName VARCHAR(50)
Address VARCHAR(100)

Figure 3.4 The updated Contact table with field information

With the addition of the field information that has been identified, the ERD for the Contact table now looks like Figure 3.4.

At this stage, be sure not to confuse values with fields. Each field name should be a **description** of the data the field will store, rather than values that will be included as data. For example, if we wanted to include a salutation (like *Mr.*, *Ms.*, *Dr.*, and so on), we would use a single field named *Salutation* that could hold at most one of those values, rather than creating a separate field for each potential salutation.

Also note that different RDBMSs use data types somewhat differently, so the exact data type you assign to each field will depend on whether you are using MySQL, SQL Server, or something else. We will use relatively generic types here, but an ERD for a specific RDBMS may need more details.

Identifying Keys

A final addition at the table level is to indicate the primary and foreign keys. This is often done by adding PK or FK (respectively) to the left of the appropriate field names in the table. It is also common to underline the primary key field (or any other field whose value must be unique within the table) to help make it even more visible.

The Contact table you are building has only one field in the primary key and no foreign keys, so the additional notation is to add PK to the left of ContactID and underline the field name. After adding the key notation, the Contact table should look like Figure 3.5.

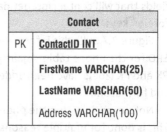

Figure 3.5 The updated Contact table with a primary key

Including Additional Tables

As mentioned in the beginning of this lesson, the ContactList database contains three tables, Contact, PhoneType, and Phone. The Contact table has been defined, but now you need to take a look at the ERD representations of the other two tables in the database. What can you tell about the fields in each table?

The PhoneType table allows information to be stored about the different kinds of phones your contacts might use so that separate work numbers, cell phone numbers, home numbers, and fax numbers can be identified for each contact. It uses PhoneTypeID as the primary key, with the INT data type. PhoneType will contain the name of the type of phone, so it will store a string, which in this case will be VARCHAR(10) to hold up to 10 characters. Both fields are required.

You can see in Figure 3.6 that the characteristics for the fields have been added to the ERD for the PhoneType table. This includes adding the PK labeling, the data types and sizes, and the bolding for required fields.

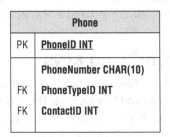

PhoneType	
PK	**PhoneTypeID INT**
	PhoneTypeName VARCHAR(10)

Figure 3.6 The PhoneType table

The phone numbers themselves are recorded in a separate Phone table. The Phone table contains PhoneID, which will hold an integer (INT) and be used as the primary key. In addition to the key, there are three fields that are included. The PhoneNumber will hold a string that contains 10 characters, which is shown using **CHAR(10)**. The other two fields, PhoneNumberTypeID and ContactID, are required fields that will contain integer data and be used as foreign keys.

Phone	
PK	**PhoneID INT**
	PhoneNumber CHAR(10)
FK	**PhoneTypeID INT**
FK	**ContactID INT**

Figure 3.7 The Phone table

Figure 3.7 pulls this information together into the ERD for the Phone table. Again, you can see that the PK and FK labels have been added to identify the keys along with the other information and formatting.

Note especially that the phone number is treated as a string, rather than as a number. This is done for multiple reasons.

- Mathematical operations are not going to be applied to the phone numbers, so they don't need to be stored as numbers.

- Phone numbers can contain non-numeric characters, such as letters or dashes, especially if there are contacts from outside the United States.

You will notice, too, that the Phone table includes two fields designated as foreign keys (FK): PhoneTypeID and ContactID. The use of foreign keys is one way that an ERD can be used to represent relationships between tables. This will be seen more clearly after creating a more formalized representation.

Showing Relationships

So far, you have seen representations of individual tables, but that's kind of like looking at a blueprint that shows only the individual rooms of a home. It is also important to see how the pieces fit together. The ERD needs to be updated to show visualizations for the relationships themselves. The first relationship to examine is with the Contact and Phone tables.

While there is variation in techniques used to represent the relationship between two tables, the simplest is to use an arrow that points *from* the **one** side of the relationship *to* the **many** side of the relationship. In this case, each contact can have many phone numbers, but each phone number is associated with exactly one contact, so the arrow points from the Contact to the Phone table, as shown in Figure 3.8.

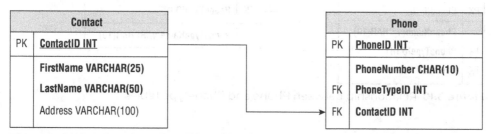

Figure 3.8 Showing the relationship that contacts can have phones

However, notations can be added to provide more details about the relationship. In Figure 3.9, we replaced the arrow. In this case, a crow's foot marking (three small lines replacing the arrowhead) has been added on the many side of the relationship to indicate that any record in the Contact table can be associated with several records in the Phone table (a contact can have multiple phone types). Additionally, there is a small vertical line on the Contact side to indicate that each record in the Phone table must have one and only one related record in the Contact table. This supports the business rules for the database that state that there must be at least one phone number for each contact.

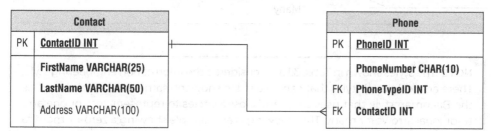

Figure 3.9 Updated relationship notation

There is also a relationship between the Phone and PhoneType tables. Figure 3.10 presents the ERD representation of this relationship. In this case, each PhoneType can be associated with any number of phone numbers, but each phone number must have exactly one type, so the crow's foot appears on the Phone table (the many side of the relationship).

Here, though, the vertical line on the PhoneType side is excluded. It's quite possible that when the database is set up, a phone type might be included that is never used (like fax numbers). As such, you don't want to force each PhoneType to be used if it isn't necessary.

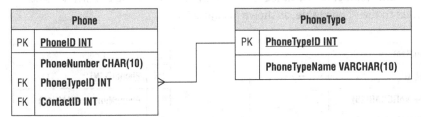

Figure 3.10 Relationship between Phone and PhoneType tables

There are other relationships that can be used in an ERD diagram as well. Table 3.1 gives the primary styles used and the relationship they represent.

Table 3.1 ERD Relationship Notations

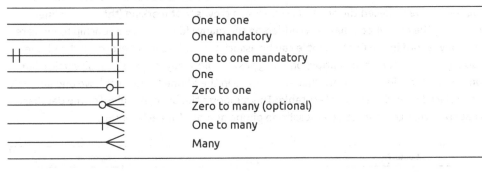

———————————	One to one One mandatory
——————————‖	One to one mandatory One
‖——————————‖	
——————————⊕	Zero to one
——————————○<	Zero to many (optional)
——————————<	One to many
——————————<	Many

> **NOTE** The styles shown in Table 3.1 are considered the information engineering style. There are additional styles that can be used to show the same relationships such as the Bachman style that uses open and closed circles to represent zero or one and traditional arrows for many. The following is an example showing a zero-or-more to a one-or-more relationship:
>
> ○————————▶●

ERD OF DATABASE

Figure 3.11 puts all the pieces of the database's ERD together into a single model of the database.

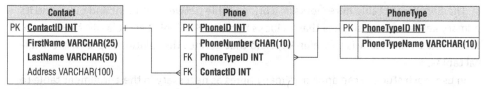

Figure 3.11 The full ERD of the database

Notice how this view allows all fields in all tables to be seen together in a single view, as well as identifies how the tables are connected. When SQL statements are written to retrieve data from the database, knowing what field is in what table is critical, as is understanding the relationships (or JOINs) between the tables. Many database developers find it useful to have an ERD on hand while writing SQL queries, especially for databases that are much more complicated than this one.

WHAT ABOUT MANY-TO-MANY RELATIONSHIPS?

When you start with an unnormalized set of data, several many-to-many relationships between tables will generally be identified as the data is normalized into the required tables. In a normalized database (normalized to at least 2NF), all relationships will be either one-to-one relationships (where each record in one of the tables corresponds to at most one record in the other table) or, more often, one-to-many relationships.

Any many-to-many relationships will be normalized to be defined as two one-to-many relationships between three tables, using a bridge table to connect the original tables. A many-to-many relationship, then, must include three separate tables: the two original tables and a bridge table. In many cases (but not all), the primary key fields of the original tables are used to create the primary key of the bridge table, in which case there are multiple fields that are both a foreign key and part of the primary key.

As an example, in a typical school database, there is a many-to-many relationship between students and classes, because each student is likely to take multiple classes (over time, if not simultaneously), and each class should include multiple students. Figure 3.12 shows a basic example of what this relationship might look like in an ERD.

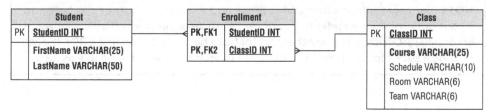

Figure 3.12 Showing the many-to-many relationship between students and classes

The Enrollment table here works as a bridge table between Student and Class, and its primary key is a composite key that includes both the StudentID and ClassID fields. Each of those fields individually is a foreign key field that defines the relationship with the original tables.

In use, each student can appear as many times as necessary in the enrollment table to represent each course they take. Similarly, each class can appear in the enrollment table as many times as necessary for each student who enrolls in the class. However, the composite key that includes both StudentID and ClassID means that no student can be enrolled in the same class more than once.

SUMMARY

Entity-relationship diagrams are important tools in relational database design because they provide a visualization of the database structure. They are useful at all levels of database administration processes, from creating the database through retrieving data from the database. Any ERD should give you the basic information needed to identify the structure of a relational database, including the following:

- Table names
- Field names
- Key fields
- Relationships between tables

This lesson showed the most basic aspects of an ERD, but ERDs can be more complicated depending on the level of detail included. For example, you can include metadata such as indexes within the table and exactly how many records can be included on the many side of a relationship. This can be useful for defining business rules such as how many classes a student can take at one time or the maximum number of phone numbers we want to store for each client.

There are several different sets of symbols in use for ERDs, and the symbols shown in this lesson are just one example. As you are exposed to different ERDs, look for a reference or ask for help if there are symbols that are not familiar to you.

> **NOTE** For more information about ERDs and examples of other symbols and layout options, you can refer to LucidChart's article at www.lucidchart.com/pages/er-diagrams. LucidChart is another tool that can be used for creating ERDs. It does include a subscription model, but there is a limited free version available as well.

EXERCISES

The following exercises are provided to allow you to experiment with concepts presented in this lesson:

Exercise 3.1: Customers and Orders

Exercise 3.2: The Relationship Between Libraries and Books

Exercise 3.3: Many to Many No More

Exercise 3.4: Diagramming the Menu

Exercise 3.5: Database Design Assessment

> **NOTE** The exercises are for your benefit. They help you apply what you learn in the lessons. Please note that these are to be done on your own, and thus solutions are not provided.

Exercise 3.1: Customers and Orders

In Lesson 2, "Applying Normalization," tables were created for customers and orders. Review those tables and make any additions needed to better track customers making orders. After completing any refinements, create an ERD for the tables. Make sure to include any primary or foreign keys, indications if the fields are optional or nullable, and data types and sizes for the fields you identified.

Exercise 3.2: The Relationship Between Libraries and Books

In Exercise 2.2 in Lesson 2, "Applying Normalization," you created and normalized tables that tracked libraries and the books within them. Create an ERD for the solution you created in that exercise. Make sure to include any primary or foreign keys, indications if the fields are optional or nullable, and data types and sizes for the fields you identified.

Exercise 3.3: Many to Many No More

In the Contact List examples, it was assumed that each phone number was associated with a single person. In reality, it is common for multiple people to share phone numbers. For example, all members of a family or a set of roommates can share the same home number, and multiple employees who work for the same business may have the same work number.

Take a look at the ERD in Figure 3.13. This shows a many-to-many relationship between contacts and phone numbers. Redesign this ERD so that the many-to-many relationship is removed.

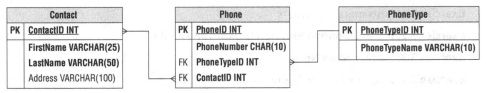

Figure 3.13 A many-to-many relationship

Exercise 3.4: Diagramming the Menu

Create an ERD for the menu database you created in Exercise 2.5 from Chapter 2.

Exercise 3.5: Database Design Assessment

This exercise has you use everything you've learned in the first three lessons of this book. Start by selecting a topic of your choice and design a database in third normal form (3NF) based on that topic. Create a report that includes the following:

- A description of the database, including specifications on how the database will be used and a general description of the data that will be stored in the database.
- A list of all entities and their attributes, including the following:
  - The primary key of the entity
  - The data type for each attribute, in generic or RDBMS-specific types
  - Foreign keys
  - Required attributes
- An ERD that corresponds to the list of entities.

Use any tool you want to create the ERD, but make sure your diagram is complete and easy to read. You can choose to use paper and pencil, but make sure that the drawing is clear and reasonably sized.

Use the following checklist to evaluate the results:

- All entities and attributes follow the same naming convention.
- Each entity has an appropriate primary key.

- All relationships between tables are one-to-many relationships, using bridge entities where necessary for many-to-many relationships.
- Each entity is related to at least one other entity, with the foreign key on the appropriate side of the relationship.
- Each attribute is assigned an appropriate data type.
- Required attributes are easy to identify in both the list and the ERD.
- The design is in 3NF.
- The number of tables is reasonable for the planned database, with no unjustified tables.

After completing the project, share it with a programmer or another person and ask for feedback. See if they notice any fields or tables that seem to be missing. If they are unfamiliar with ERDs, then explain the relationship between the tables to them so they understand what is being shown. Do they agree with the relationships you described?

Pulling It All Together: Normalizing a Vinyl Record Shop Database

As a beginning developer, you are not likely to have to normalize large databases right off the bat. Most businesses that maintain their own databases also have a team of database specialists who handle things like that. However, you are likely to have to access data stored in a database, which means that you do need to understand how a database is structured.

In this lesson, you will use everything you've learned up to this point to pull together a database and normalize it as well as create an entity-relationship diagram (ERD) to model the database.

Learning Objectives

By the end of this lesson, you'll be able to:

- Determine the fields for a database
- Identify the appropriate data type for each field
- Normalize the data to third normal form
- Create an ERD for the database

> **NOTE** Throughout this book are several lessons that help you pull together all the things you've learned in the previous chapters. These lessons take a different format that is more hands-on than others. As you work through this lesson, you should be working through the solution. Because the lessons that pull it all together are more hands-on, they will not include additional exercises.

THE VINYL RECORD SHOP DATA OVERVIEW

To pull together everything you've learned to this point, in this lesson, you will create and work with a relatively small inventory database for a vinyl music store that sells both singles and full albums. The database will support the following:

- For each album in the database, include the following:
  - A list of songs on the album
  - The name of the band and/or artists who performed on the album
  - The name of the album label
  - The price of the album
  - The album's original release date

- For each song in the database, include the following:
  - The title of the song
  - The name of the band and/or artists who performed the song
  - A URL for a video of the song
  - The album that the song first appears on
- For each band, include the following:
  - The name of the band
  - The names of the artists in the band
- For each artist, include the following:
  - The name of the artist

Normalization is a theoretical process, typically done with paper and pencil or a digital drawing tool of some sort, so no computer or specific software is required. As you work through this lesson, you are encouraged to simply use pencil and paper to design the database using ERDs.

For the sake of simplicity here, you can assume the following:

- The membership of a band will not change over time.
- Each album and song feature exactly one band.

Neither of these assumptions represents real life. Artists do move from band to band, and compilation albums include multiple artists and bands by definition. However, for this lesson things are simplified to make the normalization process more obvious at this point.

NOTE For each step, basic information will be given that you should incorporate into your design. Attempt the design on your own before continuing to the next section to see the proposed result.

STEP 1: IDENTIFY THE ENTITIES AND ATTRIBUTES

As a first step, the description of the planned database will be used to identify the entities the database will include, as well as the attributes of those entities. The term **entity** is being used to refer to an abstract concept of a person, place, thing, or event that the database will include, so an entity is a type of proto-table whose form may change during the design process. Each entity includes **attributes** that will eventually become fields in the database itself.

Look over the bulleted description in the overview in the previous section and list each entity you can identify, as well as the attributes of those entities, in the form of bulleted lists. Don't worry about applying any of the normal forms at this time. After you have your result, continue with this lesson.

Step 1 Results

You might have noticed that the bulleted list in the overview basically describes the entities that you can start with, as well as their attributes. The following is a possible solution for the entities and their attributes for the Vinyl Record Shop database:

album

- title
- song
- band/artist
- label
- price
- release date

song

- title
- videoUrl
- album
- band/artist

band

- name
- artists

artist

- name

As you can see by comparing this list to the earlier objectives, having a clear understanding of what the user wants from a database gives us a strong foundation for designing the database.

Your lists may not be identical to those shown here. For example, you may have already included ID values that could be used as the primary key in each entity, or you may have broken down the artist names into first name and last name. We know both of these will need to be added eventually, so it's fine to include them. However, the focus in this step is to create a rough outline of what the database will eventually include.

While some flexibility is allowed, it would be wrong to put a song-specific value like videoUrl in the album or band entity. Make sure that each attribute is assigned to the correct entity before going on. If you aren't sure where a specific attribute goes, put it in any and all entities where you think it might be appropriate (like *artists* in the previous example). You will use normalization rules to put it into the correct place later.

Note that each entity uses a singular noun as its name. This is part of the naming convention we will use in the database, so it is used here as well. All of the field names and data types will be finalized at the end of the process.

STEP 2: FIRST NORMAL FORM

Next, you need to make sure that each entity is in first normal form (1NF), which includes the following requirements:

- Every row can be uniquely identified.
- Every row/column intersection (field) contains only one value.

Look at your list and put each of the entities in 1NF. This means doing the following steps:

1. Make sure that each entity includes a field or a set of fields that can act as the primary key.

2. Identify any fields in the existing entities that could potentially include multiple values, based on the description given in the "Vinyl Record Shop Data Overview" section of this lesson, and create a separate entity for each of those fields. (Be sure to include the first entity's primary key as a foreign key in the new entity so that you can see the relationship between them.)

3. Repeat steps 1 and 2 until each entity is in 1NF.

You may want to do this as a new entity-relationship diagram or a set of lists. You should keep your original version for reference purposes. Before continuing, try putting the entities into 1NF.

NOTE In Lesson 2, "Applying Normalization," there were four items for 1NF.

- There is no top-to-bottom ordering to the rows.
- There is no left-to-right ordering to the columns.
- Every row can be uniquely identified.
- Every row/column intersection (field) contains only one value.

You might be wondering why only two of the four are listed in step 2. The reason the first two were not listed for this project is because the entities and fields already meet the requirements that there is no top-to-bottom or left-to-right ordering. In other words, the design describes each album, song, artist, and band as a distinct value, so items can be described within each entity without having to reference other items in the same entity. Similarly, the attributes assigned to each entity do not depend on other attributes within the same entity.

Determining Primary Keys

There are no strong candidate keys in the existing entities. videoUrl could potentially be used for the songs, but while only one URL is wanted for each song, the reality is that most songs have multiple URLs, and it's possible that a given URL could open a playlist with multiple songs.

For the sake of simplicity, you can create a surrogate key for each entity. The following shows the updated list with these keys added:

album

- albumId (PK)
- title
- song
- band/artist
- label

- price
- release date

song

- songId (PK)
- title
- videoUrl
- album
- band/artist

band

- bandId (PK)
- name
- artists

artist

- artistId (PK)
- name

Resolving Multivalued Fields

Now you need to address fields that may have more than one value. The artist entity is close. The name field can be split to include separate first and last name fields. Because the word *name* is used to reference names in multiple entities, it is good to use something more descriptive. In this case, we'll rename them to specifically refer to artists.

Artist

- artistId (PK)
- artistFirstName
- artistLastName

A given band is likely to include multiple artists, which means that artist data will need to be in a separate entity. A more descriptive name for the band name attribute is also needed. The update to the band information is now as follows:

band

- bandId (PK)

- bandName
- artistID (FK)

Now look at the relationship between artist and band. Remember that we are assuming the following for this lesson:

- Band membership is constant and will not change.
- Any band must have at least one member, but most bands have multiple members.
- Any artist can be in multiple bands. For example, Paul McCartney was a member of the Beatles, but he later led another band named Wings.

This means that there is a many-to-many relationship between artist and band, and if either entity's primary key is put into the other entity, 1NF will be violated. The only solution is to create a new bridge entity that includes the primary key from both entities as its own primary key. That results in the following entities:

band

- bandId (PK)
- bandName

bandArtist

- bandId (PK, FK)
- artistId (PK, FK)

artist

- artistId (PK)
- artistFirstName
- artistLastName

An ERD will help show the relationship of these tables clearer. At this point, the ERD would look like Figure 4.1.

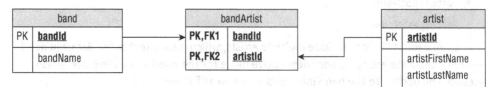

Figure 4.1 ERD for the band and artist entities as well as the bridge table

Normalizing the Song Entity

With the band entity now together, let's look at the song entity. The current song entity is as follows:

song

- songId (PK)
- title
- videoUrl
- album
- band/artist

The title field should be renamed to distinguish it from album titles. Additionally, we are working on the assumption that any given song has a single artist. Things can be further simplified by assuming that solo artists will be added as a band with one member in the database. This means that bandId will be added as a foreign key to the song entity. With these assumptions and changes, the song entity is now as follows:

song

- songId (PK)
- songTitle
- videoUrl
- album
- bandId (FK)

Is it possible for a given song to appear on multiple albums? Definitely. Bands and artists frequently release "best of" albums that include best-selling songs from earlier albums (not to mention compilation albums that are being ignored for the time being).

Let's hold that thought for now and look at the album entity. The current album entity looks like the following:

album

- albumId (PK)
- title
- song
- band/artist

- label
- price
- releaseDate

The vast majority of albums have multiple songs, so that will need to be put somewhere else. Given the assumption that there is only one band/artist per album, though, you can simply replace that field with bandId as a foreign key. The title attribute will also be updated to specifically reference albums. The updated album entity now looks like the following:

album

- albumId (PK)
- albumTitle
- label
- price
- releaseDate
- bandId (FK)

Look at the relationship between song and album. Any song can appear on multiple albums, and most albums have multiple songs. This means that there is a many-to-many relationship, and thus a bridge entity is needed. Album can be taken out of song and song out of album to create the bridge table. The net result is that the entities now look like the following:

song

- songId (PK)
- songTitle
- videoUrl
- bandId (FK)

songAlbum

- songId (PK, FK)
- albumId (PK, FK)

album

- albumId (PK)
- albumTitle
- label

- price
- releaseDate
- bandId (FK)

These entities can represent this with the ERD presented in Figure 4.2.

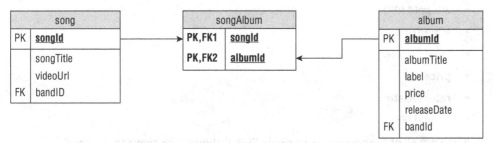

Figure 4.2 ERD for the song and album entities as well as the bridge table

Step 2 Results

At this point the entities seem to be normalized to 1NF. The following are the entities at this point:

band

- bandId (PK)
- bandName

bandArtist

- bandId (PK, FK)
- artistId (PK, FK)

artist

- artistId (PK)
- artistFirstName
- artistLastName

song

- songId (PK)
- songTitle
- videoUrl
- bandId (FK)

songAlbum

- songId (PK, FK)
- albumId (PK, FK)

album

- albumId (PK)
- albumTitle
- label
- price
- releaseDate
- bandId (FK)

If you put all of the entities into a single ERD, it should look similar to Figure 4.3.

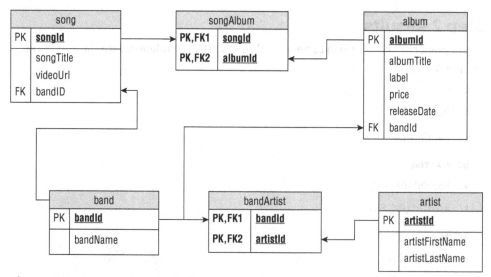

Figure 4.3 The complete ERD diagram at 1NF

If you use the checklist for 1NF, everything meets the requirements.

- Each entity has a primary key.
- Each attribute in each entity has a single value.

You might see the problem with the fact that bandID is a foreign key in both song and album, but that's why you don't stop at 1NF in the normalization process. This issue will be resolved as part of the additional normalization forms.

STEP 3: SECOND NORMAL FORM

Now that everything looks like it's in 1NF, focus can switch to second normal form (2NF). These are the primary requirements for 2NF:

- All entities are in 1NF.
- No field is partially dependent on a primary key.

Before continuing, look over the structure you have now and determine what changes, if any, should be made to meet the 2NF requirements. You should also update the ERD as necessary for 2NF before continuing.

Step 3 Results

You just finished walking through the process of 1NF in the previous section, so it should be safe to assume all entities are in 1NF. As such, 2NF will apply only to entities that have composite keys. In this case, there are two such entities.

bandArtist

- bandId (PK, FK)
- artistId (PK, FK)

songAlbum

- songId (PK, FK)
- albumId (PK, FK)

Neither of these entities includes nonkey fields, so there is nothing more that needs to be done. At this point, you can move on to the next step.

STEP 4: THIRD NORMAL FORM

Third normal form (3NF) states that all entities are in 2NF (and by extension, in 1NF) and that **no nonkey field depends on another nonkey field**. Look through the entities that have already been defined. Look at each field that is not part of the primary key for that entity and determine whether it depends on a field other than the primary key.

Based on that information, you can determine what changes, if any, should be made to meet the 3NF requirements. Try doing this review and update the ERD as necessary for 3NF before continuing.

Step 4 Results

As you start looking at the entities, you should notice that both of the bridge entities (songAlbum and bandArtist) include only key fields, so you can focus on the other entities in this step.

Take a look at the band and artist entities:

band

- bandId (PK)
- bandName

artist

- artistId (PK)
- artistFirstName
- artistLastName

These entities are fine at this point, because the names depend on the band or artist that the entity describes. No change is needed to reach 3NF.

The song and album entities need a closer look:

song

- songId (PK)
- songTitle
- videoUrl
- bandId (FK)

album

- albumId (PK)

- albumTitle
- label
- price
- releaseDate
- bandId (FK)

For the song entity, songTitle and videoURL depend on the song. For the album entity, albumTitle, label, price, and releaseDate depend on the album. This leaves just bandId.

Where bandId should go is the tricky part.

Technically, there is nothing wrong with having the same primary key act as the foreign key in multiple entities, as long as that is how the two entities are related to each other. In this case, bandId must be a foreign key in the bridge entity bandArtist, but it needs to describe the relationship between the bands and the songs and the albums. This is where 3NF can help us.

While an album can be thought of as having a single artist or band, the reality is that an album is a collection of songs that each are by a single artist or band (at least on our working assumption that only one artist or band will be listed per song and album). This means that the band on an album depends on the **songs** on that album, rather than on the album itself. If you have band information about each song and a list of songs on each album, then you can identify the artists on an album because you know what songs are on the album.

ERD in 3NF

The bandId is not needed on the album entity. This gives us the following final normalized set of entities:

band
- bandId (PK)
- bandName

artist
- artistId (PK)
- artistFirstName
- artistLastName

song
- songId (PK)

- songTitle
- videoUrl
- bandId (FK)

album

- albumId (PK)
- albumTitle
- label
- releaseDate
- price

bandArtist

- bandId (PK, FK)
- artistId (PK, FK)

songAlbum

- songId (PK, FK)
- albumId (PK, FK)

The ERD for this set of entities will now look like Figure 4.4.

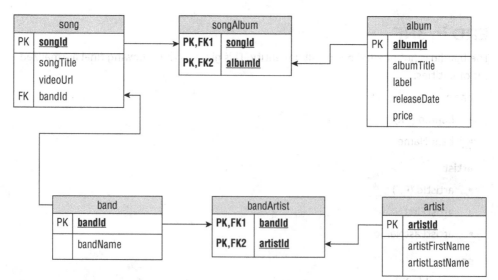

Figure 4.4 The Vinyl Record Store data in 3NF

STEP 5: FINALIZE THE STRUCTURE

After each change in the design and especially when you reach the end of the initial design steps, you want to go back through the existing entities and start over again with 1NF to be sure that the final design meets the needs of the database.

Look at the final design one more time that was presented in Figure 4.4 and the list in the previous section. At this point, the database is in 1NF: each entity has a primary key, and each attribute will store exactly one value.

It's also in 2NF. The only entities with a composite key are songAlbum and bandArtist, and neither entity includes a nonkey attribute at all.

For 3NF, each attribute describes only the entity it is in and depends on the primary key of that entity. As such, 3NF is met.

Is this the only potential design? Not really, and because database design is as much art as science, it's quite possible for two different designers to come up with slightly different designs, both in 3NF. For example, this design depends on treating solo artists as bands in their own right so that you can identify what artist performs what song. An alternative approach could be to have a songArtist bridge entity and treat bands as artists or to have two separate bridge entities, songArtist and songBand, depending on whether the song is by a single artist or a band of multiple artists.

Another consideration is the label attribute. Any given label will produce multiple albums, so there is a potential to have a separate label entity in the event that more than just the name of the label is to be included. However, given that an album is produced by exactly one label and only the name of the label is needed for this database, we can leave the structure as is and consider it a denormalization step that can make the database more efficient.

This structure does, however, allow us to account for compilation and "best of" albums relatively easily, because the association between the artist and the album depends on the songs, rather than on the artist. Another advantage is that the track number of each song on a given album could be tracked. Because the track number depends on both what song it is and what album it is on, a nonkey field can simply be added to songAlbum, as shown in Figure 4.5.

songAlbum	
PK,FK1	songId
PK,FK2	albumId
	trackNumber

Figure 4.5 Adding a trackNumber to the songAlbum entity

FINAL STEPS

The final step is to identify the data type for each attribute in each entity. While the exact data types you will use are dependent on the RDBMS that will handle the database, generic data types can be used at this point. The generic types can be converted to specific data types when you are ready to build the tables. The attributes needed to define each table can also be identified. For example, a title must be included for each song, but you might not have a URL to use for the video. For this example, we will consider the following:

- We have already identified the naming convention for tables (singular in camelCasing). We will use the same conventions for field names.
- All primary keys will be integers.
- Required fields are in bold.
- Nonkey data types will be strings, dates, or numbers, depending on the data the field will hold.
- We include the maximum field size for string columns, e.g., STRING(25) for a text field that will store a maximum of 25 characters.
- We will split the artist's name into first name and last name.

In list format, the final version of the database looks like the following:

band

- bandId (PK) int
- bandName string(50)

artist

- artistId (PK)
- artistFirstName string(25)
- artistLastName string(50)

song

- songId (PK) int
- songTitle string(100)
- videoUrl string(100)
- bandId (FK) int

album

- albumId (PK) int
- albumTitle string(100)
- label string(50)
- releaseDate datetime
- price float(5,2)

bandArtist

- bandId (PK, FK) int
- artistId (PK, FK) int

songAlbum

- songId (PK, FK) int
- albumId (PK, FK) int

Figure 4.6 shows the ERD for the final database.

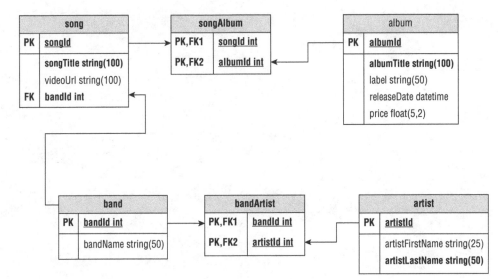

Figure 4.6 The final normalized ERD diagram

When you start using SQL to create a database, you will find it useful to have a schema like this to refer to as you write the code to build the tables.

SUMMARY

In this lesson, you walked through the process of putting together a database design. You started with a database that identified four separate entities (album, song, band, and artist) and normalized those attributes to create the foundation for a relational database with six tables.

The structure presented in this lesson is a good starting point, but because normalization is as much art as science, some parts could be different. In the long run, the goal is to get a database as close to 3NF as possible and be able to justify areas where the structure may not be fully normalized. More important, novice software developers must understand how a database is structured so that they can write programs that retrieve data from an existing database.

PART II

Applying SQL

PART I

Lesson 5
Working with MySQL Server

Up to this point you have been learning about relational database theory. Now it is time to get your hands dirty and turn theory into practice. This lesson will walk you through installing a tool that will let you enter and run SQL code. This includes installing a database, MySQL, as well as MySQL Workbench, a database management application.

Learning Objectives

By the end of this lesson, you will be able to:

- Install the MySQL database server and client
- Use a command-line interface to connect to MySQL Server
- Install the MySQL Workbench database management application
- Identify the main MySQL Workbench interface elements
- Use the Schemas panel to view database details
- Create a database from a SQL script
- Execute a SELECT query

MySQL INSTALLATION

MySQL is a relational database management system (RDBMS) that runs as a server providing multi-user access to multiple databases. This section will cover the steps of installing MySQL. During installation, you will be asked to set the MySQL **root** user password.

IMPORTANT! Do *not* forget your root password. If you forget it, you won't be able to use your tools.

MySQL's installer will be used for the installation. It installs everything needed for MySQL development and makes the 32-/64-bit decision for you.

Step 1: Get the Download

Browse to the MySQL download page at dev.mysql.com/downloads/windows/installer. If necessary, scroll down a bit until you see the downloads, similar to what is shown in Figure 5.1, which shows two options.

Either download works. The first item listed is smaller because it fetches the necessary resources from the Web during installation. This means that the initial download is fast, but the installation process will take longer and require an Internet connection throughout the process. The second includes all necessary resources. It will take longer to download, but once it is saved to your computer, you can install MySQL without being connected to the Internet. Choose the option that works best for you and click the appropriate Download button.

Step 2: Skipping the Login

The MySQL site uses a bit of a dark pattern next. The installation process wants you to believe that you need an account to download the software. While you can create an account if you think it will be useful to you, you can click the "No thanks, just start my download" link under the login buttons (as shown in Figure 5.2) and save the file to a known location on your computer.

Figure 5.1 The MySQL download page

Step 3: Starting the Install

When the download is complete, open the downloaded file to start the installer. This will be either `mysql-installer-community-[version].msi` if you downloaded the full version or `mysql-installer-web-community-[version].msi` if you downloaded the web version.

After the installation process starts, you will be prompted for a setup type, as shown in Figure 5.3. Select **Developer Default** in the left column.

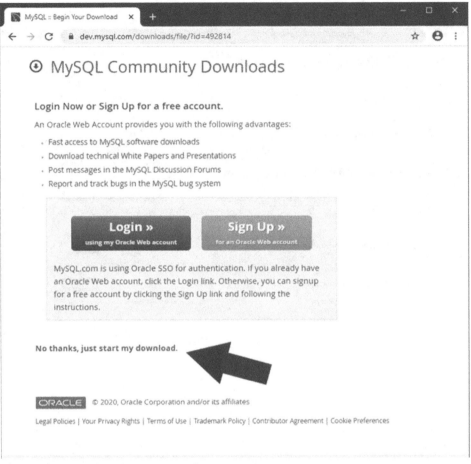

Figure 5.2 Skipping the account sign-up

The installer will automatically check for problems, such as missing utilities or path conflicts. If you see an error, you will need to resolve the error before continuing the installation. For example, the installer may identify other software that must be installed first, such as Microsoft Visual Studio.

Step 4: Tool Selection

You should be presented with a screen listing the MySQL tools, as shown in Figure 5.4. Review the tools to be installed. You should see MySQL Server and MySQL Workbench included in the list, but it also includes connectors for a variety of languages, documentation for the current version of MySQL, and sample files that you can use to experiment with MySQL.

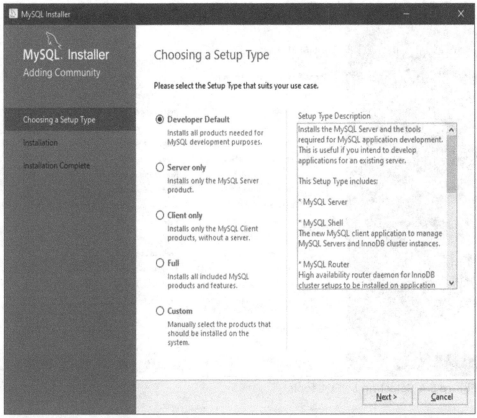

Figure 5.3 Selecting the setup type

Click Execute and relax. Installation takes a while. As the installation proceeds, you will see components being checked off the list.

If you see errors associated with any of the components, wait until everything else is installed and click the **Try Again** link for that component. If it fails a second time, click the **Show Details** button and scroll down if necessary to see the details of the error. Use that error message to research options to get help. You can also review MySQL's official instructions at dev.mysql.com/doc/mysql-installation-excerpt/5.7/en to help with problem solving.

Step 5: Product Configuration

After everything is installed, the process will move onto product configuration. You should be greeted with a screen similar to Figure 5.5.

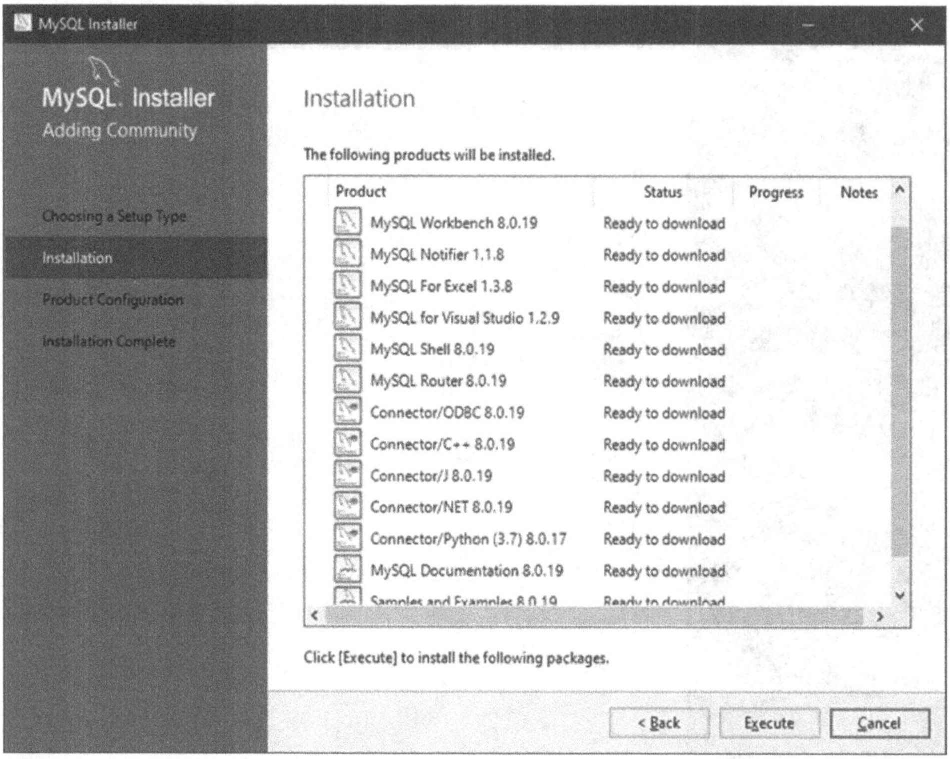

Figure 5.4 Selecting MySQL tools

This screen presents you with the products that will be configured. If you selected additional items, then you might see them listed on your screen. Simply click Next to continue to the configuration process.

For the most part, default options are sufficient. The following are a few specific options for configuring:

- Under High Availability, use the default option **Standalone MySQL Server / Classic MySQL Replication,** as shown in Figure 5.6.

- Under Type And Networking, use the default options for **Development Computer With TCP/IP,** using the port number **3306,** and open the Windows firewall port (see Figure 5.7).

- For Authentication Method, use the **Legacy Authentication method.** The stronger password encryption is a better option if you are running MySQL Server on a remote machine or if you are using sensitive data. For what you are doing within this book, you don't need that level of encryption. Figure 5.8 shows the option to select for your authentication method.

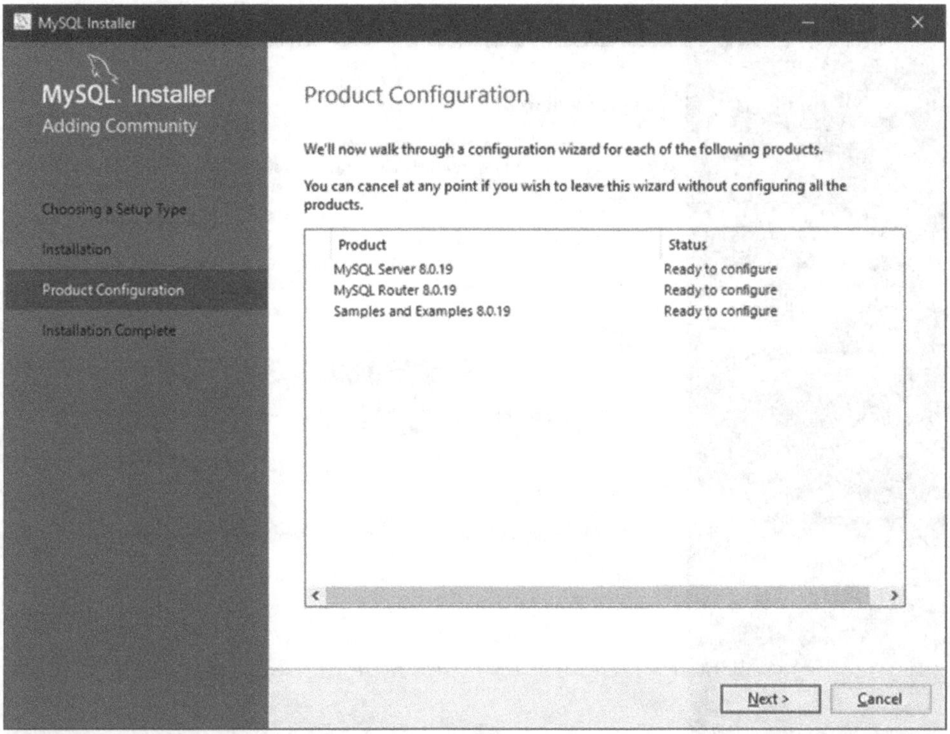

Figure 5.5 The Product Configuration screen

- Under Accounts And Roles, you will need to define a password for the root account, as shown in Figure 5.9. The root account allows the user to do anything in the database, so in a typical installation that would include many users, this password should be extremely secure. In this case, you are doing a local install that only you can access, so a simple password is fine.

NOTE Take note of this password! You will need it later when you open MySQL.

- MySQL will run as a Windows service, and the default option to use the Windows Service named **MySQL80** and the standard system account are fine. You can see these configuration settings in Figure 5.10.

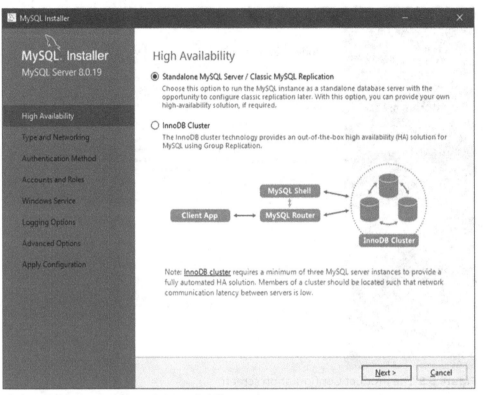

Figure 5.6 Selecting the High Availability option

After all configuration options have been defined, you will see the Apply Configuration screen similar to what is shown in Figure 5.11. Click **Execute** from this window.

You should receive a message that the configuration was successful with each item shown in Figure 5.11 being checked as completed. The buttons at the bottom of the window will be replaced with **Finish** button, which you can click to continue.

NOTE If you don't see the change just described, then review the feedback presented, look over the configuration options again, and research ways to solve the problems.

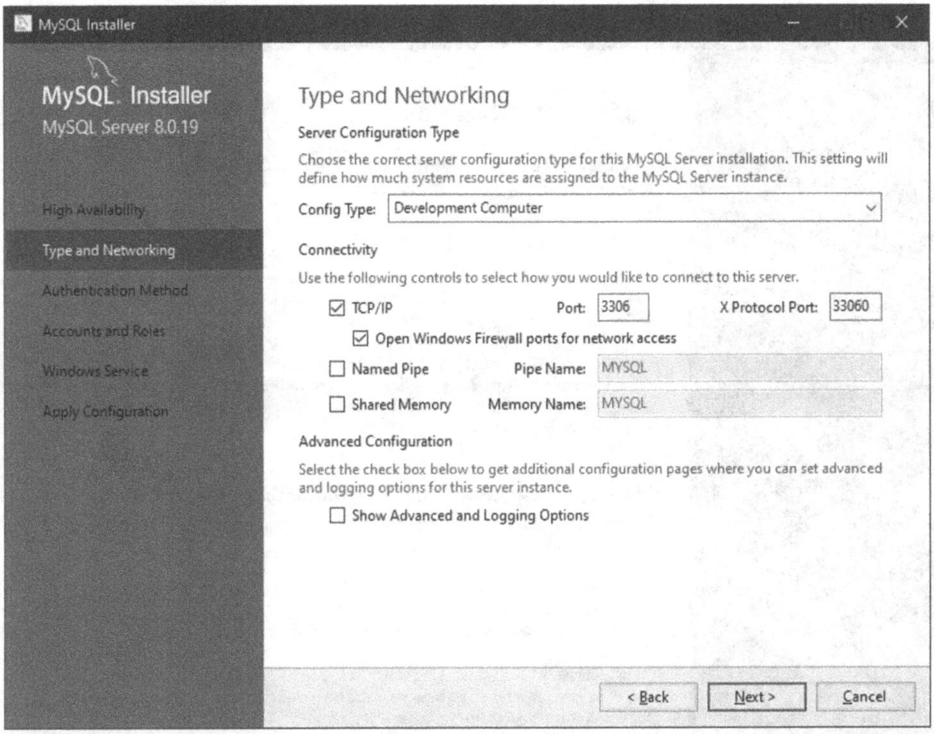

Figure 5.7 Selecting the Type And Networking options

Step 6: MySQL Router Configuration

The installation wizard will return to the Product Configuration window and show that the configuration for MySQL Server is complete similar to Figure 5.12.

Clicking the **Next** button will open the MySQL Router Configuration options, as shown in Figure 5.13. This is used only for managing a database cluster, so we won't change anything here.

The installation wizard will again return to the Project Configuration window. Click **Next** to continue. You will be prompted to connect to the server. At this point, a local MySQL Server should already be running. Enter the password you created for the root account, as shown in Figure 5.14, and then click **Check** to verify that you can connect to the server.

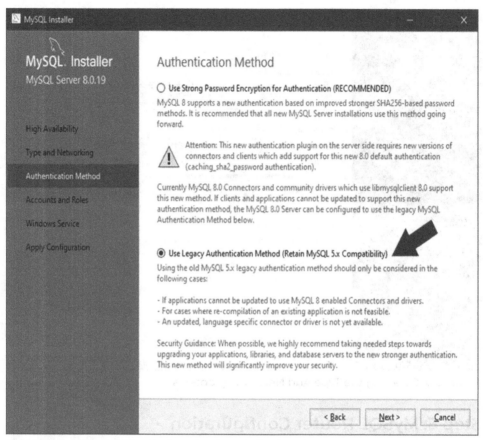

Figure 5.8 Selecting the Authentication Method option

If everything is set up correctly and you entered the correct password, you will see a "Connection succeeded" message, as shown in Figure 5.15.

Click **Next** to continue to the Apply Configuration screen, as shown in Figure 5.16. Then click **Execute** to apply the configurations you just defined.

The installation wizard will install the samples and examples files and confirm that the configuration is complete. Upon completion, the two items in Figure 5.16 should be checked off, and the buttons at the bottom of the page will be replaced with a Finish button. Click **Finish** to return to the Product Configuration window, which should look similar to Figure 5.17.

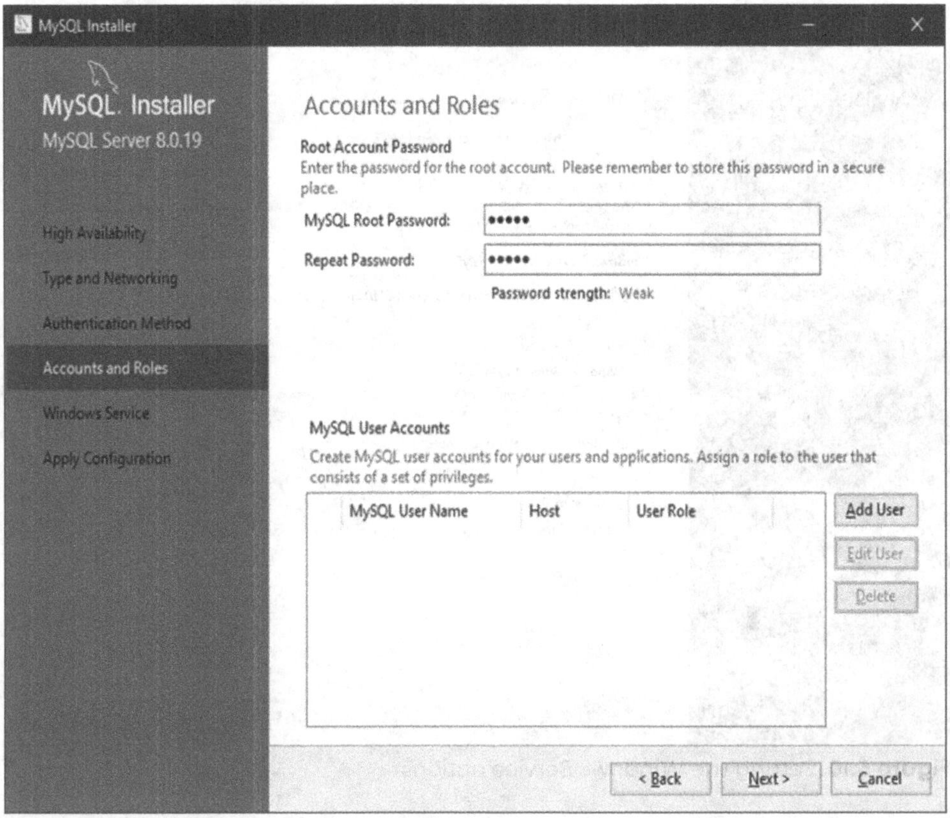

Figure 5.9 Setting the root account password

From the Product Configuration window, click Next to complete the installation. The final step shown in Figure 5.18 confirms that the installation is complete. Uncheck the boxes if you do not want to open MySQL Workbench or the MySQL shell immediately. You can then click **Finish** to close the installation wizard.

Installation and configuration are complete. You have now installed the following:

- The MySQL database server
- The MySQL shell, which is a command-line query interface
- MySQL Workbench, which is a GUI query interface and schema browser
- Documentation
- Samples
- MySQL connectors for various programming languages

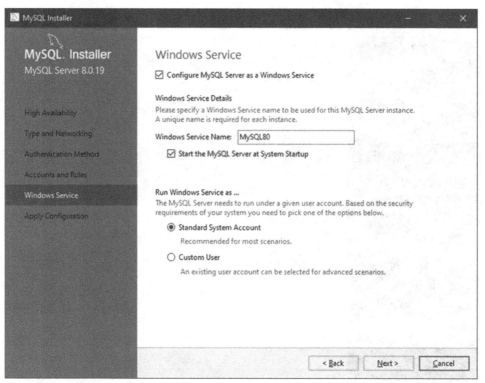

Figure 5.10 Setting the Windows Service options

MySQL NOTIFIER

The MySQL data server is configured to start when your computer boots up and always runs in the background. You should also install the MySQL Notifier. It is not required, but it is a helpful tool that gives you more control over whether MySQL is running. Download it from `downloads.mysql.com/archives/notifier` and install it using the default settings.

The Notifier installs a system tray icon that shows the status of existing MySQL database servers and allows you to start and stop them. Figure 5.19 shows a menu similar to what you should see when clicking the tray icon.

> **NOTE** Note in Figure 5.19 that the menu to the left is the submenu shown when you highlight the Actions option on the main Notifier menu.

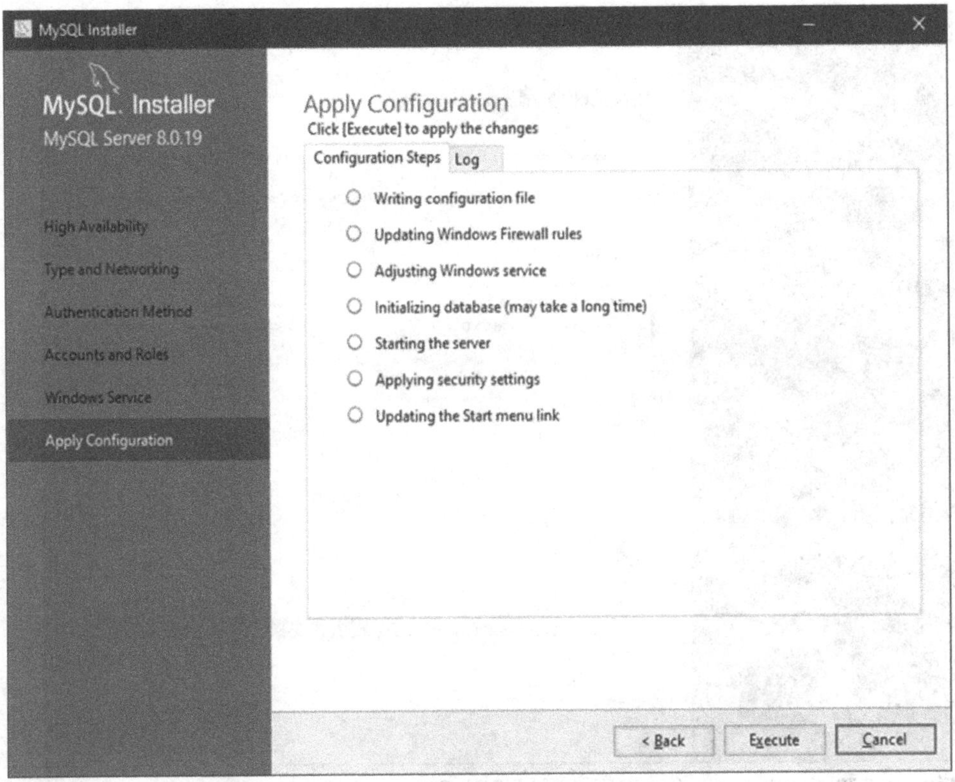

Figure 5.11 Applying the configuration options

COMMAND-LINE INTERFACE

You can use a command-line interface to verify that MySQL is installed and that you can connect to it. The MySQL Server installation includes both a basic command-line interface (MySQL Command Line Client) and a graphic user interface (MySQL Workbench). You can use either tool to perform exactly the same tasks, and in most cases, you can decide which tool makes the most sense.

You can open the MySQL Command Line Client from the Windows Start menu and then enter the password if prompted to do so. You will then see a command window with a `mysql>` prompt similar to what is shown in Figure 5.20.

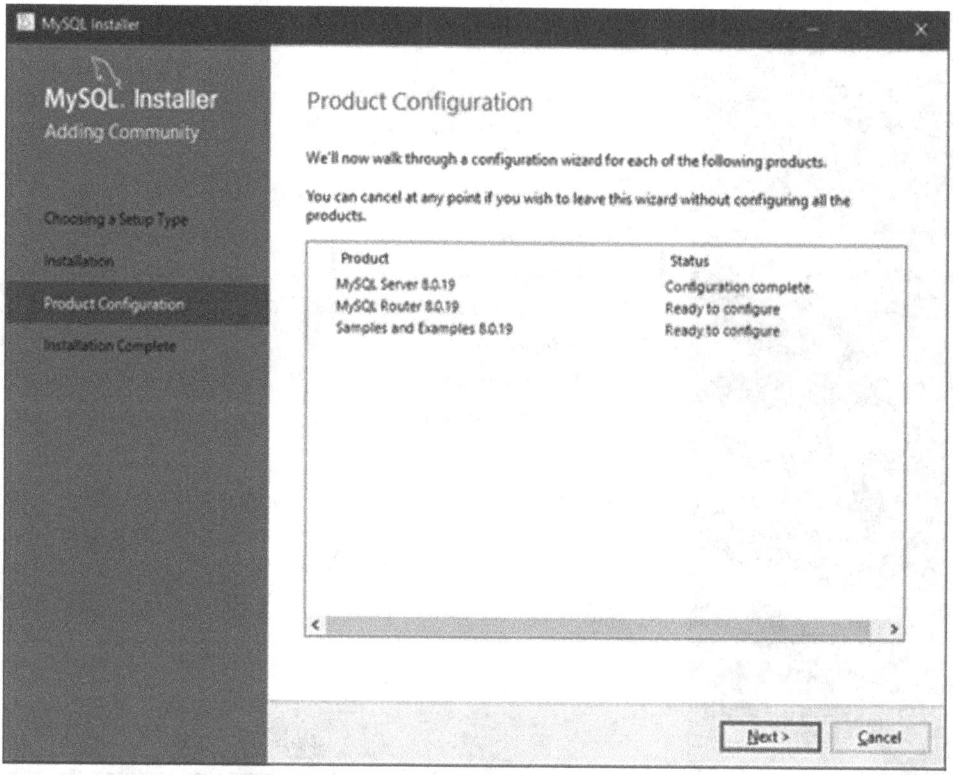

Figure 5.12 Product configuration of MySQL Server complete

As noted by the MySQL welcome statement, commands end in a semicolon (;) or \g. In this book, a semicolon will be used to end each command. Enter the following command into the window:

```
show databases;
```

This command will list all the existing databases currently managed by MySQL, as shown in Figure 5.21.

This list includes metadatabases that MySQL uses to track information about itself and how it is being used, as well as sample databases that you can use to practice using MySQL. You will create your own databases later in this lesson.

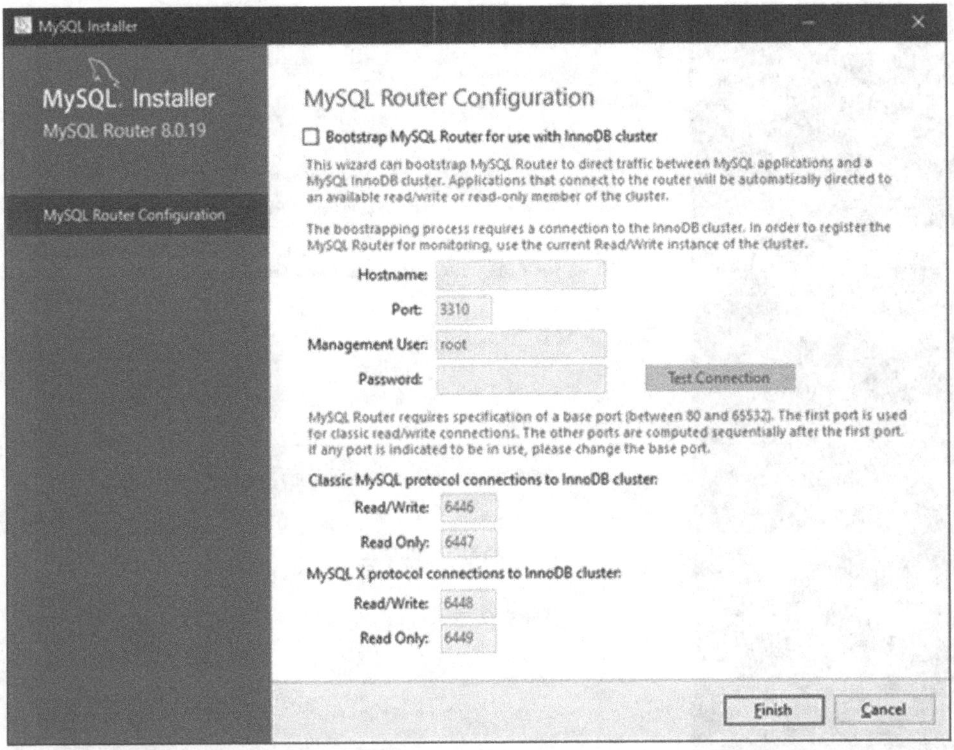

Figure 5.13 MySQL Router Configuration options

If you were able to connect to MySQL and view the existing databases, you are good to go at this point. Exit MySQL by entering `quit;` or by simply closing the command-line window.

GETTING STARTED WITH MySQL WORKBENCH

MySQL Workbench is a database management application. It allows you to connect to a database server, view the server's databases, and execute queries against those databases. It also provides a graphical interface that can generate queries based on interface actions. You don't always need to write queries by hand.

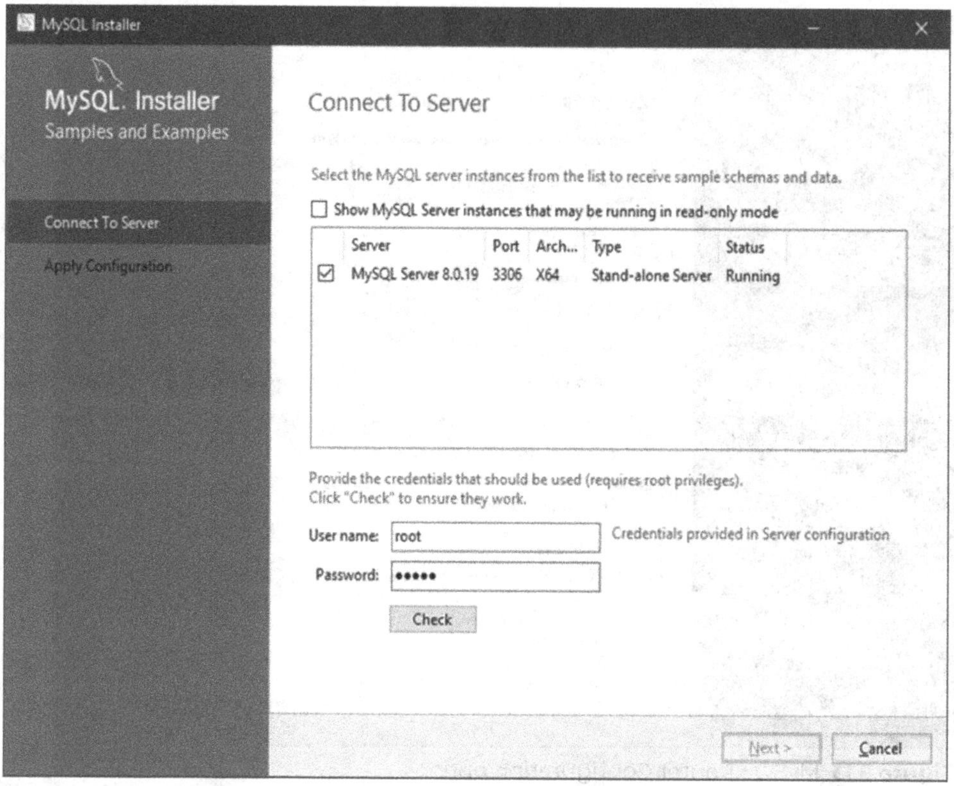

Figure 5.14 Connecting to a server

You can connect to any MySQL server by providing its hostname, port, and credentials. Once connected, you can do the following:

- Create databases and manage schemas, including tables
- Manage security for users, roles, and permissions
- Back up and restore databases
- Execute SQL

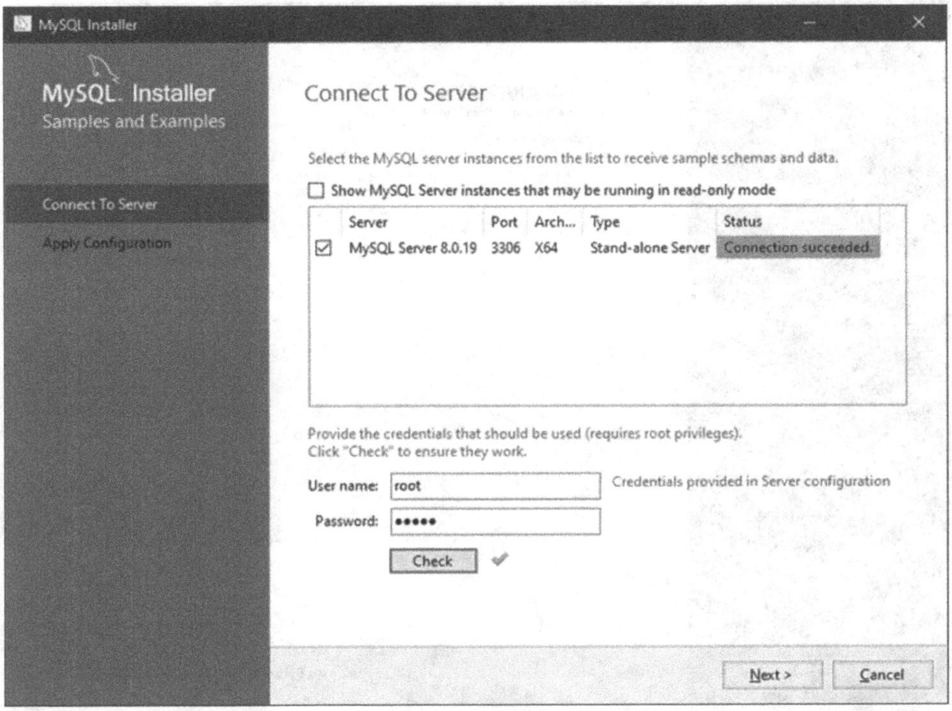

Figure 5.15 "Connection succeeded" message

Before continuing, you must have gone through the previous sections to install MySQL and test it so that you can connect to a local MySQL Server using a root account. Once you've confirmed your installation of MySQL is working, you'll be ready to continue, where you will do the following:

- Identify the main MySQL Workbench interface elements
- Use the Schemas panel to view database details
- Create a database from a SQL script
- Execute a SELECT query

NOTE MySQL Workbench was installed as part of the MySQL installation.

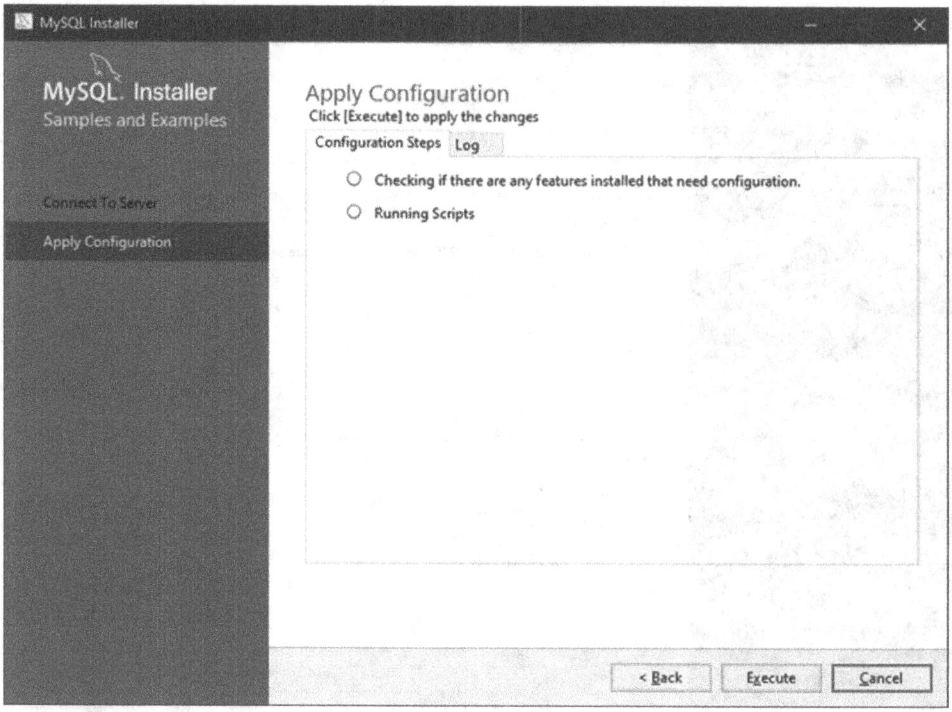

Figure 5.16 The Apply Configuration window

Use MySQL Workbench

After opening MySQL Workbench, you should see the MySQL Workbench home screen, with a button for your server's setup, as shown in Figure 5.22.

If you have already used MySQL, you may see those connections as well. If there are no connections, add one with the values shown:

```
**Local instance MySQL80**
(User) **root**
(Service) **localhost:3306**
```

Click the Local Instance MySQL80 button, as shown in Figure 5.22. You'll be asked for your root password. Enter it and click **Ok** to log in. Once logged in, you will see the MySQL Workbench environment, as shown in Figure 5.23.

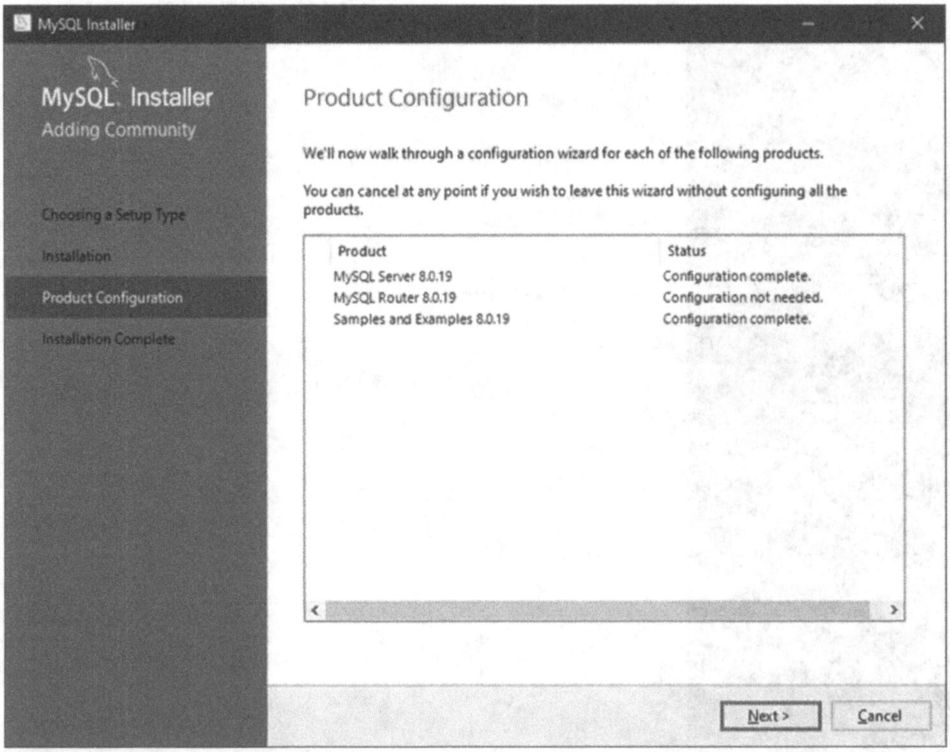

Figure 5.17 The updated Product Configuration window

This window resembles an IDE in that there are multiple panes that allow you to manage different parts of the database from the same place. Like an IDE interface, you can resize the panes to meet your needs or use the View menu to hide or show specific panels.

The main pane in the center (with the tab Query 1) is the query pane itself, and this is where SQL commands (which are typically called **queries**) can be run.

Under that pane is the Output pane. This is where the results of a query will appear.

In the left pane, you will find an Administration tab and a Schemas tab. The Administration tab includes tools to manage server connections, users, and permissions, as well as import and export tools. The Schemas tab allows you to manage the databases themselves. In fact, within MySQL, the term *schema* is simply another term for a database.

If you click the Schemas tab, as shown in Figure 5.24, you will see at least some of the database you may have seen when you tested a command-line interface with MySQL.

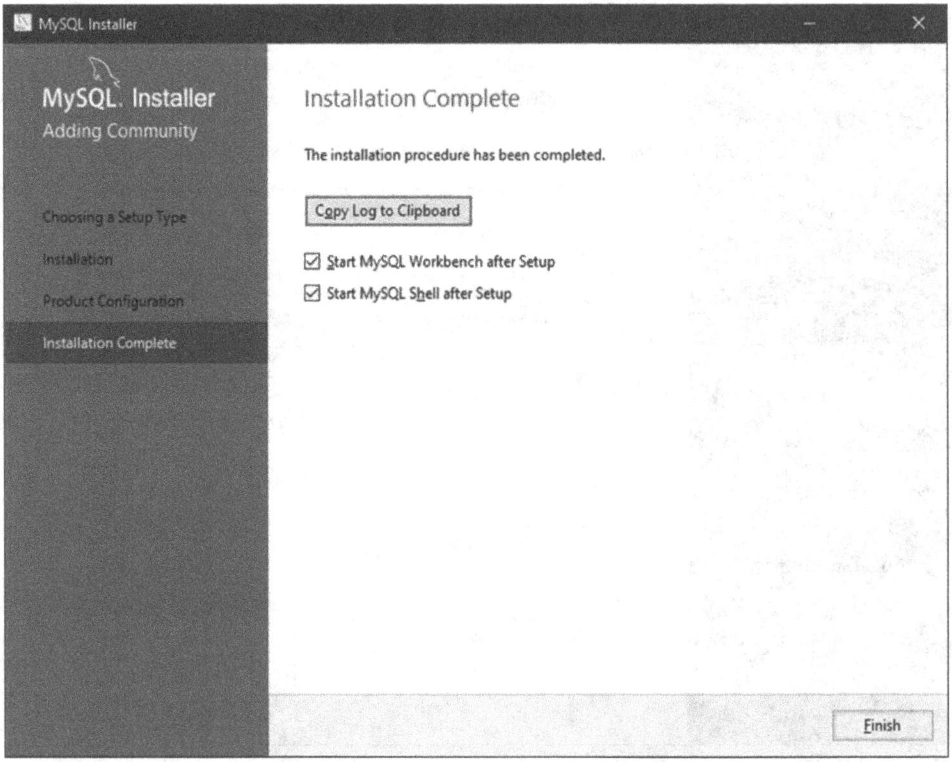

Figure 5.18 Installation complete

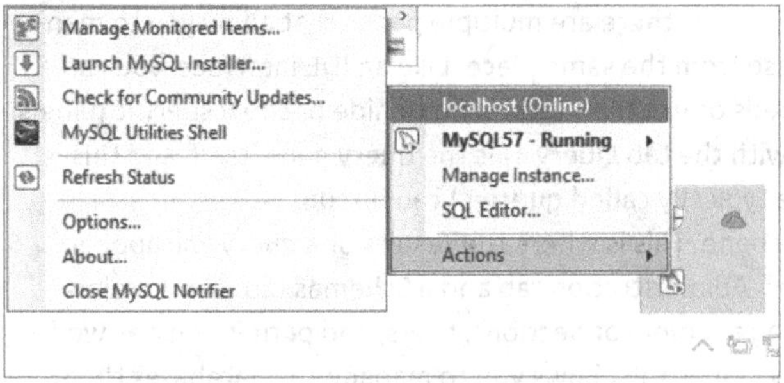

Figure 5.19 The SQL Notifier menu

In this figure, you can see schemas named sakila, sys, and world. The sakila and world databases are sample databases that can be used to practice using MySQL. The sys database is a read-only system database that MySQL uses and manages internally. Other meta-databases like mysql are typically hidden in Workbench because they are not meant to be accessed by human users.

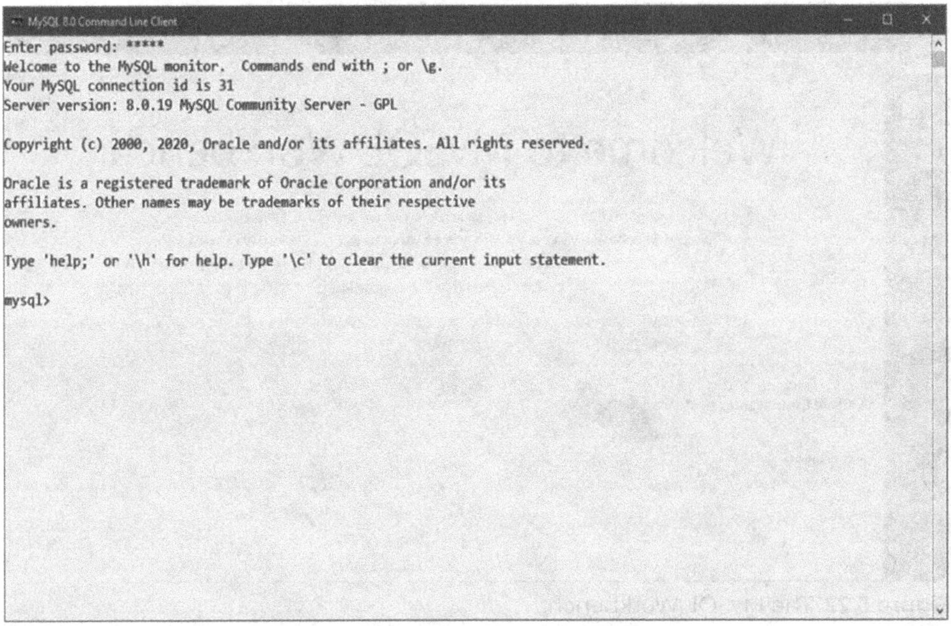

Figure 5.20 The MySQL Command Line Client prompt

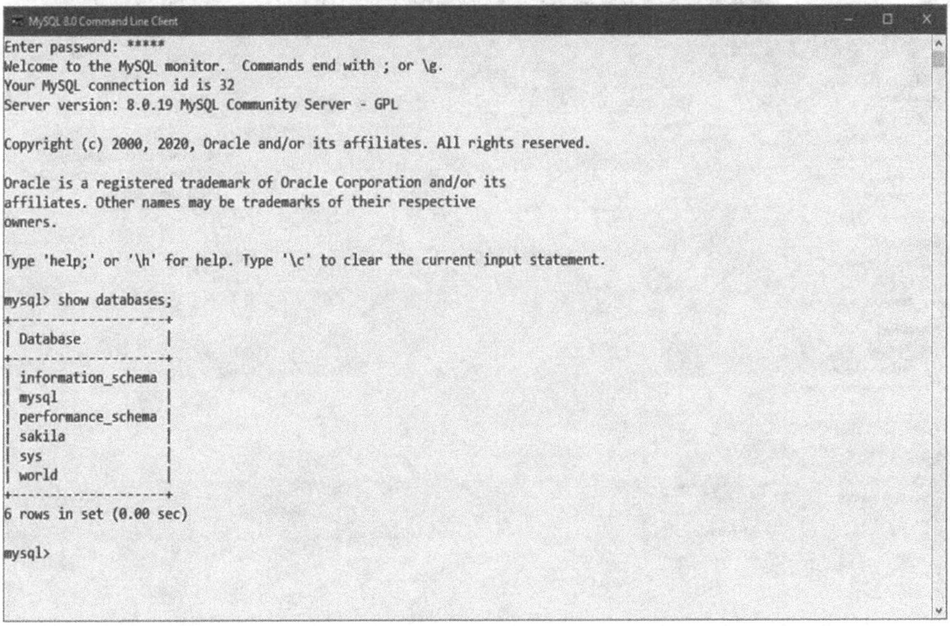

Figure 5.21 List of all existing databases currently managed

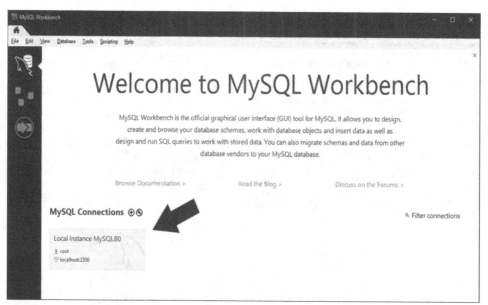

Figure 5.22 The MySQL Workbench

Figure 5.23 The MySQL Workbench environment

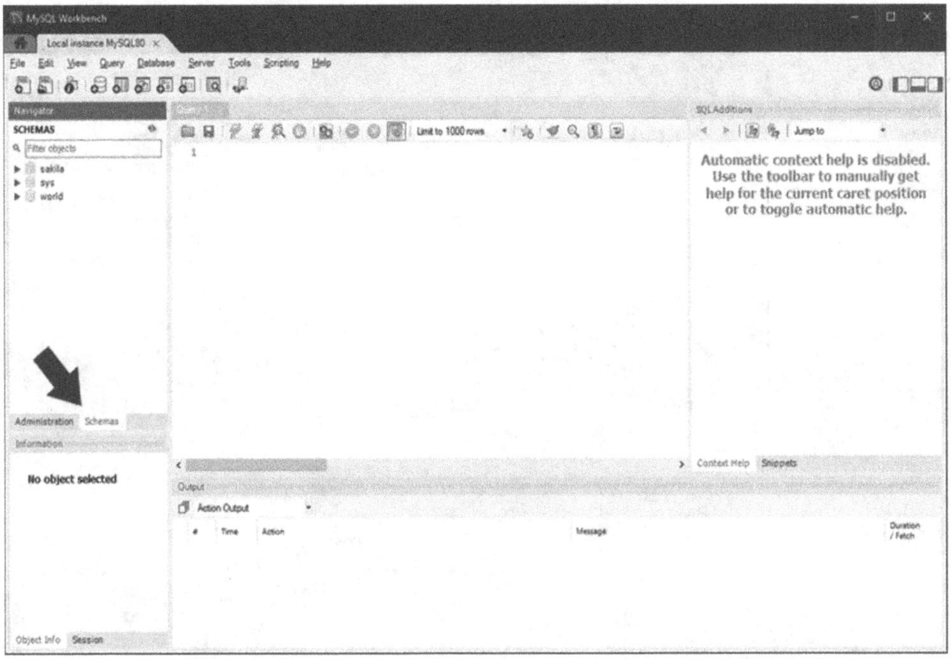

Figure 5.24 The MySQL Workbench Schema tab

Clicking the expand arrow next to a schema will allow you to view the tables, views, stored procedures, and functions associated with that schema. In Figure 5.25, the world schema has been expanded, so you can see that it includes tables for city, country, and countrylanguage. You also see that the city table includes columns for ID, Name, Country-Code, District, and Population.

Run a Test Command

You can run a quick command just to be sure that you are connected. In the Query 1 panel, enter the following command on the first line:

```
show databases;
```

Click the Execute button on the toolbar in the query window. The button looks like a lightning bolt and is shown in Figure 5.26. The results will appear in a new subpane in the query panel. The Output panel will confirm that the command executed correctly. If this query ran correctly, then you are set up in MySQL Workbench.

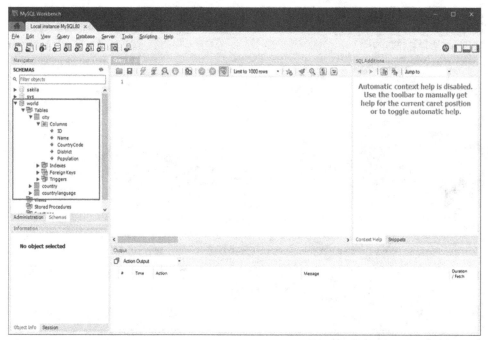

Figure 5.25 The expanded city table

SUMMARY

In this lesson you set up MySQL and the tools you'll use to access it throughout the rest of this book. This includes the server itself, the MySQL Notifier, and the MySQL command-line interface.

You also opened and saw the MySQL Workbench, which is a powerful tool for working with MySQL servers and their databases. It allows you to do the following:

- Visually explore databases and their structure
- Write SQL
- Execute SQL
- Fetch and explore data
- View query statistics such as execution time and rows affected

With your foundation in database knowledge and your tools in place, you are now ready to dive into the syntax of SQL.

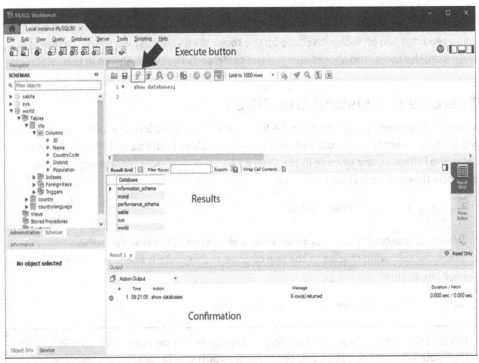

Figure 5.26 The executed query

EXERCISES

The following exercises are provided to allow you to experiment with concepts presented in this lesson:

Exercise 5.1: Running the Tools

Exercise 5.2: Listing the Cities

Exercise 5.3: Small Cities

> **NOTE** The exercises are for your benefit. The exercises help you apply what you learn in the lessons. Please note that these are to be done on your own, and thus solutions are not provided.

Exercise 5.1: Running the Tools

If you read this lesson without setting up the tools, then your first exercise is to download and install the tools. You should also run the commands that were shown in this lesson.

Exercise 5.2: Listing the Cities

In MySQL Workbench, click World in the list of schemas on the left side of the window. This will select that schema to work with and display its tables in the pane. With it selected, enter the following line of code in the Query 1 panel. This should replace any text that might be there already from the lesson.

```
select * from city limit 0,100;
```

When you execute this line of code, what is displayed in the results panel?

Make the following change to the line of code and execute it again. How does this change the output?

```
select * from city order by Name limit 0,100;
```

> **NOTE** Don't worry if you don't understand what this code is doing. This is SQL code that you will learn about as you continue through this book.

Exercise 5.3: Small Cities

In the previous exercise, you should have seen a list of 100 cities displayed in two different manners. This time enter the following code and see how it changes the output:

```
select Name, CountryCode, Population
from city
where Population < 10000
order by Population;
```

When you execute this line of code, what is displayed in the results panel? Change the test to look for large cities.

Lesson 6

Diving into SQL

SQL is designed as a universal language to manage data stored in a relational database management system. In this lesson, we will look at some of the features of SQL before jumping into using it heavily to manage data. This includes the topic of working with null values and how to use them in MySQL. We will also take a look at indexing.

Learning Objectives

By the end of this lesson, you will be able to:

- Discuss the origins of SQL
- Demonstrate syntax features of core SQL, including the use of letter case, spaces, quotation marks, and semicolons
- Explain what a null value is in a dataset
- Add null values to a table
- Explain how relational databases use indexes to improve retrieval efficiency
- Identify design features that can affect indexes

INTRODUCTION TO SQL

SQL stands for Structured Query Language, and it can be pronounced like "sequel" or using the letters S-Q-L. It is designed to work with any relational database management system (RDBMS), which includes MySQL Server, Microsoft SQL Server, and Oracle Database, among others. Because it works universally across RDBMSs, programming languages such as Java, C#, and PHP support the use of SQL to retrieve and manage data stored in an RDBMS.

As relational database systems have become more prominent and widespread, RDBMS-specific versions of SQL have been developed to extend its abilities and improve performance within those systems. As an example, Microsoft SQL Server uses a variation named Transact-SQL (T-SQL), while Oracle Database uses Procedural Language/SQL (PL/SQL). However, the standard SQL statements covered in this book will run regardless of the system you are using. The SQL variations are typically significant only for complex processes or for data types that are not universally handled across RDBMSs, such as DateTime.

Because standard SQL is universal, it is useful for any software developer in any language to understand how to use it. Having a solid foundation on the basics will also make it easier for you to learn any of the variants, should the need arise in the future.

In SQL, the term **statement** is often used to refer to any complete command. The term **query** technically refers to a statement that retrieves data from a database, but many developers also use the term *query* to refer to any SQL statement. GUIs like MySQL Workbench also typically use *query* in this way.

Additionally, similar to programming languages, SQL has a set of **keywords** that are reserved words with special meaning to SQL. For example, SELECT is a SQL keyword used to select data. Keywords are used within statements and queries. A final term to be aware of is **clause**. A clause is simply a section of a query.

SQL SYNTAX

SQL follows a rigid syntax, where each keyword and clause must be in a specific order. The most common statement is a SELECT statement, which is used to retrieve data from one or more tables in a database. The SELECT statement uses the following basic syntax:

```
SELECT field1, field2, field3
FROM table1
WHERE criteria
ORDER BY field1, field2;
```

This statement will retrieve the data from *field1*, *field2*, and *field3* whose values match the criteria statement in the WHERE clause in a table named *table1*. The results will be sorted by the values in *field1* and *field2*. Each of these clauses must be included in this order for the query to work correctly.

As SQL statements are introduced in this lesson, keep in mind that the order in which the clauses are written is part of the overall syntax, and a statement may not work if the syntax is not strictly followed.

Semicolon

A standard SQL statement always ends in a semicolon, although RDBMS-specific versions may vary.

- MySQL requires the use of a semicolon or /g at the end of each statement.
- Recent versions of T-SQL (used in Microsoft SQL Server) do not require semicolons, but they do support them, so it doesn't hurt to include them, especially since SQL Server documentation normally includes a warning that semicolons may be required in future versions.

Basically, it's a good idea to always end a SQL statement with a semicolon, even if it may not be strictly necessary. If you are using MySQL and do not include a required semicolon or /g, it will simply wait patiently until you provide the appropriate syntax.

> **NOTE** In this book, a semicolon will be used at the end of every SQL statement.

Line Breaks and Indents

Neither line breaks nor indents are required within SQL statements, although you are encouraged to use them to improve readability in the code. As an example, a table could be created using a single-line command that ends with a semicolon.

```
create table `Client` (ClientId char(36) primary key, FirstName varchar(50)
not null, LastName varchar(50) not null, BirthDate date null, Address
varchar(256) null, City varchar(100) null, StateAbbr char(2) null, PostalCode
varchar(10) null, foreign key fk_Client_StateAbbr (StateAbbr) references
State(StateAbbr));
```

However, this format is hard to read, and as a result, it's hard to verify that all the expected fields are included and set up correctly. The same statement can be written with each field on a separate line, making it much easier to verify that the table's settings are correct.

```
CREATE TABLE `Client` (
    ClientId CHAR(36) PRIMARY KEY,
    FirstName VARCHAR(50) NOT NULL,
    LastName VARCHAR(50) NOT NULL,
    BirthDate DATE NULL,
    Address VARCHAR(256) NULL,
    City VARCHAR(100) NULL,
    StateAbbr CHAR(2) NULL,
    PostalCode VARCHAR(10) NULL,
    FOREIGN KEY fk_Client_StateAbbr (StateAbbr)
        REFERENCES State(StateAbbr)
);
```

You can also see how much more readable the statement is with the line breaks. This is why each clause of a SQL statement is typically written on a separate line. For example, the following SELECT statement will retrieve data from named fields in the named table:

```
SELECT FirstName, LastName, Address FROM Client;
```

If the statement is written on two separate lines, it can be easier to read.

```
SELECT FirstName, LastName, Address
FROM Client;
```

SQL statements can be complex. When you are writing your own SQL statements, you should add line breaks and indents where they make the most sense to you. If you are working on a team, remember that the line breaks and indents should be meaningful to anyone else who will read the code.

NOTE You might look at the examples of line breaks presented here and think they are easy to understand with or without the line breaks. While that might be true for shorter queries like these, longer and more complex ones will be much easier to understand with the breaks. It is best to simply get in the habit of adding the formatting regardless of the query's complexity.

Letter Case

SQL keywords are not case-sensitive, so you can use SELECT, select, or even SeLect interchangeably when typing SQL statements. That said, it is common to write keywords in ALL CAPS as a way of distinguishing keywords from other parts of a statement, mainly to improve readability.

For example, in the following statement, it is easy to see that SELECT and FROM are keywords.

```
SELECT FirstName, LastName, Address
FROM Client;
```

When referencing parts of a database, it is best practice to use the same case used to name tables, fields, keys, or other objects in the database. Different development teams use different naming conventions within a database, and while some SQL servers are not case-sensitive at all, others require that names use the same case used in the database itself. In addition, if you are using a case-sensitive language like Java or C# to access data in a database, you will need to use a case consistent with that system.

In other words, if a table is named Client in the database, you should use Client in SQL statements that reference that table. A statement may run even if you use client instead, but it's good to get in the habit of matching the case for database objects.

> **NOTE** It is useful to know and follow the team's naming conventions so you don't have to guess.

Commas

SQL uses commas to separate like objects in a series. For example, in the following CREATE TABLE statement, there is a comma after each field definition:

```
CREATE TABLE `Client` (
    ClientId CHAR(36) PRIMARY KEY,
    FirstName VARCHAR(50) NOT NULL,
    LastName VARCHAR(50) NOT NULL,
    BirthDate DATE NULL,
    Address VARCHAR(256) NULL,
    City VARCHAR(100) NULL,
    StateAbbr CHAR(2) NULL,
    PostalCode VARCHAR(10) NULL,
    FOREIGN KEY fk_Client_StateAbbr (StateAbbr)
        REFERENCES State(StateAbbr)
);
```

Similarly, the following SELECT statement names three fields in the SELECT clause, using commas to separate the field names:

```
SELECT FirstName, LastName, Address
FROM Client;
```

Note that there is no comma after the last item in the series. If you were to add a comma after `Address` in the last statement, SQL would interpret `FROM` as another field name and throw an error because there is no field named `FROM`.

Spaces

SQL requires a space after each logical word in a statement, including keywords and object names. Spaces are not required around commas or parentheses, although they can be used to improve readability.

As a general best practice for any RDBMS, names of objects like tables, fields, and indexes should not include spaces. However, if the database designer included them anyway, the name of that object must be inside quotation marks, like this:

```
SELECT "First Name", "Last Name", Address
FROM Client;
```

Quotation Marks

When used, quotation marks may be double quotes (" ") or single quotes (' '), as long as they are used in pairs. In the previous example, you saw how quotes can be used to iden-tify fields whose names include spaces or other unusual characters, but they are also used to identify string values when adding data to a table or when using a string in a conditional statement. For example, if you wanted to find a client with the last name Smith, either of the following queries will work:

```
SELECT FirstName, LastName, Address
FROM Client
WHERE LastName = "smith";
```

or

```
SELECT FirstName, LastName, Address
FROM Client
WHERE LastName = 'smith';
```

You cannot, however, mismatch them. The following query will not work:

```
SELECT FirstName, LastName, Address
FROM Client
WHERE LastName = 'smith";
```

Spelling

We've saved spelling for the last of the SQL syntax topics because it's both the most obvious and the most common source of errors. All keywords must be spelled correctly, and all object names must be spelled exactly as they appear in the database (even if they might be misspelled in the database). If a statement doesn't run as expected, double-check the spelling of every word.

WORKING WITH NULL VALUES

In addition to understanding the syntax for SQL statements, a critical concept to understand in any database is that of null values. When a table is defined, one of the key characteristics of any field is whether a value is required for that field in each record. A variety of terms are used for that concept, including *required* (which means that there must be a value for every record), *nullable* (which means that a value is optional), and the official definition NOT NULL, which means that a value is required.

Essentially, a null value is an empty value: it contains no value at all.

Null vs. Zero

null is not the same as zero. Zero is a value, while null is not. Let's look at a couple of examples.

Suppose you are working on a candy vendor's database, and the Product table includes a Price field. Table 6.1 contains a few sample records.

Table 6.1 Product Table for Candy Vendor's Database

ProductID	ProductName	Price
001	Cherry Lollipop	0.5
002	Honey Bit	0
003	Chocolate Toffee	

In looking at the Product table, if a customer purchases a cherry lollipop, they will be charged 50 cents. From the table, you can see that honey bits are free because their price is 0. The question to ponder, however, is how much would the store charge for a chocolate toffee?

Because the price is null, we don't know what its price is. Furthermore, we don't know why there is no value. It could be that the data entry person forgot to include the price.

It could also be that for whatever reason someone chose not to determine the price when the product was added to the database. If we want to sell chocolate toffees, though, a real price will eventually need to be defined.

Nullable Fields

When a table for any RDBMS is defined, it must be determined whether each field in that table is nullable. The decision mostly lies in how the database will be used. Remember, a nullable field is a field that makes it optional to include a value.

The one hard and fast rule about nullables is that **any field used in a primary key is *not* nullable**. Entity integrity requires that there is a value for every primary key, and this is a default setting when a field is defined as a primary key.

All other fields in a table are nullable by default. In other words, if you don't set a NOT NULL attribute on a field, SQL will allow users to leave those fields empty. This means that it is part of the database designer's job to identify which fields are nullable for the purposes of that database when they define the tables.

In the previous candy shop example, the price field should be set to NOT NULL, if only so that it is known how much to charge customers for each type of candy. ProductName should also be required, to avoid entries like this:

ProductID	ProductName	Price
004		3

In this example, you can see that product 004 costs $3, but we have no idea what the name of the candy is. In this example, it should be clear that all three fields should have the NOT NULL attribute. The first field, ProductID, cannot be null because it is the primary key. Neither of the other fields should be null for the reasons just described. The table could be defined with the SQL code shown in Listing 6.1.

LISTING 6.1

Creating the Product Table

```
CREATE TABLE Product (
    ProductID INT NOT NULL PRIMARY KEY,
    ProductName VARCHAR(25) NOT NULL,
    Price FLOAT NOT NULL
);
```

The code in Listing 16.1 creates a new table called Product that is defined to have three fields: ProductID, which is a string and the primary key; ProductName, which is a variable string of characters up to 25 characters long; and Price, which contains a floating-point number. All three field definitions include NOT NULL. The inclusion of NOT NULL would not prevent someone from adding a price of 0, but it would prevent someone from not including the product name or the price.

In other cases, though, nulls are more acceptable. For example, consider a personal contact list, like the one provided for most smartphones. Because these are for individual use, all the fields are nullable, allowing the user to enter only the data they have and need for each person or company in the contact list. Here are some examples:

- John contacts Mary about an item she is selling on Craigslist. Mary wants John's phone number so that she can text him (and know who it is when he texts her), but she doesn't need a last name or address. That entry will include only a first name and a mobile number, with possibly a note about the item on Craigslist.

- Jack wants to add a plumbing company to his contact list so that he can call the company when he needs service. He doesn't have a specific person's name, so he enters the name of the company in the Company field, leaving the name fields empty. He then adds the company's phone number and website but leaves all remaining fields empty.

- Marcos finds and buys a collectible baseball card from a seller on Etsy. He wants to keep track of the seller in case they have more cards he wants to buy in the future, so he adds the seller's first and last name to his contact list, along with the name of the store, the email address, and the store's web address.

- Elizabeth adds a good friend to her contact list, including the person's first and last name, mailing address, email address, birthday, and phone number.

All of these examples include null values for fields that are not important for that entry. When designing a database, you must consider the purpose of the database itself, as well as the importance of each field to individual users of the database.

Consequences of Null Values

Choosing to allow nulls in a table has consequences on the efficiency of the database. A phone's contact list likely does not use a relational database structure (even though the concepts are the same), so it can allow as many nulls as the user wants. However, relational databases are highly structured, so nulls have more impact.

RDBMSs set aside storage space for each field in a record, based on the defined size of the field. For example, an INT field requires 4 bytes of space, while a DATETIME field requires 8 bytes of space. Taken individually, these seem like very small numbers, but when you consider that a table can have hundreds of thousands of records, it multiplies quickly.

Note that this is **reserved** space, not used space, and the RDBMS will use that much storage regardless of the actual value stored in each of those fields, and even if nothing is stored there. Each time a record is added that includes a null value, space is set aside that will not be used.

In the long run, if there are relatively few nullable fields in a table and if the data is likely to use fields even when they are nullable, this is a reasonable trade-off, because it allows data to quickly be added to those fields if they are to be used in the future.

If, however, a table has a considerable number of nullable fields, it might be worth creating a separate table that includes only those fields, allowing users to create records with those fields only as necessary.

As an example, let's extend the candy shop database. Most of the products are straightforward with a name and a price. Let's branch out the inventory a bit to sell stickers as well as candy. For candy, we want to know the name and price, but also the flavor, the size of the package, the texture, and other candy-related attributes. For stickers, we might want to know the size, but flavor and texture would be irrelevant. If all these attributes are put into one table, each record will include many null values, as shown in Table 6.2.

Table 6.2 Product Table for Candy and Stickers

ProductID	ProductName	Price	Weight	Width	Length	Flavor	Texture
001	Cherry Lollipop	0.5	1.5 oz	null	null	cherry	Hard
002	Honey Bit	0.75	3 oz	null	null	Honey	Chewy
003	Chocolate Toffee	2.50	6 oz	null	null	Chocolate	Hard
004	Sponge Bob	.99	null	3	3	null	null
005	Robot	.99	null	2	4	null	null
006	Red hots	1.19	1.2 oz			Cinnamon	hard
007	Unicorn	1.19	null	4	3	null	null

To solve this problem, the attributes could be split across multiple tables. The Product table would include the attributes common to all products.

- ProductID
- ProductName
- Price

We would also have a Sticker table, which includes only the attributes relevant to stickers.

- ProductID

- Width
- Length

Finally, we would have a Candy table that includes only the attributes for candy.

- ProductID
- Flavor
- PackageWeight
- Texture

You can see that each table includes ProductID to identify what specific product each record describes, but the result is that the number of null values is reduced by using only the table that is appropriate for each specific table. Table 6.3, Table 6.4, and Table 6.5 show the data from reorganizing Table 6.2.

Table 6.3 New Product Table

ProductID	ProductName	Price
001	Cherry Lollipop	0.5
002	Honey Bit	0.75
003	Chocolate Toffee	2.50
004	Sponge Bob	.99
005	Robot	.99
006	Red hots	1.19
007	Unicorn	1.19

Table 6.4 Sticker Table

ProductID	Length	Width
004	3	3
005	2	4
007	4	3

Table 6.5 Candy Table

ProductID	PackageWeight	Flavor	Texture
001	1.5 oz	cherry	Hard
002	3 oz	Honey	Chewy
003	6 oz	Chocolate	Hard
006	1.2 oz	Cinnamon	hard

Understanding nulls and how they impact the efficiency of a database is an important part of database design. However, as with the denormalization processes, you have to consider how much efficiency reducing null fields gives us. If you routinely pull related data from two or more tables, it might make more sense to combine those fields into a single table to improve the amount of time required to retrieve data.

Using the example given in this lesson, if the majority of the stock is candy while stickers make up a very small percentage, it might make more sense to put everything in one table anyway, knowing that some of the fields will be empty. That would improve the amount of time it takes to retrieve data from that table, while trading off the amount of empty space that the nulls will create in storage.

WORKING WITH INDEXES

Indexing is a complex but essential process in any relational database system. Experienced database developers can use indexing to improve the efficiency of retrieving data from a database, but new database designers must understand what it is and how it affects design decisions.

Chances are good that at some point in your life, you have used the index of a book to find out more information on a topic included in that book. Most textbooks include an index of major topics, for example, but recipe books use indexes to help users find recipes based on ingredient or cuisine, while atlases use indexes to help users find specific maps based on location name.

A good index has the following characteristics:

- **It is easy to find.** In printed books, the index is typically at the end of a book, but it might also appear at the beginning. It is never located in a random location somewhere in between.

- **It includes only values the user is likely to look for.** A textbook index will tell you what pages to look at for specific concepts, but it does not include every word that might appear in the book. Consider how long an index would be if every instance of the words *the* or *that* were included or if a cookbook index listed every recipe that includes salt.

- **It has the indexed values sorted in a way that makes it easy for the user to find specific values.** This sorting is normally in alphabetical order. The index values might also be grouped so that subtopics appear under major topics, such as countries in Europe or recipes that use beef as a major ingredient.

Relational databases use index values in much the same way and for the same reasons. Before covering the indexing of fields, let's first talk about storage.

Primary vs. Secondary Storage

For relational databases, it is important to understand the difference between primary storage and secondary storage. Primary storage includes memory or RAM in a computer system, which tends to store data for only a short time. Secondary storage includes things such as hard drives, flash drives, and solid-state drives, which can store things for a longer period of time including when the computer is not powered. For the sake of clarity, the term *memory* will be used to refer to a system's short-term storage and *storage* to refer to long-term storage.

Memory is the space where a computer holds the instructions and data it is currently working with. Memory is significantly faster than other forms of storage, which makes it ideal for those things that the computer needs immediately. However, memory is one of the most expensive components of a computer system, so how much is available is often limited to reduce those costs. For this reason, there is normally significantly less memory in any computer system than there is storage. Memory is also volatile, which means that as soon as the program using memory closes (or the computer is shut down for any reason), all data and instructions stored in memory are erased.

Storage, especially hard drive storage, is relatively inexpensive these days. It is also nonvolatile, meaning that anything we store there will be available the next time the computer is logged into or an application is started, barring physical damage to the drive. This makes it ideal for storing data that will be wanted for use again later. However, storage can be very slow both in terms of writing/recording data and retrieving data that is stored on the disk, which makes it less than ideal if users need to retrieve data from a large database.

To improve a database's efficiency, you need to take advantage of both technologies: data most likely to be used should be in memory when the database opens, while data that isn't likely to be used remains in storage until it is needed.

This is where indexing fields come into play.

Indexing Fields

Just like the index entries in a book tell you what page to look at for a specific term, map, or recipe, an indexed field tells the database where to look for related data when the user wants to retrieve data using an indexed value. When fields are indexed, the database engine is being told that the values in those fields need to be loaded into memory (only to the extent that memory is available) when the database opens. Unindexed data remains on the hard drive until it is retrieved by the user, and only the relevant data is retrieved at that time.

A gut reaction to finding out that data stored in memory can be accessed more quickly than data in storage is to try to index *everything*, so that everything is always immediately available to the user. Remember, though, that most systems have a limited amount of memory. If you try to add too much content to memory, that extra content goes into a **swap disk**, a portion of the hard drive that most systems use for memory overflow. Because that process puts the data back on the hard drive, you end up back where you started, and you gain no efficiency with that approach. In essence, this is equivalent to a textbook's index that includes every word that appears in the book, including minor words like *the* and *that*.

Instead, an experienced database designer will look at how each field is used and index only those fields that users are most likely to need. For example, in a customer database, a user is more likely to look up people by their last name than by their first name, so the last name field is a better candidate for indexing than the first name is. The database engine will automatically load all values in an indexed field into memory when the database is opened, making it faster to find those values. Users can retrieve the first name associated with any given last name more quickly than if the last name was not indexed.

This approach does not prevent users from searching by first name rather than by last name, but the search will be slower because the database will have to search through storage rather than through memory.

Default Indexes

By default, an RDBMS automatically indexes key fields, including primary and foreign keys. These fields are essential for retrieving data across tables, and indexing those fields helps make queries more efficient.

Guidelines state that the order of the rows themselves is not important in a table. While no table should be set up so that the values in one row are dependent on another row in the same table, indexes typically control the order in which the rows appear in a search.

When a table's indexed fields are loaded into memory, the database sorts the values in the order as specified in the index definition—alphabetically if the indexed values are strings or numerically if the values are numbers. This means that the values are in a predictable order, making searches much more efficient. You can see this when you retrieve data from a table without specifying a sort order: regardless of the order in which the records are added to a table, the results will default to being sorted by the primary key values.

This sort order serves the same purpose as putting a book's index in alphabetical order. As a user, you do not have to look at every value in the index to find the one you want. Chances are good that you skip through the index by column or page until you are close to what you want to find and then pay attention to individual values only when you are within a few records of the term you are trying to find. Database searches work the same way, using common search algorithms to quickly find specific values, rather than reading each individual value until it finds the one it needs.

This is also why having too many indexed fields slows down the write processes of saving new data to the database. Indexed fields are stored in a predictable order to make it easier to retrieve data based on those indexes. Every time a new indexed value is added to a table, the database must reorganize the data in that table to match the expected order. Adding records using an auto-incremented key helps improve write efficiency because it guarantees that each new record will be added at the end of the primary table.

Unique and Nonunique Indexes

Indexes can also be used to control allowable values in a column. For example, a primary key index by definition verifies that each value used in that field is unique within the table. A foreign key index does not check for the unique quality, but it does automatically enforce referential integrity. This means that whenever a value is entered as a foreign key, the database engine will confirm that the value references the primary key of a related table, which helps improve data integrity across tables.

Unique indexes can also be used in other fields. For example, you might want to verify that no two people in a list of employees have the same Social Security number or email address. This can be done by setting a unique index on the field that should be unique, without also defining that field as a primary key.

An index on a last name field, however, should not be unique, mainly because many people can have the same last name. If last name is frequently used for searches, the database designer can add a nonunique index to that field.

> **NOTE** For more information on indexing fields for relational databases, see Ben Nadel's blog post, "The Not-So-Dark Art of Designing Database Indexes: Reflections From An Average Software Engineer," found at bennadel.com/blog/3467-the-not-so-dark-art-of-designing-database-indexes-reflections-from-an-average-software-engineer.htm. You can also search the online documentation for specific RDBMSs for details of how to define indexes when defining tables in the database.

SUMMARY

SQL is designed to be a very human-friendly language (for English speakers, anyway), and most of its syntax rules are easy to use. While there are a few variations from one version of SQL to the next, the guidelines here will apply to virtually every version of SQL.

When creating your database's tables, it is important to review the fields that will be included. Because fields in a table can contain null values by default, a design review should include determining whether fields should be tagged as NOT NULL so that a value is required. For primary key fields, NOT NULL is required. Additionally, if your fields might contain a large number of null elements, then you might need to redesign your database to reduce the amount of storage space needed.

Relational databases generally require large amounts of long-term storage, which means that searching through databases is inherently slow. Efficiency of searches can be improved by assigning indexes to frequently used fields.

Data in indexed fields, including primary and foreign keys, is automatically loaded into memory when a database is opened, meaning that the database can quickly access those values to make searches more efficient. In addition, database designers can identify additional fields to act as indexes, especially fields that users are likely to access frequently.

EXERCISES

The following exercises are provided to allow you to experiment with concepts presented in this lesson:

Exercise 6.1: Remember Your Lines

Exercise 6.2: Contact Questions

Exercise 6.3: Missing Contact

> **NOTE** The exercises are for your benefit. They help you apply what you learn in the lessons.

Exercise 6.1: Remember Your Lines

Reformat the following line of SQL code so that it is presented with a cleaner presentation that is easier to read.

```
SELECT Last, First, Email, MobileNumber FROM Contacts WHERE Age >= 21 ORDERED
BY last, First;
```

Exercise 6.2: Contact Questions

Look at the following table:

```
CREATE TABLE Contact (
    ID    INT NOT NULL PRIMARY KEY,
    Last  VARCHAR(50) NOT NULL,
    First VARCHAR(40),
    Age   INT,
    Email VARCHAR(100),
    MobileNumber VARCHAR(12),
    HomeNumber   VARCHAR(12),
    WorkNumber   VARCHAR(12)
);
```

Answer the following questions:

- Which fields are required in the table?

- What is the data type of each field?

- What is the longest last name that can be stored in a field?

- Is age required?

- What would need to be changed to make WorkNumber required?

Exercise 6.3: Missing Contact

In this lesson, you learned about null fields. The database for contacts shown in Table 6.6 allows for null fields. This database, however, has a lot of wasted space. Redesign this database so that it uses multiple tables in a manner to be more efficient with storage space.

Table 6.6 Contacts Table

ID	Last	First	Email	MobileNumber	HomeNumber	WorkNumber	Fax
c001	Jones	John	john@bogus.com	317-555-1212	317-555-1213	317-555-1214	null
c002	Buford	Bob	Null	null	null	415-555-3333	null
c003	Smith	Sam	Sam@bogus.com	null	415-555-1212	null	null
c004	Michaels	Mitch	Null	415-555-2121	null	null	null
c005	Andrews	Adam	Adam@bogus.com	698-555-1212	null	null	null
c006	Finkel-stein	Fred	Null	null	217-555-4340	null	null
c007	Black	Brent	brent@bogus.com	null	null	null	null

Lesson 7

Database Management Using DDL

SQL comes in two flavors: data definition language (DDL) and data management language (DML). DDL is used to define and create the database and its structure, including tables, indexes, and relationships between tables. DML is primarily used to manipulate the data stored within that storage. In this lesson, we will look closely at DDL and create a database based on a defined ERD.

Learning Objectives

By the end of this lesson, you will be able to:

- Create and use a database

- Generate a list of available databases in an RDBMS

- Delete an existing database from an RDBMS

- Describe available data types and apply them to fields in a table

- Generate a list of tables in the selected database

- Show the structure of an existing table

- Update a table's structure

- Delete a table from a database

- Generate a script that can be used to rebuild/copy a database structure

- Use foreign keys to define relationships between tables

- Understand referential integrity

- Identify and compare options for deleting or updating values in primary key fields

DATABASE MANAGEMENT

As a new developer, you are not likely to have to manage data at the database level, but it is useful to understand the steps if you choose to work on your own database or in the event you do become a database administrator later.

DDL statements are used to create and manage databases. Regardless of the relational database management system (RDBMS) that will manage the database, a database must be created before tables and data can be added to it.

Create a New Database

When we create a database in an RDBMS, we are essentially creating a storage area that will hold all of the information about that database, including its objects (such as tables, views, and stored procedures) and the data itself. The RDBMS will impose some limits on the contents of a database, including the fact that each object within a database must have a unique name. This means that two tables cannot have the same name, nor can a table and a view have the same name.

This does, however, allow tables to have the same name in *separate* databases on the same RDBMS, just as fields can have the same name in separate tables in the same database.

SQL naming requirements are reasonably relaxed, and the only real requirement is that an identifier must start with a letter. Otherwise, we recommend the following:

- Include only letters, numbers, or the underscore character (_) in any identifier.
- Avoid spaces, dots, or other unusual characters.
- Follow established naming conventions for identifiers that include multiple words.

Let's create a new database that will store the data related to a bookstore's inventory. Creating a database in SQL is straightforward. After connecting to the RDBMS, run this command:

```
CREATE DATABASE books;
```

The CREATE DATABASE command will create the database. In this case, the database will be called *books*.

> **NOTE** You can enter the previous command in the Query window of MySQL Workbench.

List Existing Databases

A list of all available databases in the current RDBMS can also be generated. You can do this using the following command:

```
SHOW DATABASES;
```

Executing this command will list not only the databases you (and your team) have created but also RDBMS-managed databases that contain data related to the RDBMS setup, users, and other configurations.

If you are using MySQL and you execute this command, you might see a list of tables like what is shown in Figure 7.1, which shows the command executed in MySQL Workbench.

Except for the books database that was created in the previous section, the databases shown here are system databases that include data MySQL needs to function correctly, as well as sample databases that are normally included in a MySQL installation. You may see different tables if you are using an existing SQL server or a different RDBMS.

> **NOTE** As a general rule, you should avoid using any database you did not create!

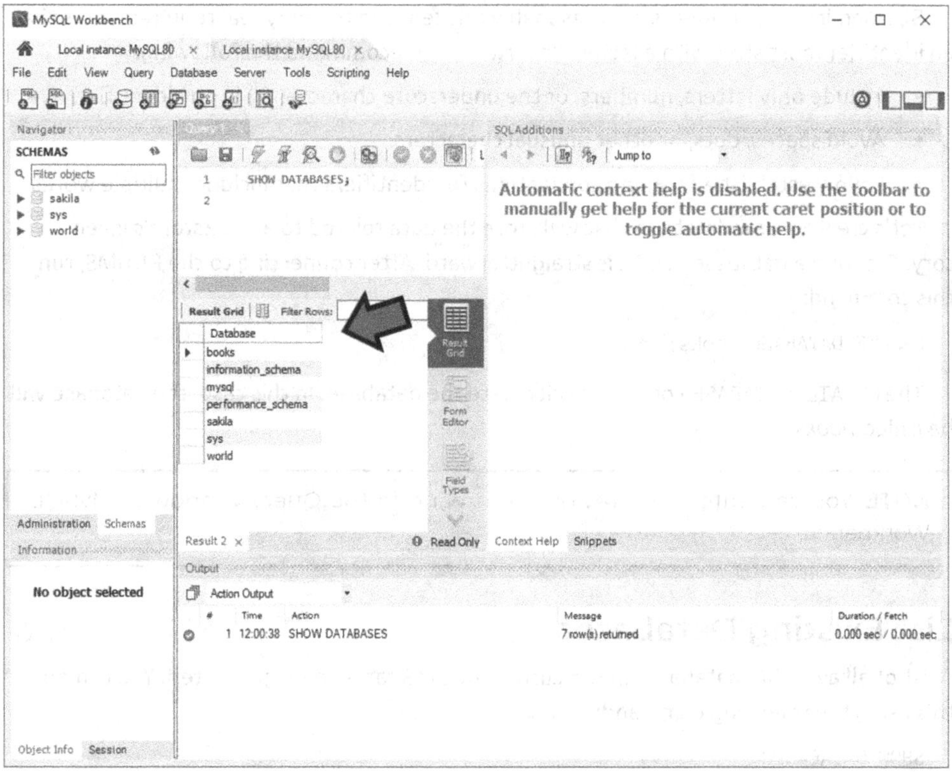

Figure 7.1 Executing SHOW DATABASES in MySQL Workbench

Use a Database

You can think of an RDBMS as an office building, where each office is a different database. When you first walk into the building (or log into the RDBMS), you are in a virtual waiting room. This means you need to tell the RDBMS which database you want to use, in the same way you would need to walk into the appropriate office to conduct your business.

The USE command will let you select a database. This command is used as follows:

```
USE books;
```

If you aren't sure what database you are using (or if you don't remember telling the RDBMS which database you want to use), you can run this command as many times as you want. In fact, you should include a USE statement at the beginning of any SQL script to be certain that the script will run in the correct database.

If you decide later that you want to use a different database in the same RDBMS session, simply run another USE command with the name of the other database.

Delete an Existing Database

You can delete an existing database using the DROP DATABASE command. This command is followed with the name of the database you want to remove. The following illustrates how to delete the books database created earlier:

```
DROP DATABASE books;
```

This Is Dangerous! When you delete a database, you delete *everything* in that database, including all tables and data.

To avoid an error that might be generated by deleting a database that doesn't exist, you can modify the comment. You can use the IF EXISTS phrase to check for a database before trying to delete it:

```
DROP DATABASE IF EXISTS database_name;
```

This command will check to see if database_name exists. If it does, it will be dropped. If it doesn't exist, nothing happens.

In a working, server-based RDBMS, only users with specific administrative permissions can delete databases to prevent accidental catastrophes, and even then, permissions to delete databases are defined only when they are needed.

You are working with your own, local database as you go through this book. You will be able to delete any database you create. You should, however, have scripts to rebuild a database you delete accidentally.

MySQL DATA TYPES

Once you have a database created, you'll need to create tables. To create tables, you'll need to create fields. You'll also need to be able to define fields in order to create them. As you saw in the previous lesson, creating fields includes assigning a data type.

While any RDBMS supports basic data types like strings and numbers, each RDBMS approaches this topic slightly differently, using different names and requirements. It is worth looking specifically at how MySQL supports different data types for field values. If you use another RDBMS in the future (such as Microsoft SQL Server or Oracle Database), you should research that RDBMS's approach to data types.

Data Types

As in programming languages, data types define the ways in which data values stored in a database can be used. With any RDBMS, one of the requirements at the table level is that each column in a table be defined to use *one* data type, and values stored in that column must be appropriate for that data type.

In this lesson, you will learn about the most common data types including the following:

- Integer types
- Decimal
- String types
- Date/time types

This list is not comprehensive, and these types can change slightly from one version of MySQL to the next. You can refer to the general MySQL documentation at dev.mysql .com/doc/refman/8.0/en/data-types.html for more information about data types.

Relational databases also tend to be more sensitive to storage requirements than general programming languages are, mainly because the data really is stored on a hard drive. As a general rule, when you select a data type for a given field, you should choose the data type that most closely meets the storage requirements for values in that field. Using a reasonably small data type will improve the efficiency of the database, both in terms of the storage space required for the data and in terms of how quickly data can be saved to and retrieved from the database.

You can change column sizes after the table has been defined, even if there is data in it. However, you should never make a column size smaller. You run the risk of losing data if you make a column smaller than the data it already contains.

> **NOTE** When in doubt, select a larger size over a smaller size when changing a column.

Numeric Data Types

Numbers can be integers or decimal values. A **signed value** allows negative and positive values while an **unsigned value** allows only positive values. Numeric data types are generally broken down between integer types, which are whole numbers, and decimal types, which can have a fractional or decimal value.

Integer Types

There are four integer types that are commonly used. These are presented in Table 7.1.

Table 7.1 Integer Data Types

Data Type	Signed Range	Unsigned Range	Storage Required
TINYINT	-128 through 127	0 through 255	1 byte
SMALLINT	-32,768 through 32,767	0 through 65,535	2 bytes
MEDIUMINT	-8,388,608 through 8,388,607	0 through 16,777,215	3 bytes
INT	-2,147,483,648 through 2,147,483,647	0 through 4,294,967,295	4 bytes

As mentioned, integer data types contain whole numbers that might be signed or unsigned. The smallest shown in Table 7.1 is a TINYINT and the largest is an INT.

Decimal Types

Numbers that might have a decimal portion can be stored in a decimal type. There are three main decimal types that you are likely to use. These are shown in Table 7.2

Table 7.2 Common Decimal Types

Data Type	Storage Required
FLOAT	4 bytes
DOUBLE	8 bytes
DECIMAL	Varies based on precision

FLOAT and DOUBLE are less precise than DECIMAL, so they should not be used where exact values are required (such as monetary calculations). Both DOUBLE and DECIMAL allow you to define the size and precision for values stored in the column, including the number of digits allowed in the value, and how many of those digits should be to the right of the decimal place. For example, the data type DECIMAL(12,4) will allow values up to 99,999,999.9999 (12 digits total, with 4 digits to the right of the decimal place). The default is DECIMAL(10,0).

> **NOTE** Be aware that the first number when defining a decimal type is the total number of digits and not the number to the left of the decimal.

String Types

String fields are used to store text values such as names or product descriptions. The most common string types are shown in Table 7.3.

Table 7.3 Common String Types

Data type	Description
CHAR(size)	A fixed-length field that can hold up to 255 characters
VARCHAR(size)	A variable-length field that can store up to 65,535 characters
TINYTEXT	A field with a maximum length of 255 characters
MEDIUMTEXT	A field with a maximum length of 16,777,215 characters
LONGTEXT	A field with a maximum length of 4,294,967,295 characters

Because CHAR is a fixed-length field, it is generally used for strings that are likely to have the same length, such as state abbreviations, ZIP codes, or other identification numbers. VARCHAR is better for storing things that are likely to have different lengths from one record to the next such as names and addresses. In both cases, a size must be specified that represents the maximum length of the strings stored in the column.

From a data storage perspective, a CHAR field will always reserve the same amount of space for each record, regardless of the value that is actually entered into the field. VARCHAR, however, will adjust the storage space required based on the current value.

Date/Time

SQL also has a special data type for storing dates and times. The common types are listed in Table 7.4. You can see that SQL provides a number of different formats that let you pick date, time, or both.

Table 7.4 SQL Date and Time Data Types

Data type	Description
DATE	A date. Default format: YYYY-MM-DD.
DATETIME	A date and time combination. Default format: YYYY-MM-DD hh:mm:ss.
TIMESTAMP	A timestamp. Default format: YYYY-MM-DD hh:mm:ss.
TIME	A time. Default format: hh:mm:ss.
YEAR	A year in four-digit format.

> **NOTE** All versions of SQL use number, text, and date/time data types, and you must assign the appropriate data type to each column when you create a table. This section has listed the most common data types for MySQL. Other versions of SQL use similar data types, but they might differ slightly in how they are used and defined.

MANAGING TABLES IN MYSQL

With an understanding of data types, you are now ready to focus on another aspect of managing and maintaining a database, which is the process of designing and defining tables that will store the data. Tables are at the heart of a relational database because they store the data in an organized way. If tables are not defined correctly, they can lead to wasted storage space and slow down data retrieval. You learned a bit about that with the discussion of nullable fields in the previous lesson. Now the focus will be on other areas related to tables, including the following:

- Creating a table in a database, including defining the fields and keys in the table
- Generating a list of tables in the selected database
- Viewing the structure of an existing table
- Changing a table's structure
- Deleting a table from a database

Create a Table

Before getting to the point of trying to code a table in SQL, you should always take the time to design the entire database on paper (real or digital), using an ERD or similar tool. Going through the design steps required to normalize and plan a database will make the SQL part of building the database much more straightforward, because you will enter the RDBMS knowing exactly what tables are needed, what fields will be in each table, what data types each field should have, and which fields should be defined as key fields. If you create tables without having all this information up front, then when you start entering data into those tables, it could be difficult to fix problems without having to delete and rebuild the database from scratch.

The following is the basic syntax to create a table:

```
CREATE TABLE tableName (
    field1 datatype,
    field2 datatype,
    field3 datatype
);
```

When a table is defined, you must include both a name and a data type for each column (field) in the table at minimum. You can also define additional parameters on individual fields, including indexes, how values are assigned to primary keys, whether the field is nullable, and any constraints that are to be applied to specific fields.

Create a simple table with the following description from an ERD:

Table name: book

Field list:

- bookId INT PK
- bookTitle VARCHAR(100) required
- numPages SMALLINT
- origPubDate YEAR

The data types for the book table were selected for the following reasons:

- bookId:
    - The primary key value will be a randomly assigned integer. INT allows for a large collection of books.
    - By default, any primary key field is also required, so there is no need to take the extra step of stating that it is required.
- bookTitle:
    - Each book has a different length title, so VARCHAR should be used instead of CHAR.
    - While it's possible that a book's title could have more than 100 characters, using 100 is a reasonable maximum for expected book titles.
    - There should be a title included for each book in the database, so this field is required.
- numPages:
    - SMALLINT was chosen here, which has a maximum unsigned value of 65,535. No book in the collection should have more than that many pages, and SMALLINT requires less storage space than INT.
    - This field is not required. There might be books in the collection for which the number of pages is unknown. In those cases, the value can be left empty.
- origPubDate:
    - This field is used to store the year the book was originally published, which may be different from the publication date of actual books in the collection.
    - Only the YEAR value is needed rather than a specific day and time.

Note that author information or format data has not been included in this table. In the design phase of creating this database, it was determined that there is a many-to-many relationship between book and author, which is reflected in separate bookAuthor and Author tables. Similarly, the format and ISBN values for a book are specific to the physical book, so this data would also appear in a different table.

Because the table is defined in an ERD, it is simple to write a SQL statement to create this table. For now, only the column names and data types are included. Listing 7.1 shows the SQL needed to create the book table.

LISTING 7.1

Creating the book Table

```
USE books;

CREATE TABLE book (
    bookId INT,
    bookTitle VARCHAR(100),
    numPages SMALLINT,
    origPubDate YEAR
);
```

In this SQL code, you can see that the USE command is applied to make sure the books database is being used. The CREATE TABLE command follows with each of the columns being defined as described in the list.

List Tables

You can verify that the table was created using the SHOW TABLES statement.

```
SHOW TABLES;
```

This command will list all tables available in the current database. At this point, if you have created the book table in the books database, the results from MySQL Workbench will look like Figure 7.2.

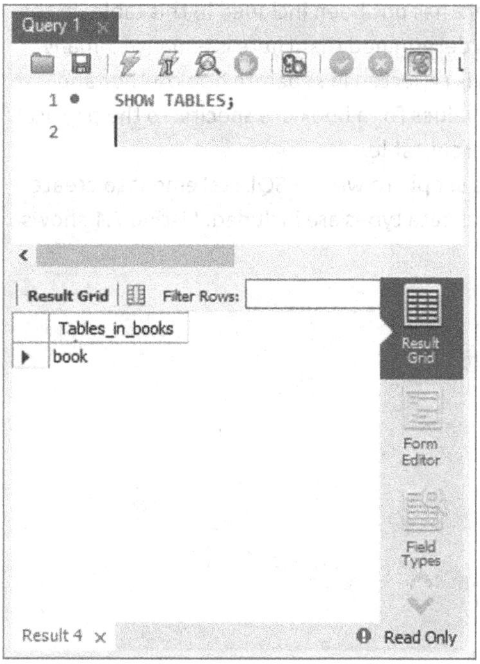

Figure 7.2 Executing SHOW TABLES

View a Table

There are many different options in MySQL for seeing how a table is structured, but the most straightforward is the DESCRIBE keyword with the name of the table. To use with the book table, you would enter this:

```
DESCRIBE book;
```

The results of entering this are shown here:

Field	Type	Null	Key	Default	Extra
bookId	int	YES		NULL	
bookTitle	varchar(100)	YES		NULL	
numPages	smallint	YES		NULL	
origPubDate	year	YES		NULL	

Note that at this point, all the fields in the table are nullable, which is the default setting. You must specify which fields are not nullable.

Change a Table

You may realize that you missed something when you first created a table. For example, you may realize later that another field is needed, that one of the fields you started with is no longer needed because of how the database is used, or that some other setting is missing, such as defining a field to be required. For this reason, SQL includes the ALTER TABLE statement. The ALTER TABLE statement will allow you to make a number of different changes to a table including the following:

- Dropping a field
- Setting a key value
- Modifying a field
- Adding a field

Dropping a Field

In looking at the table you just created, the numPages isn't really needed. The actual number of pages will depend on the format, not on the abstract version of the book that this table represents, so you can use ALTER TABLE to remove it.

```
ALTER TABLE book
    DROP numPages;
```

In this example, the ALTER TABLE statement drops (or removes) the field named numPages. If you describe the table again, the field is missing.

Field	Type	Null	Key	Default	Extra
bookId	int	YES		NULL	
bookTitle	varchar(100)	YES		NULL	
origPubDate	year	YES		NULL	

Setting a Key Value

The ALTER TABLE command can also be used to change almost any field in the table. In this case, you know that bookId should be the primary key. Ideally, you should have defined this when the table was first created, but since that didn't happen, you can change it now.

Keys (both primary and foreign) create constraints on how the fields and table behave, and they need names just like the fields do. As a matter of convention, primary key names typically start with PK and include the name of the table for which it is the primary key. In this case, the key will be named PK_book. You also have to identify what kind of constraint it is and which field(s) it applies to.

You can set a primary key on the book table using the following statement:

```
ALTER TABLE book
    ADD CONSTRAINT PK_book PRIMARY KEY (bookId);
```

If you run DESCRIBE book again, the table now includes the primary key on bookId.

Field	Type	Null	Key	Default	Extra
bookId	int	NO	PRI	NULL	
bookTitle	varchar(100)	YES		NULL	
origPubDate	year	YES		NULL	

Note, too, that the Null status for bookId changed from YES to NO in the same step. By definition, primary key fields cannot be null, so this setting is applied automatically when a field is designed as a primary key.

Modifying a Field

In the original description of the table from the ERD, bookTitle was also expected to be required. You can use ALTER TABLE to adjust that as well by using MODIFY followed by the change:

```
ALTER TABLE book
    MODIFY bookTitle VARCHAR(100) NOT NULL;
```

This will add the NOT NULL attribute to the bookTitle. Note that when a field is modified, you must modify all aspects of that field, even those that are not changing. If you once again describe the table, you will see this:

Field	Type	Null	Key	Default	Extra
bookId	int	NO	PRI	NULL	
bookTitle	varchar(100)	NO		NULL	
origPubDate	year	YES		NULL	

You can see that from the new description of the table that the bookTitle can now not be Null.

Adding a Field

The one other thing that might occur is the need to add a field. Granted, if your database was designed appropriately, this should not need to happen. To add a field, you can use the ADD statement with the ALTER TABLE command to add the field. The following adds a field called *genre* to the book table:

```
ALTER TABLE book
    ADD genre VARCHAR(20);
```

As you can see, the genre field is defined after the ADD in the same manner fields were defined when creating a table. In this case, genre will be a VARCHAR up to 20 characters. If you use DESCRIBE to view the book table again, the result should look like this:

Field	Type	Null	Key	Default	Extra
bookId	int	NO	PRI	NULL	
bookTitle	varchar(100)	NO		NULL	
origPubDate	year	YES		NULL	
genre	varchar(20)	YES		NULL	

> **NOTE** For more details on other options for changing existing tables, see TechOn-TheNet's page, MySQL: ALTER TABLE Statement, at techonthenet.com/mysql/tables/alter_table.php.

Altering Tables with Existing Data

If a table contains data, it may not be possible to modify a column. If you declare a column NOT NULL and your data contains nulls, the MODIFY operation will fail. Likewise, if you MODIFY a column to use a more restrictive data type such as VARCHAR(10) versus VARCHAR(50) and your column contains values longer than 10 characters, your MODIFY will fail. If this happens, then to force the modification, update the data to conform to restrictions and then MODIFY.

Delete a Table

If you have created a table that you no longer need, you can delete it using a DROP TABLE command.

```
DROP TABLE book;
```

You can use the SHOW command to verify that the table has been removed from the database.

```
SHOW TABLES;
```

In this case, the only table in the books database is being deleted, so the result of showing the tables is an empty set. Be aware that when you delete a table, not only is the table being removed, but so is all the data that it might have contained.

THIS IS DANGEROUS! When you delete a table, you delete *everything* in that table, including any data stored in the table.

Summarizing the book Table Changes

While MySQL does allow you to change a table's definition after the table has been created, you should ideally create the table with the appropriate structure with the first CREATE TABLE statement, making changes later only out of necessity. Once data has been saved to a table, you run the risk of deleting or altering that data when you change the table.

An appropriate CREATE TABLE statement for the scenario described in this lesson would include only the appropriate fields (defined during the design stages and reflected in the resulting ERD), as well as all keys and indexes. For the book table used as an example, Listing 7.2 shows the appropriate CREATE TABLE statement that should have originally been used.

LISTING 7.2

Creating the book Table

```
CREATE TABLE book (
    bookId INT NOT NULL,
    bookTitle VARCHAR(100) NOT NULL,
    origPubDate YEAR,
    CONSTRAINT PK_book PRIMARY KEY (bookId)
);
```

MANAGING RELATIONSHIPS IN MySQL

During the design phase of creating a database, not only were the tables and columns that will hold the data identified, but the relationships between those tables were also defined. In a standard relational database design, the relationships themselves are defined by foreign keys in tables, not as a separate object. However, it is helpful to understand how managing those keys can work in conjunction with managing the database itself. This includes understanding how foreign keys are defined, how entity integrity is applied, and how referential integrity affects data stored. It is also worth understanding how to identify and compare options for deleting or updating values in primary key fields and how changing those options impacts data in related tables.

Define a Foreign Key

A relationship between two tables is defined by using the primary key of one table as a foreign key in the second table. As an example, a person in a contact list may have multiple phone numbers. To represent that fact in a relational design, one table is created for the person, and a separate table is created for phone numbers, using the primary key person_id in the person table as a foreign key in the phone table. The ERD would look like what is shown in Figure 7.3.

In MySQL, the statement in Listing 7.3 can be used to create the person table.

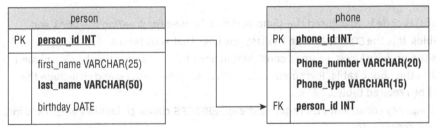

Figure 7.3 The primary-foreign key relationship

LISTING 7.3

Creating the person Table

```
CREATE TABLE person (
    person_id INT,
    first_name VARCHAR(25),
```

```
    last_name VARCHAR(50) NOT NULL,
    birthday DATE,
    CONSTRAINT PK_person PRIMARY KEY (person_id)
);
```

You can see that this creates the person table in the same manner that the book table was created earlier. Several fields are created including a primary key called person_id. With the person table created, you can then create the phone table using the code in Listing 7.4.

LISTING 7.4

Creating the phone Table

```
CREATE TABLE phone (
    phone_id INT,
    phone_number VARCHAR(20) NOT NULL,
    phone_type VARCHAR(15) NOT NULL,
    person_id INT NOT NULL,
    CONSTRAINT PK_phone PRIMARY KEY (phone_id),
    CONSTRAINT FOREIGN KEY FK_person_phone (person_id)
        REFERENCES person (person_id)
);
```

Most of this code is structured the same as the code used for creating the book and person tables. It is the CONSTRAINT in the last few lines that is different.

Just as the primary key is a named constraint in both tables, the foreign key is a named constraint in the phone table. It is common to prefix the name with FK and to include the names of both related tables.

The foreign key constraint also requires the REFERENCES clause to identify what field in what table it represents.

```
CONSTRAINT FOREIGN KEY constraint_name (local_fieldname)
    REFERENCES remote_tablename (remote_fieldname)
```

In most cases, the related field will have the same name in both tables, but there are times when a different field name is required for the foreign key, including self-referential tables that have the primary key and foreign key fields in the same table.

Entity Integrity

When a primary key is defined, the RDBMS will apply entity integrity constraints to new records automatically, including the following:

- No other existing record in the table has the same primary key value as the new entry.
- There is a value entered for each field of the primary key.

If a new record fails to meet either of these criteria, the RDBMS will reject the record and prevent it from being added to the table. For this reason, primary keys are often set up to use integer values (of which there is an infinite number of values to use), which resolves the first rule.

The field is also often set up to auto-number records as they are added to the table. This means that the RDBMS assigns a value to the primary key field automatically, assigning a new number to each record. This helps resolve the second rule.

Note that while auto-numbering fields is a useful way to ensure that the data in a table technically meets the rules of entity integrity, it does not prevent someone from entering the same logical record multiple times using different primary key values. This means it does not guarantee against duplicate data, only against duplicate records.

Referential Integrity

While entity integrity applies to the records in only one table, referential integrity applies to records added to a related table: specifically, to values used in a foreign key field. Referential integrity states:

Any value used as a foreign key must exist as a primary key in the related table.

Adding Data to a Foreign Key Field

When a foreign key constraint is added, the RDBMS will check that each value entered into the foreign key field already exists in the related primary key in the other table. This means that when data is added to a database, data must first be added to the primary table(s) before it can be added to the related table(s).

In the earlier example, a person must first be created in the person table before that person's phone numbers can be added to the phone table, and that for each phone number, a valid `person_id` value must be included.

Updating Data in a Primary Record

Updating data in a primary record is not a common problem, but it can happen that your database group decides to change the primary key values in a primary table. However, changing those values would violate relational integrity, because the foreign key values would no longer match the values in the primary key fields.

Deleting Data from a Primary Record

Along the same lines, if a person is deleted from the person table, any related phone numbers must first be removed from the phone table. From a data management perspective, this is important: what good is a phone number if you don't know who it belongs to?

Work-Arounds for Referential Integrity

There are times when referential integrity interferes with the ability to complete tasks in an RDBMS. For example, you might need to delete multiple records in a primary table, which would typically mean identifying and deleting all related records in the related table first. Because these options are destructive and difficult to recover from, they are generally only used by database administrators, and appropriate settings are applied for only as long as necessary. The following are options that can be used:

- Removing the foreign key constraints
- Using ON UPDATE
- Using ON DELETE

Remove the Foreign Key Constraints

One option is to simply remove the foreign key constraints temporarily and reapply them after making necessary changes to the data. However, when you reapply the constraint later, you may find that some of the foreign key values no longer match existing primary key values, and it can take time to find and correct the errors. It is always better to have foreign key constraints in place when adding data to a database to ensure that all foreign key values meet referential integrity requirements.

Using ON UPDATE

A better option is to include the ON UPDATE CASCADE option on a foreign key constraint when making changes to existing primary key values. When this option is set up, the RDBMS will automatically update related foreign key values when a primary key value is changed in existing data so that the changes automatically take place everywhere a given primary key value is used.

While this is less destructive than other options, in most cases, you should choose primary key fields such that their values are not likely to be changed. A meaningless, surrogate key is typically better than something like a username that reflects the person's real name so that if the person changes their name, you can change the username without changing the primary key.

Using ON DELETE

The `ON DELETE CASCADE` option is destructive in that if you delete a record from a primary table, all related records based on that primary key will also be deleted from the related tables. You can instead use `ON DELETE SET NULL`, which deletes only the foreign key values in the related records. However, this option effectively removes the relationships between the tables, and it is not allowed if the relationship between the tables is required and the foreign key field is set to `NOT NULL`.

> **NOTE** For more information, see MySQL's documentation on foreign key constraints at dev.mysql.com/doc/refman/5.6/en/create-table-foreign-keys.html.

Ultimately, software developers who work with relational databases must understand how the RDBMS defines and manages relationships between tables. From that perspective, when adding data to a database, you should follow these guidelines:

- Verify that the relationships are defined in each table prior to adding data to the database. This is done by defining foreign keys in related tables as part of the design process.
- When adding new data to a database, data must be added to primary tables before data is added to related tables to avoid violating referential integrity.

In most enterprise-level database systems, there is a database admin team that will handle more complicated situations, including deleting and updating existing data as necessary.

SUMMARY

In this lesson, a lot of information was presented. You learned that SQL comes in two flavors: data definition language (DDL) and data management language (DML). DML is used primarily to manipulate the data stored within that storage. This lesson dove into DDL, which is used to define and create the database and its structure, including tables, indexes, and relationships between tables.

Using DDL, you learned the core way to create a database and add tables and fields. You also learned how to assign data types to those fields as well as learned how to make them required or not. Finally, you learned how to manage relationships between tables within your database by defining and using primary and foreign keys.

EXERCISES

The following exercises are provided to allow you to experiment with concepts presented in this lesson:

Exercise 7.1: Book Database

Exercise 7.2: Movie Database

> **NOTE** The exercises are for your benefit. They help you apply what you learn in the lessons.

Exercise 7.1: Books Database

SQL scripts are used as a way to back up and restore relational databases. This exercise is broken into three parts to guide you through creating and testing a script that can be used (and reused!) to create the books database structure, including all tables and relationships, as defined in an ERD shown in Figure 7.4.

In list format, the database structure looks like this:

- **Author**
  - **AuthorID INT PK**
  - **FirstName STRING(25)**
  - MiddleName STRING(25)
  - **LastName STRING(50)**
  - Gender STRING(1)
  - **DateOfBirth DATE**
  - DateOfDeath DATE
- **AuthorBook**
  - **AuthorID INT PK, FK**
  - **BookID INT PK, FK**

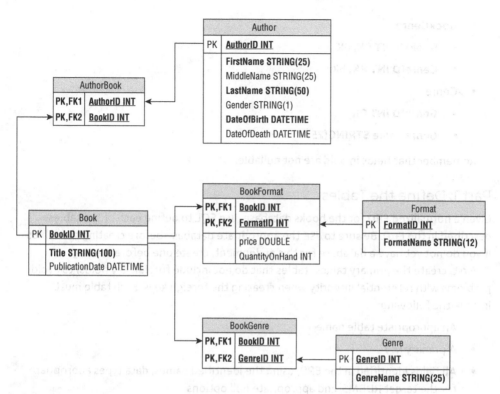

Figure 7.4 The books database ERD

- **Book**
  - **BookID INT PK**
  - **Title STRING(100)**
  - PublicationDate DATETIME
- **BookFormat**
  - **BookID INT PK, FK**
  - **FormatID INT PK, FK**
  - Price DOUBLE
  - QuantityOnHand INT
- **Format**
  - **FormatID INT PK**
  - **FormatName STRING(12)**

- **BookGenre**
  - **BookID INT PK, FK**
  - **GenreID INT PK, FK**
- Genre
  - **GenreID INT PK**
  - **GenreName STRING(25)**

Remember that fields in bold are not nullable.

Part 1: Define the Tables

Given a normalized ERD for the books database, use SQL to define each of the tables described in the ERD. Be sure to USE the appropriate database before creating the tables. If you do not yet have a database for this assignment, create one before starting.

First, create the primary tables (tables that do not include foreign key fields) to avoid problems with referential integrity when creating the foreign keys. Each table must include the following:

- An appropriate table name
- A primary key
- All fields identified in the ERD, using the identified names, data types appropriate for the target RDBMS, and appropriate null options

All foreign keys must be defined as foreign keys in the initial CREATE TABLE statement. Use SHOW TABLES and DESCRIBE table_name; frequently to make sure that each table exists with the correct structure.

Do not use ALTER TABLE statements to make changes to the initial version of the table. Instead, DROP the table, update the SQL statement to include the appropriate change, and run the statement again. As you work, save each CREATE TABLE statement to a file in a text or code editor so that you have them available for the next exercise.

Part 2: Books Database SQL Scripts

After you have confirmed that the SQL statements to create the tables work as expected, create a script that you can reuse as necessary to rebuild the database structure.

1. Create a SQL script file by creating a new text file (using any text or code editor) and saving the file with the .sql extension.

2. The first line of the script should drop the database if it exists. Remember that this will delete *everything* in the database, so verify that you have a way to re-create the database before dropping it.

   ```
   DROP DATABASE IF EXISTS database_name;
   ```

3. The second line of the script should create a database with the same name as the dropped database.

```
CREATE DATABASE database_name;
```

4. The third line of the script should USE the new database.

```
USE database_name;
```

Add the series of statements used to create the tables following the USE statement. Make sure that each CREATE TABLE statement ends in a semicolon. Save the file after making the changes.

Part 3: Test the Script

Before marking this exercise done, verify that you can run the script in your RDBMS. Most RDBMSs include an option to open and run a .sql file, but if you can't find it easily, you can open the script you just created, select and copy everything in the file, and then paste the script at a SQL prompt. After running the script, use SHOW TABLES and DESCRIBE to verify that all of the tables exist and that their structure matches that of the ERD included at the beginning of this exercise.

Exercise 7.2: DDL Activity: Movies Database

In this exercise, you will practice DDL skills by scripting a new database, tables, and relationships in a script file. The database should keep track of movies, using the structure described here.

Write SQL statements to create each of the following tables. You will put these statements in a script, so save them as you finalize them. The tables are already normalized. Your job is to determine what data type to assign to each field, as well as create appropriate keys and required fields. You may use the following list on its own or create an ERD if the visualization helps you. The tasks for this exercise are broken into three parts.

- **Movie**
  - **MovieID: Primary key, Identity**
  - GenreID: Foreign key, Genre table, Required
  - DirectorID: Foreign key, Director table, Not required
  - RatingID: Foreign key, Rating table, Not required
  - **Title: Required, Extended character set, Length: 128**
  - ReleaseDate: Not required

- **Genre**
  - **GenreID: Primary key, Identity**
  - **GenreName: Required, Extended character set, Length: 30**
- **Director**
  - **DirectorID: Primary key, Identity**
  - **FirstName: Required, Extended character set, Length: 30**
  - **LastName: Required, Extended character set, Length: 30**
  - BirthDate: Not required
- **Rating**
  - **RatingID: Primary key, Identity**
  - **RatingName: Required, Standard character set, Length: 5**
- **Actor**
  - **ActorID: Primary key, Identity**
  - **FirstName: Required, Extended character set, Length: 30**
  - **LastName: Required, Extended character set, Length: 30**
  - BirthDate: Not required
- **CastMembers**
  - **CastMemberID: Primary key, Identity**
  - **ActorID: Foreign key, Actor table, Required**
  - **MovieID: Foreign key, Movie table, Required**
  - **Role: Required, Extended character set, Length: 50**

Part 1: Define the Tables

Given a normalized schema for the database, use SQL to define each of the tables described earlier. Be sure to USE the appropriate database before creating the tables. If you do not yet have a database for this assignment, create one before starting.

First, create the primary tables (tables that do not include foreign key fields) to avoid problems with referential integrity when creating the foreign keys. Each table must include the following:

- An appropriate table name
- A primary key
- All fields identified in the ERD, using the identified names, data types appropriate for the target RDBMS, and appropriate null options

All foreign keys must be defined as foreign keys in the initial CREATE TABLE statement. Use SHOW TABLES and DESCRIBE table_name; frequently to make sure that each table exists with the correct structure.

Do not use ALTER TABLE statements to make changes to the initial version of the table. Instead, DROP the table, update the SQL statement to include the appropriate change, and run the statement again. As you work, save each CREATE TABLE statement to a file in a text or code editor so that you have them available for Part 2 of this exercise.

Part 2: Create the Script

After you have confirmed that the SQL statements to create the tables work as expected, create a script that you can reuse as necessary to rebuild the database structure.

1. Create a SQL script file by creating a new text file (using any text or code editor) and saving the file with the .sql extension.

2. The first line of the script should drop the database if it exists. Remember that this will delete *everything* in the database, so verify that you have a way to re-create the database before dropping it.

   ```
   DROP DATABASE IF EXISTS database_name;
   ```

3. The second line of the script should create a database with the same name as the dropped database.

   ```
   CREATE DATABASE database_name;
   ```

4. The third line of the script should USE the new database.

   ```
   USE database_name;
   ```

Add the series of statements used to create the tables following the USE statement. Make sure that each CREATE TABLE statement ends in a semicolon. Save the file after making the changes.

Part 3: Test the Script

Like with the previous exercise, before marking this exercise done, verify that you can run the script in your RDBMS. Most RDBMSs include an option to open and run a .sql file, but if you can't find it easily, you can open the script you just created, select and copy everything in the file, and then paste the script at a SQL prompt. After running the script, use SHOW TABLES and DESCRIBE to verify that all of the tables exist and that their structure matches that of the ERD included at the beginning of this exercise.

Lesson 8

Pulling It All Together: Building the Vinyl Record Shop Database

In this code-along lesson, you will work through the steps to create a database for a Vinyl Record Shop, a small business that specializes in vinyl albums. As you go through each step of creating the database structure, you should save the step to a SQL script. By the end of this lesson, you will have pulled together all the ideas learned to this point, and you will have a script that you can use (and reuse!) to create the Vinyl Record Shop database structure, including all tables and relationships, as defined in an ERD.

> **NOTE** SQL scripts can be used for a variety of things including to back up an existing database or to transfer a database to another server.

Learning Objectives

By the end of this lesson, you will be able to:

- Review a database structure
- Build a database using SQL
- Determine the primary tables within a database
- Construct the related tables within a database
- Show the tables you have created and their fields

As you walk through this project and code along, you will go through the following steps, which align with the objectives:

Step 1:   Examine the database's structure and organize the tables.

Step 2:   Create the database.

Step 3:   Create the primary tables.

Step 4:   Create the related tables.

Step 5:   Finalize the script.

STEP 1: EXAMINE THE STRUCTURE

Before starting to build any database, you should go through the steps to normalize the structure and create an ERD or a list of tables and fields that you can use as a road map for this process. For this lesson, this step has already been done for you. Figure 8.1 shows the ERD for the Vinyl Record Shop database that will be built.

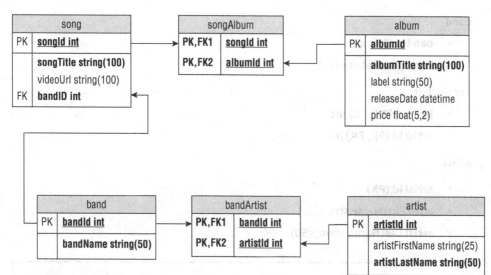

Figure 8.1 The Vinyl Record Shop database ERD

In list format, the database structure looks like this:

song

- **songId (PK) int**
- **songTitle string(100)**
- videoUrl string(100)
- **bandId (FK) int**

songAlbum

- **songId (PK, FK) int**
- **albumId (PK, FK) int**

album

- **albumId (PK) int**
- **albumTitle string(100)**
- label string(50)
- releaseDate date
- price float(5,2)

band

- **bandId (PK) int**
- **bandName string(50)**

bandArtist

- **bandId (PK, FK) int**
- **artistId (PK, FK) int**

artist

- **artistId (PK)**
- artistFirstName string(25)
- **artistLastName string(50)**

> **NOTE** Remember that fields in bold are not nullable.

The following are additional expectations for this database:

- All primary key fields are auto-incrementing integer fields.
- The data types defined in the design steps must be converted to appropriate MySQL data types. For example, strings will use VARCHAR, and floats must use DECIMAL in MySQL.

Organize the Tables

Because of referential integrity, you must create the primary tables (tables that do not include foreign keys) before you can create the related tables that depend on existing primary keys. Scan through the tables described in the ERD or the previous list and identify the ones you believe should be created first.

The primary tables are as follows:

- album
- artist
- band

These are primary tables because they do not have any foreign keys. The related tables in the database include foreign keys that depend on other tables.

- song references band.
- songAlbum references both song and album.
- bandArtist references both band and artist.

Note that the related tables must be prioritized as well. In this case, the songAlbum table depends on the song table, so the song table must be created before you can create the songAlbum table. Because song depends on band, the band table must be created before you can create the song table.

You can create the primary tables in any order, as long as all of them are created before you create the dependent related tables. In this lesson, the tables will be created in the order they were listed earlier.

Create the Script File

The end result of this lesson will be a script that can be used to rebuild the database structure anytime it is needed. To this end, create a new file in a code editor or text editor and save the file as vinylrecordshop-schema.sql.

Note that the term *schema* references the structure of the database. Including this in the filename indicates the purpose of the file. The .sql extension is used for SQL scripts. Relational database management system (RDBMS) interfaces (like MySQL Workbench) can recognize these files and open them automatically. You can run the script directly in the RDBMS interface after saving any changes.

For basic documentation, you should add your name in a comment on the first line of the script, with a current date on the second line. There are two ways to comment within a SQL script. The first way is to start a line with a double hyphen, which is simply a double dash (--). This will cause the rest of the line to be treated as a comment.

```
-- This is a comment in a SQL Script
```

The second way to comment is to use /* and */. The comment will start with the use of /* and then end when */ is reached. All text in between, which can be on multiple lines, will be treated as a comment. The following is an example of a multiline comment for a SQL script:

```
/*
Script written by: John Smith
Date written: March 21, 2023
*/
```

STEP 2: CREATE THE DATABASE

> **NOTE** For the remaining steps in this lesson, you should write the SQL statement in your SQL interface (such as MySQL Workbench). You can then test your SQL to verify that it runs correctly. Once it works as expected, copy and paste it at the end of the script. You can then run the script to set up the database for the next SQL statement.

Before you can create tables, a database space must be created to hold the tables. In this case, name the database **vinylrecordshop**. You will want to be sure that you are starting with an empty database. For this reason, you want to remove an existing database with that name before creating the new one.

Run the following command in MySQL:

```
DROP DATABASE vinylrecordshop;
```

This statement will delete an existing database named *vinylrecordshop*. If you have this database in your MySQL instance, the statement will run without problem, but if the database does not exist, MySQL will throw an error because you cannot delete a database that does not exist.

The script needs to be flexible enough that anyone can use it, even if they are creating a new database rather than replacing an existing database. For this reason, you should modify the statement to the following:

```
DROP DATABASE IF EXISTS vinylrecordshop;
```

The IF EXISTS clause tells MySQL to ignore the DROP command if the named database does not exist, so it will not throw an error.

Try both statements a few times to see how they work and what they do before going on. Remember that you can use the SHOW DATABASES; statement to see a list of available databases in MySQL to verify that the vinylrecordshop database is deleted or doesn't exist.

Next, let's create the database.

```
CREATE DATABASE vinylrecordshop;
```

Use SHOW DATABASES to verify that the database was created. Once its existence is confirmed, make it the active database.

```
USE vinylrecordshop;
```

Add the three statements under the comments you added to the .sql file you created in step 1. Execute the script to make sure it works without error before continuing to the next step. Your vinylrecordshop-schema.sql file should look similar to Listing 8.1.

LISTING 8.1

`vinylrecordshop-schema.sql` with the Create Logic

```
/*
 * Script written by: John Smith
 * Date written: March 21, 2023
*/

DROP DATABASE IF EXISTS vinylrecordshop;

CREATE DATABASE vinylrecordshop;

USE vinylrecordshop;
```

STEP 3: CREATE THE PRIMARY TABLES

At this point, you have a script that can delete an existing database named *vinylrecordshop* and replace it with a new (empty) database with the same name. The next step is to create the tables themselves. Because the organizational step was done first, you know the order in which the tables should be created to avoid problems with referential integrity. For each table, you will define the table name and all fields in the table, along with appropriate field properties (data type, size, and NULL status) and key fields.

Start with the album table, which looks like this:

album

- **albumId (PK) int**
- **albumTitle string(100)**
- label string(50)
- releaseDate date
- price float(5,2)

You will use the CREATE statement in MySQL to create the album table. The statement will look like the code in Listing 8.2.

LISTING 8.2

Creating the album Table

```
CREATE TABLE album (
    albumId INT AUTO_INCREMENT,
    albumTitle VARCHAR(100) NOT NULL,
    label VARCHAR(50),
    releaseDate DATE,
    price DECIMAL(5,2),
    CONSTRAINT pk_album
        PRIMARY KEY (albumId)
);
```

This statement defines the table using the expected parameters.

- The albumId field auto-increments, which means that the database engine will automatically assign a sequential number to each new record, if no value is specified. This ensures that each record will have a different primary key value.

- The string values are defined using VARCHAR, specifying the maximum number of characters.

- releaseDate is a DATE field. In MySQL, the default format for a date is yyyy-mm-dd. This format is important to know when data is going to be added to the field, but right now, you can simply specify the field as DATE.

- The price is a DECIMAL field with a maximum value of 999.99, which is appropriate for the data that will be stored for this solution.

- price, releaseDate, and label are nullable fields.

- The PRIMARY KEY constraint is defined on albumId.

Use DESCRIBE to verify that the table is defined correctly. If the statement works as expected, add it at the bottom of your script, save the script, and run it to make sure it works to delete and re-create the database and rebuild the table.

Column Order

Does the column order matter?

One of the basic rules of relational database design is that the column order is not important. That said, primary keys are generally put first because this helps speed up retrieval from the table. This placement is less important for foreign keys, but some database designers will add foreign key fields immediately after the primary key.

The CONSTRAINT definitions can also appear in any order, as long as the column the constraint references is defined first. This means the statement shown in Listing 8.3 could be used to define the album table instead of the one used in Listing 8.2.

LISTING 8.3

Modified SQL for Creating the album Table

```
CREATE TABLE album (
    albumId INT AUTO_INCREMENT,
    CONSTRAINT pk_album
        PRIMARY KEY (albumId),
    albumTitle VARCHAR(100) NOT NULL,
    label VARCHAR(50),
    releaseDate DATE,
    price DECIMAL(5,2)
);
```

Remember to put a comma after each column and constraint defined in a table (except the last one), because that is how MySQL differentiates each item in the table.

On Your Own

Use the model for the album table to create the other primary tables (artist and band) on your own. Here are the table descriptions again:

artist

- **artistId (PK)**
- artistFirstName string(25)
- **artistLastName string(50)**

band

- **bandId (PK) int**
- **bandName string(50)**

Remember that you can use DESCRIBE tableName; to verify that a table's structure is correct, as well as DROP TABLE tableName; to delete an existing table if you need to rebuild it. After verifying that each CREATE TABLE statement works, add them to your SQL script.

NOTE If you have trouble creating the tables, you can find the complete script near the end of this lesson in Listing 8.10.

STEP 4: CREATE THE RELATED TABLES

The related tables in the database include foreign keys that depend on other tables. These tables and their references are as follows:

- song references band.
- songAlbum references both song and album.
- bandArtist references both band and artist.

Because these tables depend on the primary tables, the primary tables must be created first. However, the songAlbum table also depends on the song table, so the song table must be created before the songAlbum table can be created.

Create the song Table

The song table is the first that we will tackle of the three. This table includes the following fields:

song

- **songId (PK) int**
- **songTitle string(100)**
- videoUrl string(100)
- **bandId (FK) int**

The first three columns include a primary key (songID), a required field (songTitle), and a nullable field (videoUrl). In Listing 8.4, the SQL script to create the table with these three fields is presented.

LISTING 8.4

Creating the First Three Fields in the song Table

```
CREATE TABLE song (
    songId INT NOT NULL AUTO_INCREMENT,
    songTitle VARCHAR(100) NOT NULL,
    videoUrl VARCHAR(100),
    CONSTRAINT pk_song
        PRIMARY KEY (songId)
);
```

You can see in the script that each of the three fields is created with its data type and the attributes defined for the field. The songID is automatically incremented and is required. The songTitle is also required as indicated with NOT NULL and can be up to 100 characters long. The video URL is simply defined as a string of up to 100 characters, and because NOT NULL isn't included, you know the field is optional. The last of the code defines the primary key using songId.

The last column is a foreign key that references the bandId field in the band table. If you have not yet created the band table, you must do so before you can define the foreign key that references that table.

In MySQL, you need to complete two steps to define a foreign key.

Step 1: Define the field as a normal field in the table. In this case, add it after the videoUrl column, as shown in Listing 8.5.

LISTING 8.5

Adding the Normal Field to the Table

```
DROP TABLE IF EXISTS song;
CREATE TABLE song (
    songId INT NOT NULL AUTO_INCREMENT,
    songTitle VARCHAR(100) NOT NULL,
    videoUrl VARCHAR(100),
    bandId INT NOT NULL,
    CONSTRAINT pk_song
        PRIMARY KEY (songId)
);
```

Step 2: Add a foreign key constraint following the primary key constraint. This tells MySQL to enforce referential integrity on the bandId field in this table so that any value entered in this field in the song table must first exist in the band table. Add this after the primary key constraint, as shown in Listing 8.6.

LISTING 8.6

The song Table Script with the Added Foreign Key Constraint

```
DROP TABLE IF EXISTS song;
CREATE TABLE song (
    songId INT NOT NULL AUTO_INCREMENT,
    songTitle VARCHAR(100) NOT NULL,
    videoUrl VARCHAR(100),
    bandId INT NOT NULL,
    CONSTRAINT pk_song
        PRIMARY KEY (songId),
    CONSTRAINT fk_song_band
        FOREIGN KEY (bandID)
        REFERENCES band(bandId)
);
```

Note that the foreign key constraint is named using both tables: the current table and the primary table. This ensures that the constraint name is unique, but it also helps document its purpose.

Verify that the table exists and that it includes the appropriate columns and settings. You can then add the code including the CREATE TABLE statement to your script.

Create the songAlbum Table

Now you're ready for the songAlbum table, which includes the following fields:

songAlbum

- **songId (PK, FK) int**
- **albumId (PK, FK) int**

Note the following:

- The table has a composite key: the primary key includes both fields.
- Both of the fields are foreign keys related to separate tables.

Start by defining the columns. While both columns are included in the primary key, their values depend on the related fields in the song and album tables. *This means you do not want MySQL to number the columns automatically*, so just define them as integers, as shown in Listing 8.7.

LISTING 8.7

The Initial songAlbum Table Script with Columns Defined as Integers

```
CREATE TABLE songAlbum (
    songId INT,
    albumId INT
);
```

The fields could be specified as being required, but because they are included in the primary key, entity integrity will enforce this. The next step is to add the primary key constraint. When the primary key is a single field, just that field is added into the constraint. For a composite key, all fields are listed in the primary key, separated by commas.

While an ALTER TABLE statement could be used here, the goal is to have a script that can rebuild the database. As such, drop the existing table and rebuild it to include the primary key, as shown in Listing 8.8.

LISTING 8.8

The songAlbum Table Script with Primary Key Contraint

```
DROP TABLE IF EXISTS songAlbum;
CREATE TABLE songAlbum (
    songId INT,
    albumId INT,
    CONSTRAINT pk_songAlbum
        PRIMARY KEY (songId, albumId)
);
```

Finally, both foreign key constraints need to be added, as shown in Listing 8.9.

LISTING 8.9

The full songAlbum Table Script with Foreign Key Contraints Added

```
DROP TABLE IF EXISTS songAlbum;
CREATE TABLE songAlbum (
    songId INT,
    albumId INT,
    CONSTRAINT pk_songAlbum
       PRIMARY KEY (songId, albumId),
    CONSTRAINT fk_songAlbum_song
        FOREIGN KEY (songId)
        REFERENCES song(songId),
    CONSTRAINT fk_songAlbum_album
        FOREIGN KEY (albumId)
        REFERENCES album(albumId)
);
```

Once again, verify that the table exists and that it includes the appropriate columns and settings. Once you've confirmed this, add the code to the `vinylrecordshop-schema.sql` script.

Create the bandArtist Table on Your Own

Use the model for the songAlbum table to create the bandArtist table. The model is as follows:

bandArtist

- **bandId (PK, FK) int**
- **artistId (PK, FK) int**

Add the statement to your script once you have verified that it works as expected. If you have trouble creating the SQL for this, you can find the code included in the full solution presented in Listing 8.10.

STEP 5: FINALIZE THE SCRIPT

At this point, you should have a complete script that will perform the following tasks:

- Drop the vinylrecordstore database, if it exists.
- Re-create the database.
- Use the database.

- Define all tables in the database, including the appropriate primary and foreign key fields.

  - album
  - artist
  - band
  - song
  - songAlbum
  - bandArtist

Verify that you can run the script in MySQL. Most database systems (including MySQL Workbench) include an option to open and run a `.sql` file, but if you can't find it easily, you can open the script you just created, select and copy everything in the file, and then paste the script at a MySQL prompt.

After running the script, use `SHOW TABLES` and `DESCRIBE` to verify that all the tables exist and that their structure matches that of the ERD included at the beginning of this exercise. Listing 8.10 shows the version of the completed script.

LISTING 8.10

The Complete `vinylrecordshop-schema.sql` Script

```
/*
 * Script written by: John Smith
 * Date written: March 21, 2023
 */
-- Running this script will DELETE the existing database and all data
-- it contains.
-- Use with caution.

DROP DATABASE IF EXISTS vinylrecordshop;

CREATE DATABASE vinylrecordshop;

USE vinylrecordshop;
```

```
CREATE TABLE album (
   albumId INT AUTO_INCREMENT,
   albumTitle VARCHAR(100) NOT NULL,
   label VARCHAR(50),
   releaseDate DATE,
   price DECIMAL(5,2),
   CONSTRAINT pk_album
      PRIMARY KEY (albumId)
);

CREATE TABLE artist (
   artistId INT NOT NULL AUTO_INCREMENT,
   fname VARCHAR(25) NOT NULL,
   lname VARCHAR(50) NOT NULL,

   CONSTRAINT pk_artist
      PRIMARY KEY (artistId)
);

CREATE TABLE band (
   bandId INT AUTO_INCREMENT,
   bandName VARCHAR(50) NOT NULL,
   CONSTRAINT pk_band
      PRIMARY KEY (bandId)
);

CREATE TABLE song (
   songId INT NOT NULL AUTO_INCREMENT,
   songTitle VARCHAR(100) NOT NULL,
   videoUrl VARCHAR(100),
   bandId INT NOT NULL,
   CONSTRAINT pk_song
      PRIMARY KEY (songId),
   CONSTRAINT fk_song_band
      FOREIGN KEY (bandID)
      REFERENCES band(bandId)
);

CREATE TABLE songAlbum (
   songId INT,
   albumId INT,
   CONSTRAINT pk_songAlbum
      PRIMARY KEY (songId, albumId),
```

```
    CONSTRAINT fk_songAlbum_song
        FOREIGN KEY (songId)
        REFERENCES song(songId),
    CONSTRAINT fk_songAlbum_album
        FOREIGN KEY (albumId)
        REFERENCES album(albumId)
);

CREATE TABLE bandArtist (
    bandId INT,
    artistId INT,
    CONSTRAINT pk_bandArtist
        PRIMARY KEY (bandId, artistId),
    CONSTRAINT fk_bandArtist_band
        FOREIGN KEY (bandId)
        REFERENCES band(bandId),
    CONSTRAINT fk_bandArtist_artist
        FOREIGN KEY (artistId)
        REFERENCES artist (artistId)
);
```

SUMMARY

This lesson has pulled together what you learned in previous lessons and walked you through the process of converting an ERD into SQL code for creating a database and its tables for a Vinyl Record Shop, a small business that specializes in vinyl albums. Because you created the code in a .sql file, you now have a script that can be shared with others to create the database. Of course, you should be careful because you also included code to drop any existing database by the same name, which will clear any data as well.

PART III

Data Management and Manipulation

Applying CRUD: Basic Data Management and Manipulation

I n lesson 7, "Database Management Using DDL", you learned how to create a database and set up the tables. The vast majority of work done in a database, however, involves retrieving and manipulating the data itself. While these tasks often require understanding how the database is structured, most of the people who use a database will never be expected to design a database or create a database structure.

Learning Objectives

By the end of this lesson, you will be able to:

- Create new data within existing tables in a relational database using SQL
- Retrieve existing data from a database
- Update existing data within a relational database
- Delete data from a relational database

DATA MANIPULATION LANGUAGE

In this lesson, four activities involved in working with data will be reviewed. These center on **creating**, **retrieving**, **updating**, and **deleting** data from a database using SQL. It is common to use the acronym **CRUD** to refer to these activities.

Before data can be retrieved, it has to be created. In this lesson, the Data Manipulation Language (DML) will specifically be used to show how standard SQL can add data to existing tables, update existing data, and delete data.

REQUIREMENTS As with the previous lesson, you will need MySQL installed and running on your computer to run the examples in this and future lessons.

CREATE A DATABASE

Before DML operations can be performed on a database, the database needs to exist. For this lesson, the TrackIt database will be used, whose structure is defined in the entity-relationship diagram (ERD) shown in Figure 9.1.

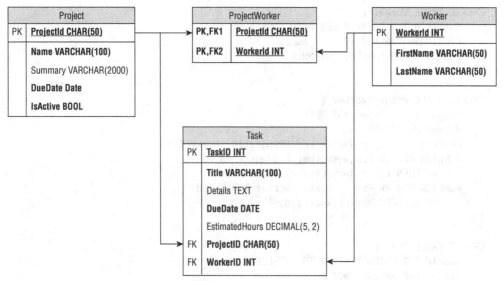

Figure 9.1 The TrackIt database ERD

If you apply what you learned from the previous lesson, you should be able to write the SQL script to create this database. Listing 9.1 makes this easier for you by presenting the SQL script to create the database.

LISTING 9.1

SQL Script to Create the TrackIt Database

```
DROP DATABASE IF EXISTS TrackIt;

CREATE DATABASE TrackIt;

-- Make sure we're in the correct database before we add schema.
USE TrackIt;

CREATE TABLE Project (
    ProjectId CHAR(50) PRIMARY KEY,
    ProjectName VARCHAR(100) NOT NULL,
    Summary VARCHAR(2000) NULL,
    DueDate DATE NOT NULL,
    IsActive BOOL NOT NULL DEFAULT 1
);
```

```
CREATE TABLE Worker (
    WorkerId INT PRIMARY KEY AUTO_INCREMENT,
    FirstName VARCHAR(50) NOT NULL,
    LastName VARCHAR(50) NOT NULL
);

CREATE TABLE ProjectWorker (
    ProjectId CHAR(50) NOT NULL,
    WorkerId INT NOT NULL,
    PRIMARY KEY pk_ProjectWorker (ProjectId, WorkerId),
    FOREIGN KEY fk_ProjectWorker_Project (ProjectId)
        REFERENCES Project(ProjectId),
    FOREIGN KEY fk_ProjectWorker_Worker (WorkerId)
        REFERENCES Worker(WorkerId)
);

CREATE TABLE Task (
    TaskId INT PRIMARY KEY AUTO_INCREMENT,
    Title VARCHAR(100) NOT NULL,
    Details TEXT NULL,
    DueDate DATE NOT NULL,
    EstimatedHours DECIMAL(5, 2) NULL,
    ProjectId CHAR(50) NOT NULL,
    WorkerId INT NOT NULL,
    FOREIGN KEY fk_Task_ProjectWorker (ProjectId, WorkerId)
        REFERENCES ProjectWorker(ProjectId, WorkerId)
);
```

Read through the script to see how it reflects the ERD. Note the following features in particular:

- `WorkerId` and `TaskId` are set up as auto-incrementing integer fields. This means that MySQL will automatically assign values to those fields when data is added to the Worker and Task tables.

- `ProjectId` is a CHAR(50) field. This allows us to use meaningful values (like db-milestone) to identify projects rather than integers that have no inherent meaning. Using integers is fine in this case, but since each project name is unique, we can define the projectID as a string where each project has a unique projectID (project name).

- The primary key of a table can be defined as part of the field definition when there is only one field in the primary key, like this:

```
WorkerId INT PRIMARY KEY AUTO_INCREMENT
```

- When there is a composite key, we must use a different format. A composite key is a key that is composed of several columns. For instance, we can't use the name of a person as a unique index since two people can have the same name. However, if we use the name and the birthdate together as a key, we can potentially identify uniquely people using the name and the birthdate. A separate PRIMARY KEY definition must be used that includes all appropriate fields. In this case, the ProjectWorker table acts as a bridge table between Project and Worker, because each project can have multiple workers, and each Worker can be assigned to multiple projects. We create the primary key using the statement:

```
PRIMARY KEY pk_ProjectWorker (ProjectId, WorkerId)
```

- In the Project table, a default value of 1 is set to the Boolean IsActive field.

```
IsActive BOOL NOT NULL DEFAULT 1
```

This means that when a value is not specified, MySQL will automatically set that default value in each new record.

Create the Database

You can run the script to create the TrackIt database in one of two ways.

- Enter the text in the script from Listing 9.1. After connecting to MySQL, type the text at the MySQL prompt (if you are using a command-line interface, like Windows Command Prompt or Mac Terminal) or in the code editor window (if you are using a GUI like MySQL Workbench). Run the code after entering it. This will run each statement individually until it reaches the last statement.

- Enter the text to a new text file using a text or code editor. Save the file with the name TrackIt.sql. Open the file in your MySQL interface to run it. This will run all statements in the script until there is an error or it reaches the end of the script. If there is an error, the script will stop at that point and not run any subsequent statements.

If you choose to use the first method, it can be useful to have a local copy of the script saved to your computer. You can use the instructions in the second method to create the file.

> NOTE If you don't want to enter the text, you can find the TrackIt.sql file included in the files you can download for this book at www.wiley.com/go/jobreadysql.

IMPORTANT! This script *deletes* the existing TrackIt database from the MySQL server before rebuilding it, including any data that you may have added since creating the database. You should run this script only if you need to rebuild the database to start this lesson over again from the beginning.

Check That the Database Exists

After creating the database, perform the following steps to make sure that the script works as expected:

1. Execute the SHOW DATABASES; command. This will show the available databases. You should see the TrackIt database in the list.

2. Execute the USE trackit; command. This will ensure you are using the new database.

3. Execute the SHOW TABLES; command. This will allow you to check that the database includes the appropriate tables. You should see the results shown in Table 9.1.

Table 9.1 The Results of Running SHOW TABLES;

Tables_in_trackit
Project
ProjectWorker
Task
Worker

If any of these steps do not work as expected, confirm that you have entered the code correctly for Listing 9.1. You will not be able to complete the remaining steps in this lesson if you do not have a working TrackIt database.

INSERT DATA

To manipulate the data in a database, you must first create data. The TrackIt script provided in Listing 9.1 creates the structure (also sometimes called the **schema**) of the database, but it does not add data to any of the tables.

The INSERT statement can be used to add data to an existing table. The basic structure of the INSERT statement is as follows:

```
INSERT INTO TableName [( column list... )]
    VALUES ( value list... );
```

> **NOTE** Square brackets mark an optional clause.

This boils down to two basic options for inserting data into your tables:

- Adding without columns identified
- Adding with column names

Adding Without Columns Identified

The first option is to use the `INSERT` statement to add values to the table without explicitly identifying the columns the values should be added to. In this case, the RDBMS will map each value to existing fields in the same order the fields appear in the table, from left to right.

For example, assume you have a table that includes fields named SandwichName, Cheese, and IsFried, in that order; then you could use the following statement to add a row of data:

```
INSERT INTO Sandwich VALUES ('Monte Cristo', 'Emmental', 1);
```

With this option, you must provide a value or specify a null value for each column in the table, except for auto-increment fields. For example, if the Cheese column is nullable, you could use this:

```
INSERT INTO Sandwich VALUES ('PB&J', '', 0);
```

This specifies that no value will be added to the Cheese column for that record. To enter a null value into a string field, you simply include an empty pair of quotation marks. For other data types, use a comma before and after the empty spot, but do not include anything between the commas.

```
'value1',,'value3'
```

Adding Columns with Column Names

The second option is to include column names as well as values. In this case, the RDBMS will map each column to each value in the same order they are presented in the `INSERT` statement, even if this is not the order in which the columns appear in the table. For example, consider the following statement:

```
INSERT INTO Sandwich (SandwichName, Cheese, IsFried)
    VALUES ('Monte Cristo', 'Emmental', 1);
```

This statement will work regardless of the order in which the columns are defined in the table. However, if you name a field, you must provide a value or specify a null value for that field in the list of values.

The Better Option

This second option is generally the better choice because tables change over time and your INSERT assumptions will grow stale; however, before writing an INSERT statement, ask these questions:

- Does the table have auto-incremented columns?
- Which columns allow nulls?
- Are there foreign key columns?
- Are foreign key values nullable?

If you omit the value for an auto-incremented column, the database engine generates the value for you. If you include a value, MySQL allows insertion without safeguards. Other database systems, like Microsoft SQL Server, prevent insertion without temporarily disabling auto-increment.

If a column is defined NOT NULL and does not have a DEFAULT value, you must provide a value in your INSERT statement. If a column is a foreign key, any value you provide must already exist in the related primary table. If that column is nullable, you can choose to leave these values out when adding data, but if the column is not nullable, you must provide an allowed value.

For example, in the ProjectWorker table, both the ProjectId and WorkerId must be set to values that exist in the Project and Worker tables. If the values don't exist in the related tables, the INSERT will fail because of referential integrity. Because the columns are not nullable, you must provide a value or the INSERT will fail because of the column settings.

Use the following INSERT to add a Worker to your table:

```
INSERT INTO Worker (WorkerId, FirstName, LastName)
    VALUES (1, 'Rosemonde', 'Featherbie');
```

As long as WorkerId 1 doesn't exist, Rosemonde is inserted without error and is given the WorkerId value 1. On success, the message "1 row(s) affected." is displayed.

If you run the same statement a second time, however, you will see an error message like "Error Code: 1062. Duplicate entry '1' for key 'PRIMARY'." This is because two records cannot have the same primary key value in the same table.

Because auto-increment has been set up on WorkerId, you don't need to include a value for that field.

```
INSERT INTO Worker (FirstName, LastName)
    VALUES ('Kingsly', 'Besantie');
```

If Kingsly is the second worker inserted, they receive the WorkerId value 2. You can view the contents of the table using the following SELECT statement:

```
SELECT *
FROM Worker;
```

The SELECT statement is selecting the columns (fields) listed after the command. In this case, an asterisk is used to indicate all columns are being selected. If both records were inserted correctly, you will see results like the following:

WorkerId	FirstName	LastName
1	Rosemonde	Featherbie
2	Kingsly	Besantie

Pay attention to output messages you get from MySQL. If your data doesn't INSERT, the message will point you in the right direction. Other common problems include trying to add a value with the wrong data type, such as adding a string to a number field.

Inserting Multiple Rows

To insert multiple rows with one query, comma separate two or more **value lists**, including parentheses. The following INSERT statement adds three records to the database:

```
INSERT INTO Worker (FirstName, LastName) VALUES
    ('Goldi','Pilipets'),
    ('Dorey','Rulf'),
    ('Panchito','Ashtonhurst');
```

You can see there are three pairs of values that will be added. The WorkerId will be auto-incremented. To confirm the records were added, you can see all the records by again using a SELECT statement.

```
SELECT *
FROM Worker;
```

You should see the output like the following:

WorkerId	FirstName	LastName
1	Rosemonde	Featherbie
2	Kingsly	Besantie
3	Goldi	Pilipets
4	Dorey	Rulf
5	Panchito	Ashtonhurst

You can see in the output that the three records were added. You can also see that the new records were assigned unique WorkerIds.

Incrementing Auto-Increment Out of Order

What happens when a WorkerId is inserted with a value that is higher than the next auto-increment value? The following code adds a new record with a value of 50 for WorkerId:

```
INSERT INTO Worker (WorkerId, FirstName, LastName)
    VALUES (50, 'Valentino', 'Newvill');
```

This INSERT will add Valentino and Newvill to a record with a WorkerId of 50. No issue will be caused. Now add a new record without specifying a WorkerId.

```
INSERT INTO Worker (FirstName, LastName)
    VALUES ('Violet', 'Mercado');
```

Will this record have WorkerId 6 or 51? Run a SELECT statement on the Worker table to find out.

```
SELECT *
FROM Worker;
```

The output should be as follows:

WorkerId	FirstName	LastName
1	Rosemonde	Featherbie
2	Kingsly	Besantie
3	Goldi	Pilipets
4	Dorey	Rulf
5	Panchito	Ashtonhurst
50	Valentino	Newvill
51	Violet	Mercado

What you will see is that MySQL uses the next value after the current max value for the next auto-increment value. The new record you added has a `WorkerId` of 51.

Inserting a Foreign Key

Worker is a primary table, so it does not have any foreign key columns. It is, however, worth understanding how foreign key values work. Start by adding a record to the Project table. You can do that with the following code:

```
INSERT INTO Project (ProjectId, ProjectName, DueDate)
    VALUES ('db-milestone', 'Database Material', '2022-12-31');
```

- A `ProjectId` is assigned, not generated, so the value must be specified.
- Summary is nullable, so the column name and value can safely be omitted.
- `IsActive` has a `DEFAULT` value of 1, so again the column name and value can be omitted if the default is okey to use.

Now to assign a Worker to a project, you `INSERT` values into the ProjectWorker table.

```
INSERT INTO ProjectWorker (ProjectId, WorkerId)
    VALUES ('db-milestone', 75);
```

Because `WorkerId` 75 does not exist in the Worker table, the database engine rejects the query with the following error message:

```
Error Code: 1452. Cannot add or update a child row: a foreign key constraint
fails (`trackit`.`projectworker`, CONSTRAINT `fk_ProjectWorker_Worker` FOREIGN
KEY (`WorkerId`) REFERENCES `worker`(`workerid`))
```

The message is a mouthful. In plain English, it says you tried to insert a `WorkerId` value that doesn't exist in the Worker table and therefore violated the `fk_ProjectWorker_Worker` constraint.

Change the `WorkerId` value from 75 to 2 and run the query again. This time it should work properly because 2 is a valid, existing `WorkerId`.

This is one way relational databases protect you from bad data. ProjectWorker requires a `ProjectId` that exists in Project and a `WorkerId` that exists in Worker, to conform to referential integrity.

Add a second project and assign workers. You can do that with the following code:

```
INSERT INTO Project (ProjectId, ProjectName, DueDate)
    VALUES ('kitchen', 'Kitchen Remodel', '2025-07-15');
```

```
INSERT INTO ProjectWorker (ProjectId, WorkerId) VALUES
    ('db-milestone', 1), -- Rosemonde, Database
    ('kitchen', 2),      -- Kingsly, Kitchen
    ('db-milestone', 3), -- Goldi, Database
    ('db-milestone', 4); -- Dorey, Database
```

Run SELECT statements for Project and ProjectWorker to verify that the data was added to the tables correctly.

```
SELECT *
FROM Project;

SELECT *
FROM ProjectWorker;
```

You should see the following output:

ProjectIdWorkerId	Name	Summary	DueDate	IsActive
db-milestone	Database Material	Null	2022-12-31	1
Kitchen	Kitchen Remodel	Null	2025-07-15	1

ProjectId	WorkerId
db-milestone	1
db-milestone	2
Kitchen	2
db-milestone	3
db-milestone	4

UPDATE DATA

The UPDATE statement is used to change record values in a table. Its basic structure is as follows:

```
UPDATE TableName SET
    Column1 = [Value1],
    Column2 = [Value2],
    ColumnN = [ValueN]
WHERE [Condition];
```

In looking at the structure of the UPDATE statement, you should note the following:

- UPDATE `TableName` limits changes to the named table.
- One or more columns are assigned values, separated by commas, following the SET keyword.
- [`Value`] can be a value literal, another column, or even a query result.
- The WHERE [`Condition`] clause is a Boolean expression, using AND, OR, or any Boolean operators in any combination to limit records to be modified.

Watch that WHERE clause. The WHERE clause is important. Without it, you impact the whole table: *every record*. Databases do not have an "undo" command, so if you forget the WHERE clause on a query that updates a million records, you are going to have a humbling conversation with your database administrator!

Updating One Row

Because primary key values are unique to each row of a table, you can use the WHERE clause to specify the primary key value to affect only that row. This is recommended whenever possible. Listing 9.2 shows how to use UPDATE to add information to a Project record and to add a last name to a Worker record.

LISTING 9.2

Updating Rows

```
-- Provide a Project Summary and change the DueDate.
UPDATE Project SET
    Summary = 'All lessons and exercises for the relational database
milestone.',
    DueDate = '2023-10-15'
WHERE ProjectId = 'db-milestone';

-- Change Kingsly's LastName to 'Oaks'.
UPDATE Worker SET
    LastName = 'Oaks'
WHERE WorkerId = 2;
```

In this code, two updates are being executed. First, the Project table is being updated to change the Summary and DueDate for the record where the ProjectId is equal to db-milestone. For the second update, the LastName is being updated in the Worker table for the WorkerId equal to 2.

Preview Before You Update

If a query is likely to impact many rows (as any query can), it's a good practice to estimate the affected rows and make sure your WHERE condition is correct. For example, if you are updating customers in Louisiana and you know there are more than 10,000, a row count of 15 should raise a red flag.

DBAs often run SELECT statements with the same WHERE clause they plan to use in an UPDATE (or DELETE) statement before they execute the UPDATE or DELETE. If the SELECT results are suspicious, there's likely something wrong with the condition. Remember, *there's no undo in SQL*! Listing 9.3 shows SELECT statements that could be executed to preview what will be changed before you execute Listing 9.2.

LISTING 9.3

Previewing Records to Be Changed

```
SELECT *
   FROM Project
   WHERE ProjectId = 'db-milestone';

SELECT *
   FROM Worker
   WHERE WorkerId = 2;
```

You can see that the WHERE conditions from Listing 9.2 are simply used to see the records from the tables. The result should show a single record from each table, which confirms what you want.

Updating Multiple Rows

A WHERE clause can also capture many rows if it does not use a primary key field or if a range of values is selected. For example, let's say that all of Oaks' (WorkerId 2) projects are to be reassigned to Ashtonhurst (WorkerId 5). In the ProjectWorker table, WorkerId is a foreign key, so you can see in the following table that two records currently have that value.

ProjectId	WorkerId
db-milestone	1
db-milestone	2
kitchen	2
db-milestone	3
db-milestone	4

If the following UPDATE statement is executed, then only those WorkerId values will be affected:

```
UPDATE ProjectWorker SET
    WorkerID = '5'
WHERE WorkerId = 2;
```

If you run a SELECT statement to display the ProjectWorker table, you can see that only those two records are updated.

ProjectId	WorkerId
db-milestone	1
db-milestone	3
db-milestone	4
db-milestone	5
kitchen	5

WHY DID THE RECORD ORDER CHANGE? One of the foundations of relational databases is that the order of records is not important. As a result, the database engine normally uses index values to sort output unless the SELECT statement specifies a different sort order. In the ProjectWorker table, the index of kitchen + 5 is higher than the index of kitchen + 2, so it appears later in the results.

Disabling SQL_SAFE_UPDATES

If you want to update every row in a table, omit the WHERE clause. Some MySQL instances are configured to prevent an UPDATE without a WHERE. You can disable the safe updates configuration with a statement like this:

```
SET SQL_SAFE_UPDATES = 0;
```

Be sure to re-enable safe updates after you're done by using the following:

```
SET SQL_SAFE_UPDATES = 1;
```

Be aware that `SQL_SAFE_UPDATES` also prevent broad `WHERE` conditions (nonidentifying). You'll have to disable them. Listing 9.4 shows how to disable and enable `SQL_SAFE_UPDATES`.

LISTING 9.4

Disabling `SQL_SAFE_UPDATES`

```
-- Disable safe updates.
SET SQL_SAFE_UPDATES = 0;

-- Deactivate active Projects from 2022.
UPDATE Project SET
    IsActive = 0
WHERE DueDate BETWEEN '2022-01-01' AND '2022-12-31'
AND IsActive = 1;

-- Enable safe updates.
SET SQL_SAFE_UPDATES = 1;
```

In this code, you can see that safe updates are being turned off by setting `SQL_SAFE_UPDATES` to 0. The code then does an update of the `IsActive` field for any projects where the `DueDate` is between `2022-01-01` and `2022-12-31`. The listing ends by turning the safe updates back on by setting `SQL_SAFE_UPDATES` to 1.

It's also possible to `UPDATE` based on a column value. Consider the following code:

```
-- Update all of Kingsly's Task estimates to include 25% more time.
UPDATE Task SET
    EstimatedHours = EstimatedHours * 1.25
WHERE WorkerId = 2;
```

Do you need safe updates disabled for this code to work? As long as you are working in your own private database and you have a way to restore the database and its data, you can disable safe updates at your own risk. In a real working database, however, you would not want to do this. In fact, in an enterprise-level database, user permissions will likely prevent anyone other than admins from changing this setting.

DELETE DATA

The DELETE statement is used to delete rows from a table. Its basic structure is as follows:

```
DELETE FROM TableName
WHERE [Condition];
```

In looking at the structure of the DELETE statement, you should note the following:

- DELETE FROM TableName limits row removal to the named table.
- Just like SELECT and UPDATE, the WHERE [Condition] clause evaluates to a Boolean. If the result is true for a record, the record is deleted. If not, the record is ignored by the DELETE statement.

Deletes are all or nothing: they delete an entire row or they delete nothing. There is no "partial row" delete option. If you simply want to delete a couple of values in the record, use an UPDATE statement to set those values to null (assuming the columns are nullable).

REMEMBER: THERE IS NO UNDO IN SQL! As with UPDATE statements, you should execute a SELECT statement with the same WHERE clause you plan to use in a DELETE statement before running the DELETE statement to make sure you are identifying those records correctly before you delete them.

As with UPDATE statements, it is best to use primary key values to identify specific records in the WHERE clause of the DELETE statement. The following is a simple example of deleting WorkerId 50 from the Worker table:

```
DELETE FROM Worker
WHERE WorkerId = 50;
```

If the delete works as expected, a confirmation message will be given stating that one row was affected and that row will no longer appear in the table. You can run a SELECT statement to show all rows after doing the previous delete:

```
SELECT * FROM Worker;
```

As you can see in the following table, the output from this command will show that the row with WorkerId 50 is now gone.

WorkerId	FirstName	LastName
1	Rosemonde	Featherbie
2	Kingsly	Oaks
3	Goldi	Pilipets
4	Dorey	Rulf
5	Panchito	Ashtonhurst
51	Violet	Mercado

Now try deleting Panchito, whose WorkerId is 5. The code for this could be as follows:

```
DELETE FROM Worker
WHERE WorkerId = 5;
```

This code, however, causes an error message similar to the following:

```
ERROR 1451 (23000): Cannot delete or update a parent row: a foreign key
constraint fails (`trackit`.`projectworker`, CONSTRAINT `projectworker_ibfk_2`
FOREIGN KEY (`WorkerId`) REFERENCES `worker` (`WorkerId`))
```

If you look carefully, you'll see that it is exactly the same error message you saw earlier when the UPDATE statement was used that violated referential integrity. Because WorkerId 5 appears in the WorkerProject table as a foreign key, that record cannot be removed from the associated primary table without violating referential integrity.

DELETE is a form of UPDATE, so maybe SQL_SAFE_UPDATES will let us work around the problem. Listing 9.5 attempts to disable SQL_SAFE_UPDATES to see if we can then remove the worker.

LISTING 9.5

Disabling SQL_SAFE_UPDATES to Delete

```
-- Safe updates also prevent DELETE.
SET SQL_SAFE_UPDATES = 0;

DELETE FROM Worker
WHERE WorkerId = 5;

SET SQL_SAFE_UPDATES = 1;
```

When you run Listing 9.5, you might expect it to delete the row, but instead, referential integrity wins.

```
Error Code: 1451. Cannot delete or update a parent row: a foreign key
constraint fails (`trackit`.`projectworker`, CONSTRAINT `fk_ProjectWorker_
Worker` FOREIGN KEY (`WorkerId`) REFERENCES `worker` (`workerid`))
```

> **WARNING!** When you execute a SQL script (as opposed to running individual SQL statements) and any statement in the script results in an error, the database engine stops running the script immediately. Because our DELETE failed, the statement SET SQL_SAFE_UPDATES = 1; never ran. Our safe updates are still disabled! Be careful after an error. Be sure your data, schema, and database configuration are what you assume.

If you truly want to delete Panchito, you must delete all records that reference their primary key in the related tables first. Once those records are gone, referential integrity no longer applies, and you can remove the record from the primary Worker table. This is shown in Listing 9.6.

LISTING 9.6
Deleting Panchito

```
SET SQL_SAFE_UPDATES = 0;

-- Delete any Tasks first because Task references ProjectWorker.
DELETE FROM Task
WHERE WorkerId = 5;

-- Delete ProjectWorker next.
-- That removes Panchito from all Projects.
DELETE FROM ProjectWorker
WHERE WorkerId = 5;

-- Finally, remove Panchito.
DELETE FROM Worker
WHERE WorkerId = 5;

SET SQL_SAFE_UPDATES = 1;
```

Looking at this code, you can see that the first step is deleting `WorkerId` 5 from the Tasks table. This is followed by removing `WorkerId` 5 from the ProjectWorker table. Finally, `WorkerId` 5 is removed from the Worker table without error. This is all done within turning off `SQL_SAFE_UPDATES` at the beginning and then turning it back on at the end.

View the table contents by running Listing 9.7 to verify that the data has been deleted and that Panchito no longer is listed.

LISTING 9.7

Confirming Table Contents

```
SELECT *
FROM Task;

SELECT *
FROM ProjectWorker;

SELECT *
FROM Worker;
```

This code is simply selecting all the columns in the tables and displaying them. This is done for the Task, ProjectWorker, and Worker tables. You can see by the output shown here that Panchito and all constrained items are now gone:

Here is the Task table, which is empty:

TaskId	Title	Details	DueDate	EstimatedHours	ProjectId	WorkerId

Here is the ProjectWorker table:

ProjectId	WorkerId
db-milestone	1
Kitchen	2
db-milestone	3
db-milestone	4

Finally, here is the Worker table:

WorkerId	FirstName	LastName
1	Rosemonde	Featherbie
2	Kingsly	Oaks
3	Goldi	Pilipets
4	Dorey	Rulf
51	Violet	Mercado

SUMMARY

Data Manipulation Language is a subset of SQL. In this lesson, four commands provided by DML were presented that can be used to manipulate data.

- SELECT reads data from a table (or tables).
- INSERT adds rows to a table.
- UPDATE modifies values in one or more rows.
- DELETE removes one or more rows.

Within the database word, these actions are often referred to with the acronym CRUD: create, retrieve, update, and delete. You learned to create with the INSERT command. You retrieved using the SELECT command. You updated with the similarly named UPDATE command. And you deleted using the also similarly named DELETE command.

Selecting (or retrieving) data includes a wider variety of considerations, so it deserves more coverage in detail, which is what the next lesson will focus on.

Finally, it cannot be stressed enough. *There is no undo command in SQL!* You learned that you should always write a SELECT query to verify that your WHERE clause works as intended before running a DELETE or UPDATE statement. A missing or invalid WHERE clause can do a lot of damage to your data! No one wants to have that conversation with their DBA.

EXERCISES

The following exercises are provided to allow you to experiment with concepts presented in this lesson:

Exercise 9.1: Setting Up a Book List

Exercise 9.2: Updating Books

Exercise 9.3: Removing a Book

Exercise 9.1: Setting Up a Book List

In Exercise 7.1 you created a Books database. A portion of that database is presented in Figure 9.2. This version contains the book table with the book title, publication date, and a book ID. There is also a table for author names to be listed along with additional descriptive author information. If you did not create the larger database presented in the Lesson 7 exercise, then create a script that will build this smaller version now.

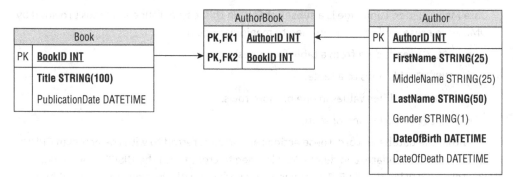

Figure 9.2 A simplified Books database

Once the database has been created, make the following additions:

- Add at least 10 books to the book table. Include the following five as part of your ten:
  - *Great Gatsby* published on April 10, 1925
  - *1984* published on June 8, 1949
  - *Pride and Prejudice* published on January 28, 1813
  - *The Hobbit* published on September 21, 1937
  - *Dad Jokes: Getting Your Kids to Laugh* published on December 2, 2020
- Add the following authors in addition to any authors from the book you added:
  - F. Scott Fitzgerald born September 24, 1896, died December 21, 1940, author of *The Great Gatsby*
  - George Orwell born June 25, 1903, died January 21, 1950, author of *1984*
  - Jane Austen born December 16, 1775, died July 18, 1817, author of *Pride and Prejudice*

- J.R.R. Tolkien born January 3, 1892, author of *The Hobbit*
- Bradley Jones born August 11, 1999, author of *Dad Jokes: Getting Your Kids to Laugh*.

Exercise 9.2: Updating Books

Use the database and tables you created in Exercise 9.1. Instead of adding new data, make the following updates to the existing records:

- Change the title of *Great Gatsby* to *The Great Gatsby*.
- Change the date of Death of J.R.R. Tolkien to September 2, 1973.
- Change the author of one of the books.

For each of these changes, which table or tables need to be updated?

Exercise 9.3: Removing a Book

If you decide to remove the book *Dad Jokes: Getting Your Kids to Laugh*, what table (or tables) will be impacted? Write and run the code to remove the book.

The author of *Dad Jokes: Getting Your Kids to Laugh* is Bradley Jones. They have no other books in the database. Should this author be removed?

The answer is dependent upon the rules for your system. Do the business or system rules allow for authors to be included in the Author table if they don't have a book in the Book table?

For this exercise, it has been determined that there should be an author stored only if they are associated to a book. Write any necessary code to remove authors who are not associated to a book.

Lesson 10

Working with SELECT Queries

While understanding DML actions such as inserting, updating, and deleting data is important, the vast majority of work that most people do in a relational database is running queries to *retrieve* data: the R in CRUD. Even novice developers who are not likely to perform administrative functions in a database should be able to use standard SELECT statements to retrieve data. These statements can also be used in conjunction with programming languages such as Java, C#, and Python, even if the developer never personally connects directly to a database. While you learned a little bit about using SELECT in the previous lesson, in this lesson, you'll dive deeper into its use.

Learning Objectives

By the end of this lesson you will be able to:

- Read data with the SELECT statement

- Filter string, number, and date values in a WHERE clause

- Use the LIKE operator to filter based on a pattern

- Describe the NULL value and strategies for using it

SETTING UP A DATABASE

To effectively learn how to use `SELECT`, you need to have a database with data that can be retrieved. One possible place to find a database you can use is a consumer complaint dataset from Data.gov (`www.data.gov`). The Data.gov site includes more than a quarter million open datasets from federal, state, local, and tribal governments. The data is interesting in its own right, but it is also excellent for practice. Without too much trouble, you can import real-world, meaningful data; decide how to model it; write complex queries; and optimize.

For this lesson, we will use a dataset of consumer complaints. The consumer complaints are anonymous in the original dataset. To keep both sides anonymous, in this lesson a dataset will be used where actual companies have been replaced with fictional companies. To create the database, follow these steps:

1. Download `consumer-complaints-schema-and-data.sql` from `the-software-guild.s3.amazonaws.com/bootcamp-v2.5/database/consumer-complaints-schema-and-data.sql`. You can also find this script in the download file for this book available at `www.wiley.com/go/jobreadysql`.

2. Execute the script in MySQL using MySQL Workbench or a MySQL command line.

Take a moment to review the script. The script uses the code presented in Listing 10.1 to create the database and then adds values to the database. The full script that you will need to download is big.

> **NOTE** Listing 10.1 contains the code to create the ConsumerComplaints database and includes the insertion of only two rows of data. For this lesson, you will need to download the script to obtain all of the records.

LISTING 10.1

A Portion of the Downloaded Script

```
drop database if exists ConsumerComplaints;

create database ConsumerComplaints;

use ConsumerComplaints;

create table Complaint (
    ComplaintId int primary key,
    DateReceived date not null,
    Product varchar(100) not null,
    SubProduct varchar(100) null,
    Issue varchar(100) not null,
    SubIssue varchar(100) null,
    ComplaintNarrative text null,
    PublicResponse varchar(250) null,
    Company varchar(100) not null,
    `State` char(2) null,
    ZipCode varchar(10) null,
    Tags varchar(100) null,
    ConsumerConsent bit null,
    SubmissionMethod varchar(50) null,
    DateSentToCompany date not null,
    ResponseToConsumer varchar(50) not null,
    TimelyResponse bit not null,
    ConsumerDisputed bit not null
);

insert into Complaint (
    ComplaintId,
    DateReceived,
    Product,
    SubProduct,
    Issue,
    SubIssue,
    ComplaintNarrative,
    PublicResponse,
    Company,
    `State`,
    ZipCode,
    Tags,
    ConsumerConsent,
    SubmissionMethod,
```

```
        DateSentToCompany,
        ResponseToConsumer,
        TimelyResponse,
        ConsumerDisputed
) values
(759217, '2014-03-12', 'Mortgage', 'Other mortgage', 'Loan modification,collection,
foreclosure', null, null, null, 'Goyette, Huel and Fadel', 'MI', '48382', '',
null, 'Referral', '2014-03-17', 'Closed with explanation', 1, 0),
(2141773, '2016-10-01', 'Credit reporting', null, 'Incorrect information on
credit report', 'Account status', 'I have outdated information on my credit
report that I have previously disputed that has yet to be removed this
information is more then seven years old and does not meet credit reporting
requirements', 'Company has responded to the consumer and the CFPB and chooses
not to provide a public response', 'Rath, Torphy and Trantow', 'AL', '352XX',
'', 1, 'Web', '2016-10-05', 'Closed with explanation', 1, 0);
```

Although you should have downloaded this script, it is worth stepping through what is being done. As you've seen before, this listing starts by using the DROP command. This removes any existing ConsumerComplaints database along with all of its data. After making sure any existing ConsumerComplaints database is gone, the CREATE DATABASE command is used to create a new ConsumerComplaints database, which is then used for the rest of the listing.

The database will have only one table called Complaint that is created using CREATE TABLE. You can look through the list of fields and see that what you learned before is being applied. The only new things you might notice is that there are several fields that are a BIT type.

Once the table is created, an INSERT is called to add all the fields to the database. The values to be added are then listed after. In this case, two records are shown. Each contains the fields that align with those listed in the INSERT statement. If you look at the down-loaded script, you'll see that there is a lot more data that will be inserted—more than makes sense to list here.

Make sure you look at the SQL syntax. You should also note the semicolons and flexible whitespace that is used. Additionally, you likely noticed that SQL isn't case sensitive, and this script uses lowercase for a lot of the commands. As mentioned, you should write your scripts in a style that is consistent and matches any organizational standards.

Database Context: Remember that because a DBMS can handle multiple databases, you must explicitly tell the DBMS which database you want to use, even if you have only one database available. You do this with a USE statement:

```
USE ConsumerComplaints;
```

Technically, the DBMS will continue to use the same database until you issue another USE statement for another database, but it is recommended that you start each query tab and .sql file with a USE statement. This reduces confusion about what database the queries reference and avoids problems that might occur if you accidentally run the queries with a different database.

With the USE statement on top, the SQL execution engine switches the database context to ConsumerComplaints before anything else executes. This is a good habit to get into, especially if your script changes a database's schema or writes data. A little bit of caution goes a long way in preventing unnecessary mistakes.

Many teams and database administrators require a leading USE. Even if they don't, it makes sense to protect yourself. Always put a USE statement at the top of your queries.

USING THE SELECT KEYWORD

The SELECT keyword is used to retrieve data from one or more tables in a database. SELECT statements are queries (or requests) for information, and they can be as simple as retrieving all data from a single table or as complex as performing functions on the data to create new data.

SELECT statements are generally safer than the other DML keywords INSERT, UPDATE, and DELETE because they do not change data in any way. At worst, you will get an error or other unexpected results because you failed to name a table or field correctly or formatted the WHERE clause incorrectly.

Using Single-Table SELECT

The simplest query is a SELECT statement written for a single table. Its structure is as follows:

```
SELECT ColumnName1, ColumnName2, ColumnNameX
FROM TableName;
```

You can apply this pattern to your own database. First, examine the Complaints table in the ConsumerComplaints database using either of the following options:

1. Run a `DESCRIBE` command at a MySQL prompt or within MySQL Workbench.

```
USE ConsumerComplaints;

DESCRIBE Complaint;
```

2. Find the MySQL Workbench Schemas panel and navigate to ConsumerComplaints ➤ Tables ➤ Complaints ➤ Columns. You can then expand the Columns node to display the columns.

With either method, you should see 18 columns, including ComplaintId, DateReceived, Product, ComplaintNarrative, and more. If you are using MySQL Workbench, then running the script in the first bullet will show the columns in the middle of the screen in a grid. This is shown in Figure 10.1.

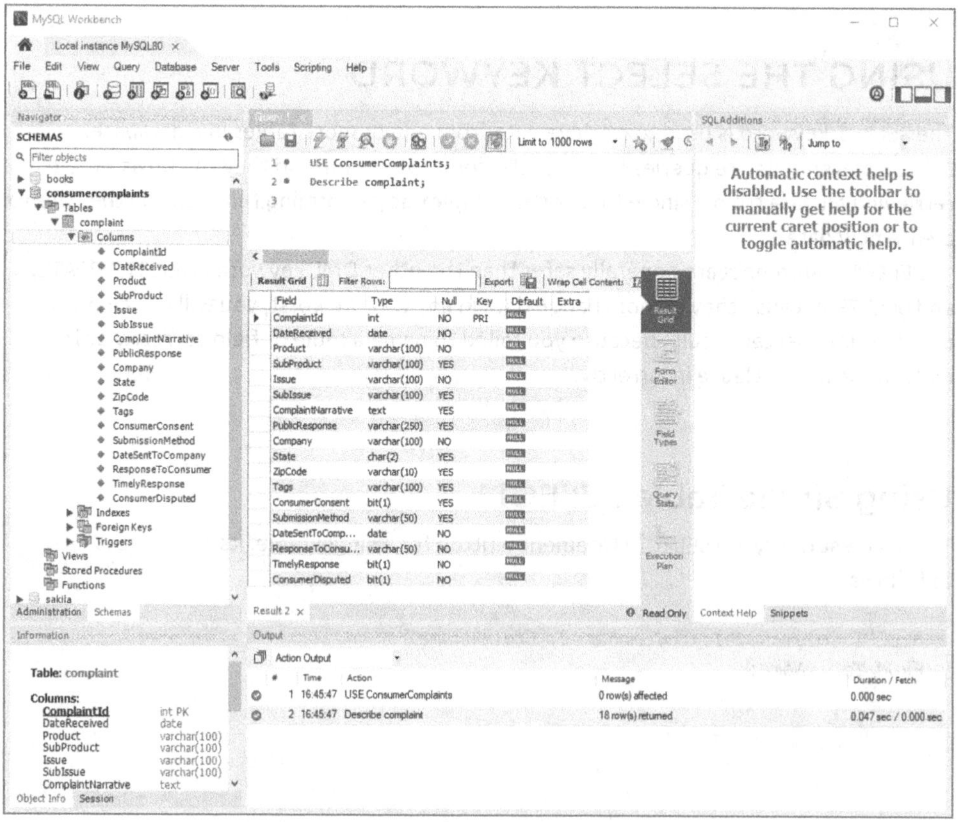

Figure 10.1 The Complaint table columns

To view a list of the dates received, products, companies, and states, you write the statement in Listing 10.2 and execute it.

LISTING 10.2

Listing Data for Some of the Columns in ConsumerComplaints

```
USE ConsumerComplaints;

SELECT DateReceived, Product, Company, State
FROM Complaint;
```

When you execute this against the data that was created from the downloaded script mentioned earlier, you will see a large number of results. The following table shows only five of the records included in the table that is displayed:

DateReceived	Product	Company	State
2012-05-21	Mortgage	Goyette, Champlin and Padberg	IL
2012-05-21	Credit card	Legros, Heathcote and Wisoky	AZ
2012-05-21	Mortgage	Little, Crist and Terry	MN
2011-12-23	Credit card	Veum Group	MD
2011-12-30	Credit card	Legros, Heathcote and Wisoky	WA

Your top five results may be different because the output is based on the data's **natural order**, or the order the data is stored on disk. SQL execution engines don't guarantee an order unless you specifically ask. More on that will be covered later in this lesson.

Using SELECT *

If you want to view or select all columns in a table, you don't have to list each column name explicitly. SQL provides a shortcut notation. This shortcut is to use the asterisk (*) symbol, as shown in Listing 10.3.

LISTING 10.3

Listing All Columns

```
USE ConsumerComplaints;

SELECT *
FROM Complaint;
```

Be careful with queries using *. They're great for a quick look at all columns in a table, but in live applications, it's wasteful to select *everything* when you don't need it. Consider an example where you need three columns from a table with 10,000 rows and 30 columns. If you use SELECT *, you are selecting 27,000 extra values for nothing. That's a lot of network traffic, server processing, and client processing.

USING THE WHERE CLAUSE

So far, our queries fetch every row in Complaints. There are 1,000 records, but 1,000 records might not be as useful as you may imagine. To see why, consider a search engine. How many times have you clicked to the second page of your search results? How about the third? Search engines display between 10 and 25 results per page. That means you'd have to click through at least 40 pages of results to see all 1,000. No one is that patient.

There needs to be a way to focus in on what's relevant. Maybe records are needed only for a specific state, specific company, or a limited date range. SQL uses the WHERE clause to filter the output to relevant results.

The WHERE clause is a conditional expression, which means it resolves to a Boolean, TRUE or FALSE, for each record in the table. If the expression is true for a record, the record is included in the result. If not, it is excluded. You can build complex Boolean expressions using AND, OR, and NOT. Table 10.1 shows the common WHERE operators you can use to build your Boolean expressions.

Table 10.1 Common WHERE Operators

Expression	Usage	Example
=	Equals	State = 'LA'
!= , <>	Not equals	State != 'LA' State <> 'LA'
AND	And (both conditions must be true)	State = 'LA' AND Product = 'Mortgage'
OR	Or (at least one condition must be true)	State = 'LA' OR Product = 'Mortgage'
IN	Match a list of values; this is a shorter way of writing a long list of OR conditions	State IN ('LA', 'AZ', 'TX')
NOT IN	Not in a list of values	State NOT IN ('LA', 'AZ', 'TX')

The WHERE clause follows the FROM clause in a SELECT statement. Listing 10.4 shows an example of using the WHERE clause to select user complaints that came from the State of Louisiana.

LISTING 10.4

Using WHERE

```
USE ConsumerComplaints;

-- Two hyphens is a SQL comment. This line is ignored.
-- If your query has many columns, you may want to stack them for readability.
-- Whitespace is ignored.

SELECT
    DateReceived,
    Product,
    Issue,
    Company
FROM Complaint
WHERE State = 'LA';
```

Looking at this code, you can see that the ConsumerComplaints database is being used. You are selecting four fields from the database that are in the Complaint table. The WHERE statement is then filtering out any records so that only the ones where State is equal to 'LA' are displayed. The result should include 13 records.

DateReceived	Product	Issue	Company
2013-03-26	Mortgage	Loan servicing, payments, escrow account	Cartwright, Sporer and Nader
2014-04-04	Bank account or service	Making/receiving payments, sending money	Cassin-VonRueden
2014-04-09	Credit reporting	Incorrect information on credit report	Welch, Bashirian and Bauch
2014-08-27	Bank account or service	Account opening, closing, or management	Medhurst-Cole
2015-06-24	Debt collection	Cont'd attempts collect debt not owed	Jacobi, Adams and Prosacco
2015-09-22	Bank account or service	Making/receiving payments, sending money	Herman-MacGyver
2015-09-30	Consumer Loan	Applied for loan/did not receive money	O'Hara-Raynor
2016-04-06	Bank account or service	Account opening, closing, or management	Veum Group
2016-05-11	Money transfers	Wrong amount charged or received	Walker LLC
2016-08-05	Debt collection	Disclosure verification of debt	Beer Inc
2016-11-26	Mortgage	Application, originator, mortgage broker	Schiller, Larkin and Orn
2017-03-17	Debt collection	Disclosure verification of debt	Zemlak-Aufderhar
2017-04-03	Debt collection	False statements or representation	Corkery-Predovic

> **NOTE** For practice, you should enter other common WHERE conditions. Try some of the following and look at the results:
>
> - Use different states.
> - Limit results by Product, Issue, or SubmissionMethod.
> - Build a complex expression using AND or OR.

Listing 10.5 contains another query for the ConsumerComplaints database. Enter this query and see how many records are fetched.

LISTING 10.5

A Query to Fetch Records from the ConsumerComplaints Database

```
USE ConsumerComplaints;

SELECT *
FROM Complaint
WHERE State = 'LA'
AND (Product = 'Mortgage' OR Product = 'Debt collection');
```

If you look at the WHERE statement, you can see that the order that Boolean operators are evaluated (Boolean precedence) can be forced by using parentheses, just like math. You should see six rows displayed as a result of running Listing 10.5.

In Listing 10.6, the parentheses have been removed. Run this listing and see how the results differ.

LISTING 10.6

Dropping the Parentheses

```
USE ConsumerComplaints;

SELECT *
FROM Complaint
WHERE State = 'LA'
AND Product = 'Mortgage' OR Product = 'Debt collection';
```

How many records are fetched with the parentheses removed? It is quite a few more: 194 rows to be exact.

Filtering Numbers

Different columns can hold different types of data, and the types may have different conditional operators. Numeric columns can be filtered using math comparison operators like < (less than) or >= (greater than or equal). There's also a keyword BETWEEN for value ranges. Table 10.2 contains some of the common comparison operators that can be used with numbers.

Table 10.2 Common Numeric Comparison Operators

Expression	Usage	Example
=	Equals	`ComplaintId = 1653822`
!=, <>	Not equals	`ComplaintId != 1653822`
		`ComplaintId <> 1653822`
>	Greater than	`ComplaintId > 10000`
>=	Greater than or equal to	`ComplaintId >= 10000`
<	Less than	`ComplaintId < 10000`
<=	Less than or equal to	`ComplaintId <= 10000`
BETWEEN	Column value in an inclusive range	`ComplaintId BETWEEN 1000 AND 30000`

Note that BETWEEN is *inclusive*, which means that both values entered in the statement will be included in the results. In the example included in Table 10.2, `ComplaintId BETWEEN 1000 AND 30000` will include both Complaint 1000 and Complaint 30000, as well as every record in between.

Comparison operators can be used to answer questions like the following:

- Does ComplaintId 1200385 exist?

- How many Complaints are there with a ComplaintId less than 100,000?

- What is the most common Product between ComplaintId 100,000 and 200,000?

Based on what you think the column titles mean, what does the query in Listing 10.7 do? How many rows does it return? Try to answer these questions before entering and running the code.

LISTING 10.7

Using Math Comparisons

```
USE ConsumerComplaints;

SELECT
    Product,
    Issue,
    Company,
    ResponseToConsumer
FROM Complaint
WHERE ConsumerDisputed = 1
AND ConsumerConsent = 1
AND Product NOT IN ('Mortgage', 'Debt collection');
```

You should see 23 rows returned as a result of running this query. You'll notice that the NOT IN operator was used, which means that only products that are not "Mortgage" or "Debt collection" will be included—assuming they are not filtered by any of the other WHERE conditions.

Filtering Dates

Relational databases store dates as a specific data type. The DATE type is small and fast, two attractive qualities for a data storage system. Dates can use many of the numeric operators; conceptually, you can think of a date as bigger or smaller than another date. Table 10.3 shows comparison operators that can be used with dates.

Table 10.3 Date Comparison Operators

Expression	Usage	Example
=	Equals	DateReceived = '2017-07-04'
!= , <>	Not equals	DateReceived != '2017-07-04'
		DateReceived <> '2017-07-04'
>	Greater than	DateReceived > '2017-07-04'
>=	Greater than or equal to	DateReceived >= '2017-07-04'
<	Less than	DateReceived < '2017-07-04'
<=	Less than or equal to	DateReceived <= '2017-07-04'
BETWEEN	Column value in an inclusive range	DateReceived BETWEEN '2017-01-01' AND '2018-01-01'

Date literals, e.g., '2017-07-04', are delimited with single ticks like strings. However, they are *not* strings under the hood. The SQL execution engine converts these date literal values to the date type if they have the proper format. The format 'yyyy-MM-dd' is understood by MySQL and most other databases.

Date filters can be used to answer questions like the following:

- Did anyone submit a complaint on New Year's Day 2014?

- Are there complaints in 2018?

- How many complaints were reported in July 2015?

- Do any complaints claim to have been sent to the company (DateSentToCompany) *before* the complaint was received (DateReceived)?

Pattern Matching Text

SQL can match patterns in strings and text. The LIKE operator works from a string example. If a column value matches the example, the record is included. The example string may contain characters with special meaning, which differentiates LIKE from simple string comparisons. Special characters include the following:

- **% (percent):** Matches any number of characters, including *no* characters
- **_ (underscore):** Matches any single character

Table 10.4 shows a number of examples of how pattern matching can be used. Note that if you want to match the literal value '%' or '_', you must precede the character (sometimes referred to as *escaping them*) with a backslash. For example, '\%' would translate to a percent sign, '%'.

Table 10.4 Examples of Pattern Matching

Expression	Description	Does Not Match	Matches
LIKE 'A%'	Matches strings that start with the letter *A* (case insensitive by default)	• Banana • @#&?! • cream corn	• Apple • A • atom • Antagonist
LIKE 'a%c'	Matches strings that start with *a*, end with *c*, and have any number of characters in between	• a brick • atom • bucolic	• abc • AC • Al's bric-a-brac • All is quiet. Calm yourself. Don't be dogmatic
LIKE '%space%'	Matches strings that contain the value *space* anywhere	• apostrophe ace	• outerspace • spaceship • tab, space, and newline
LIKE '%'	Matches all strings. Therefore, it's not particularly useful		• a spaceship • Any value works!
LIKE '_at'	Matches strings that start with any single character and end with *at*	• brat • spaceship • phat	• cat • bat • sat • rat
LIKE '___'	Matches any string exactly three characters long	• 1 • spaceship • too long	• abc • !!! • cat • too

There are a number of ways you could use pattern matching with the ConsumerComplaints database you've been using. For example, using wildcards, you could search to find answers to the following:

- Consumer complaints about companies with names that start with *V*
- Complaints that use the word *whom* in their ComplaintNarrative
- SubmissionMethods with exactly three characters
- Complaints that mention *loan* in their Issue

NULL: The "Billion-Dollar Mistake"

The value NULL is special. It represents an unset value or missing information. Any table column can be configured to accept or reject NULL values, even columns that store numbers. Unfortunately, NULL is impervious to many operators in the WHERE clause. For example, if you run a SELECT * query on the Complaint table, you will see that multiple records in the table include a NULL value in the SubProduct field, as evidenced by the sample records shown here:

ComplaintId	DateReceived	Product	SubProduct
37	2012-05-21	Mortgage	Other mortgage
105	2012-05-21	Credit card	NULL
110	2012-05-21	Mortgage	Other mortgage
7887	2011-12-23	Credit card	NULL
8908	2011-12-30	Credit card	NULL
9052	2012-01-02	Credit card	NULL
10001	2012-01-05	Mortgage	Conventional fixed mortgage

However, *none* of these WHERE statements in Listing 10.8 will work to identify the records that have a NULL value for the SubProduct field.

LISTING 10.8

Invalid WHERE Statements

```
USE ConsumerComplaints;

-- This query does not return any records at all.
SELECT *
FROM Complaint
WHERE SubProduct = NULL;
```

```
-- But neither does this!
SELECT *
FROM Complaint
WHERE SubProduct != NULL;

-- Still empty.
SELECT *
FROM Complaint
WHERE ComplaintId BETWEEN 15000 AND NULL;

-- No NULLS included in results.
SELECT *
FROM Complaint
WHERE SubProduct IN ('Other mortgage', NULL);
```

To find NULL values, the special operator IS needs to be used. You can express that a value IS NULL or IS NOT NULL. As such, the queries in Listing 10.8 can be rewritten as shown in Listing 10.9.

LISTING 10.9

Valid WHERE Statements Using IS NULL or IS NOT NULL

```
USE ConsumerComplaints;

-- Returns 278 rows
SELECT *
FROM Complaint
WHERE SubProduct IS NULL;

-- Returns 722 rows
SELECT *
FROM Complaint
WHERE SubProduct IS NOT NULL;

-- Returns 991 rows
SELECT *
FROM Complaint
WHERE ComplaintId > 15000 OR ComplaintId IS NULL;

-- Returns 391 rows
SELECT *
FROM Complaint
WHERE SubProduct = 'Other mortgage'
OR SubProduct IS NULL;
```

```
-- All Complaints with a value for ComplaintNarrative.
-- Exclude null values.
SELECT *
FROM Complaint
WHERE ComplaintNarrative IS NOT NULL;
```

In looking at this listing, you can see that IS NULL and IS NOT NULL are being used. As a result, you will see the various records displayed for each of the five different SELECT statements that contain results filtered by the corresponding WHERE clause.

> **NOTE** "Null References: The Billion Dollar Mistake" is an interesting article to read, which can be found at www.infoq.com/presentations/Null-References-The-Billion-Dollar-Mistake-Tony-Hoare.

PERFORMING CALCULATIONS

A SELECT query can also be used to perform calculations on existing data and produce new data. Calculations can be done on numbers as well as dates.

In the current dataset, there are two DATE fields: the date on which the complaint was received (DateReceived) and the date on which the complaint was sent to the company (DateSentToCompany). As shown in Listing 10.10, you can use a SELECT query to calculate the number of days between those dates.

LISTING 10.10

Calculating the Number of Days Between Two Dates

```
USE ConsumerComplaints;

SELECT
    ComplaintId,
    DateReceived,
    DateSentToCompany,
    (DateSentToCompany - DateReceived) AS DateDifference
FROM Complaint;
```

Because the database engine treats dates as numbers, you can use a simple subtraction operation to calculate the difference between the dates. This is a new value, so you can name the column DateDifference using the AS keyword. The parentheses are optional, but you should include them to improve readability.

When you run the listing, you'll see results from all the records in the database. Five sample records include the following:

ComplaintId	DateReceived	DateSentToCompany	DateDifference
37	2012-05-21	2012-05-29	8
105	2012-05-21	2012-05-21	0
110	2012-05-21	2012-05-21	0
7887	2011-12-23	2011-12-27	4
8908	2011-12-30	2012-01-03	8873

You can also use a calculation in the WHERE clause. This is shown in Listing 10.11, which has a WHERE clause that shows only the results that have dates with a difference greater than 365 days.

LISTING 10.11

Using a Calculated Value in a WHERE Clause

```
USE ConsumerComplaints;

SELECT
    ComplaintId,
    DateReceived,
    DateSentToCompany,
    (DateSentToCompany - DateReceived) AS DateDifference
FROM Complaint
WHERE (DateSentToCompany - DateReceived) > 365;
```

This code selects a number of fields from the ConsumerComplaints database based on the difference between DateSentToCompany and DateReceived. If the difference is greater than 365, the record is selected. This should generate results for 11 records. Five sample results include the following:

ComplaintId	DateReceived	DateSentToCompany	DateDifference
8908	2011-12-30	2012-01-03	8873
42864	2012-03-30	2012-07-12	382
78668	2012-05-15	2012-11-06	591
209482	2012-12-12	2013-01-18	8906
283132	2013-01-31	2013-08-09	678

In Listing 10.11, you might have noticed that the subtraction calculation was done twice, once to display the difference and again within the WHERE clause. In Listing 10.12, the code is adjusted to show an alternative.

LISTING 10.12

Using a Calculated Field in a WHERE Clause

```
USE ConsumerComplaints;

SELECT
    Newtable.ComplaintId,
    Newtable.DateReceived,
    Newtable.DateSentToCompany,
    Newtable.DateDifference
FROM (SELECT
        ComplaintId,
        DateReceived,
        DateSentToCompany,
        (DateSentToCompany - DateReceived) AS DateDifference
    FROM Complaint) as Newtable
WHERE Newtable.DateDifference > 365;
```

This time, the FROM statement from the primary SELECT is adjusted so that it is using records that are being SELECTed from the Complaint table along with the calculation to determine the date differences. The FROM clause is creating a new table called Newtable that will have a new field called DateDifference. This new table is then used in the first SELECT where the calculated field, DateDifference, is checked to determine whether it is greater than 365. The output from this listing is the same as that from Listing 10.11 with 11 records being displayed.

> **NOTE** You should note that the Newtable created in Listing 10.12 is a temporary table that can be used only within the query where it was created. The table and any fields it creates will not be accessible once the query has completed.

SUMMARY

A SELECT statement tells the SQL execution engine to read from a database. It fetches data from one or more tables and can filter the result.

You can list the columns to be included or use the asterisk (*) to select all columns. The FROM clause follows columns and indicates which table (or tables) contains the columns.

The WHERE clause follows FROM. It is a conditional, Boolean expression. If the expression is true for a record, the record is included in the result. If it is false, the record is excluded. Multiple operators can be combined using AND, OR, and other operators.

You can perform calculations using existing data in a table to create new data. The AS keyword can be used to name columns that contain calculated data.

EXERCISES

The following exercises are provided to allow you to experiment with concepts presented in this lesson:

Exercise 10.1: Complaints

Exercise 10.2: Personal Trainer

> **NOTE** The exercises are for your benefit. They help you apply what you learn in the lessons.

Exercise 10.1: Complaints

Within this lesson there were a number of suggested questions that you could answer using SELECT statements and the ConsumerComplaints database. If you did not do these while reading the lesson, then you should write the appropriate SELECT statements now.

Write corresponding SELECT statements to answer each of the following questions:

- Does ComplaintId 1200385 exist?
- How many Complaints are there with a ComplaintId less than 100,000?
- What is the most common Product between ComplaintId 100,000 and 200,000?
- Did anyone submit a complaint on New Year's Day 2014?
- Are there complaints in 2018?
- How many complaints were reported in July 2015?
- Do any complaints claim to have been sent to the company (DateSentToCompany) *before* the complaint was received (DateReceived)?
- Find consumer complaints about companies with names that start with *V*.
- Find complaints that use the word *whom* in their ComplaintNarrative.
- What are the SubmissionMethods with exactly three characters?
- Which Complaints mention *loan* in their issue?

Exercise 10.2: Personal Trainer

In these exercises, you will complete a series of SELECT queries using the PersonalTrainer schema. That sets up the Personal Trainer database.

You will need to run the `personaltrainer-schema-and-data.sql` script to create this database. You can find this with the downloaded files for this book available at www .wiley.com/go/JobReadySQL, or you can find it at `the-software-guild.s3.amazonaws` `.com/sql/v1-2003/data-files/personaltrainer-schema-and-data.sql`.

You can use any of the following methods to run this script after saving the file to your computer:

1. Open MySQL Workbench and connect to your local MySQL Server. Double-click the saved .sql file, and it should open automatically in MySQL Workbench. Use the Execute button in the toolbar to run the script and create the database.

2. In MySQL Workbench, use the Open SQL Script command in the File menu or toolbar. Navigate to the file saved on your computer, open the file, and use the Execute button to run the script.

3. Open the .sql file and copy its contents to the system clipboard. Open a new query window in MySQL Workbench or connect to MySQL Server through a command-line interface (such as Windows Command prompt or Terminal). Paste the script at the prompt and hit Enter to run it.

> **WARNING!** If you already have a database named PersonalTrainer in MySQL Server, this script will DELETE that database before rebuilding a new one. If you want to keep the existing database, you can rename the existing database before running this script, or you can modify the script to use a different name for the new database.

The PersonalTrainer schema models data for a professional personal trainer. Important concepts are described next. You will SELECT from only one table at a time in these exercises, but consider how each table might relate to another. When is more than one table required to represent a concept?

- **Client:** A personal trainer's customers. Each client has a name, an address, and a unique identifier.
- **Workout:** A themed schedule of exercises with a set of goals.
- **Exercise:** A physical activity (e.g., running, lifting weights, or stretching) that can be configured per workout. You might run a little or a lot. Weight amounts and repetitions might differ.
- **Goal:** A desired physical or emotional outcome for a client or workout.

- **Login:** Credentials for the personal trainer application. Clients may or may not have a login.
- **ExerciseCategory:** A logical group of exercises. Each exercise has a category. Categories can have parent categories.
- **Invoice:** A dated bill for a client.
- **InvoiceLineItem:** An itemized charge on an invoice.

Instructions

For each of the following activities, write and execute a SQL SELECT statement that will produce the correct results. For each activity, the first two records are provided as well as the total number of records you should see in the results. Use this information to verify your results.

Remember to USE the PersonalTrainer database. Keep in mind that there's usually more than one correct way to write a query.

Activity 1

Select all rows and columns from the Exercise table.

Here are the first 2 of 64 rows:

ExerciseID	Name	ExerciseCategoryId
1	Squat	2
2	Deadlift	2

Activity 2

Select all rows and columns from the Client table.

Here are the first 2 of 500 rows:

ClientId	FirstName	LastName	BirthDate	Address	City	StateAbbr	PostalCode
00268ec4-cdb6-4643-8e94-3aa467419af6	Ingrid	Colquitt	1982-11-11	63 Mayer Hill	Hammond	LA	70147
028f6b4d-a40c-4c6e-b285-3f12b596a461	Filberte	Beurich	1978-10-21	4 Hauk Parkway	Metairie	LA	70117

Activity 3

Select all columns from Client where the City is Metairie.

Here are the first 2 of 29 rows:

ClientId	FirstName	LastName	BirthDate	Address	City	StateAbbr	PostalCode
028f6b4d-a40c-4c6e-b285-3f12b596a461	Filberte	Beurich	1978-10-21	4 Hauk Parkway	Metairie	LA	70117
054db61d-fd8d-4de8-b5f0-ade14ac29a20	Arvy	Zorn	1994-12-08	521 Cambridge Place	Metairie	LA	70180

Activity 4

Is there a Client with the ClientId '818u7faf–7b4b–48a2–bf12–7a26c92de20c'? (0 rows.)

Activity 5

How many rows are in the Goal table?

Here are the first 2 of 17 rows:

GoalId	Name
1	Weight Loss
2	Strength

Activity 6

Select Name and LevelId from the Workout table.

Here are the first 2 of 26 rows:

Name	LevelId
Get In Shape Beginners Cardio	1
The "I don't have time…" Workout	1

Activity 7

Select Name, LevelId, and Notes from Workout where LevelId is 2.

Here are the first 2 of 11 rows:

Name	LevelId	Notes
Mindfulness, Calm, Strength, Affirmation	2	Become more by being less distracted. This yoga-based program helps you grow by shrinking your ego and anxieties.
Swimming Is Sexy	2	Swimming is low-impact, builds endurance, and makes you look and smell nice.

Activity 8

Select FirstName, LastName, and City from Client where City is Metairie, Kenner, or Gretna.

Here are the first 2 of 77 rows:

FirstName	LastName	City
Filberte	Beurich	Metairie
Arvy	Zorn	Metairie

Activity 9

Select FirstName, LastName, and BirthDate from Client for Clients born in the 1980s.

Here are the first 2 of 72 rows:

FirstName	LastName	BirthDate
Ingrid	Colquitt	1982-11-11
Son	Bullough	1988-08-09

Activity 10

Write the query from Activity 9 in a different way.

- If you used BETWEEN, you can't use it again.
- If you didn't use BETWEEN, use it!

The results should be the same as for the previous query, with 72 rows.

Activity 11

How many rows in the Login table have a .gov EmailAddress?

Here are the first 2 of 17 rows:

ClientId	EmailAddress	PasswordHash	FailedAttempts	IsLocked
0d660a51-8a2b-4b8e-be88-65a99f7e0d74	emaddoxcz@whitehouse.gov	afgLBEMAuhNqCxkAaL97pzsc42LOHkX4hvD2m9iXlQFTnE7zTm+bxi1bFnnKyYcmiZvwy97u33ObyrPbppcOa8ePwR30Eufi/0JKFWDCvvqJ2HvqSwppRkvHJDwo9hRHCUxQCi+m7	0	0x00
2ab89d12-69ed-474b-ba1b-1241947566a7	aryancw@cdc.gov	LzJOfgT0YnbK4Wh2rPaLgiK-WU2eD1FlPJXODqVpp3u77NotImQnxTPWRV13qqRa8/iC1q2rwB327v/SBflhcOd+XBhqgqjl9J11XQuE	0	0x00

Activity 12

How many Logins do *not* have a .com EmailAddress?

Here are the first 2 of 122 rows:

ClientId	EmailAddress	PasswordHash	FailedAttempts	IsLocked
03c203ea-d45d-4c35-8a04-150002ae8128	bgreenless9k@jugem.jp	mzIW8boWO2yMJvr4RU/NKsH/UZrqKK04AHidPXSQMbYNym-2O/06jMEPi697BikSglzSPOBxM9tBp7cn2t7uGcC9b1FbTmDsc4kY1YdfQwlrXbfuBE3viJ3uDyX	0	0x00
054db61d-fd8d-4de8-b5f0-ade14ac29a20	azorndu@arizona.edu	5quwr0YUzldyEOElYMCma2QbFXkScb+Hg7b8rx2aTQq3QhYwZCSi56TmEZh9LzO1db2BEhaHGf/lPTYwrv	0	0x00

Activity 13

Select the first and last names of Clients without a BirthDate.

Here are the first 2 of 37 rows:

FirstName	LastName
Andy	Sawell
Chantalle	MacGrath

Activity 14

Select the Name of each ExerciseCategory that has a parent (ParentCategoryId value is not null).

Here are the first 2 of 12 rows:

Name
Free Weights
Kettlebells

Activity 15

Select Name and Notes of each level 3 Workout that contains the word *you* in its Notes.

Here are the first 2 of 4 rows:

Name	Notes
Explosive Power: Contact Sports Training	Be the best version of yourself when you make contact.
Body Sculpting	Name the shape and we'll help you achieve it. This program will make you the master of your body.

Activity 16

Select FirstName, LastName, City from Client whose LastName starts with L, M, or N, and who live in LaPlace.

Here are the first 2 of 5 rows:

FirstName	LastName	City
Riannon	Larderot	LaPlace
Brody	Lorenc	LaPlace

Activity 17

Select InvoiceId, Description, Price, Quantity, ServiceDate, and the lineitem total, a calculated value, from InvoiceLineItem, where the line item total is between 15 and 25 dollars.

Here are the first 2 of 667 rows:

InvoiceId	Description	Price	Quantity	line_item_total
1	Individual Instruction	75.0000	0.2500	18.75000000
4	Equipment	11.9700	2.0000	23.94000000

Activity 18

Does the database include an email address for the Client, Estrella Bazely? To answer this question, it will require two queries:

- Select a Client record for Estrella Bazely. Does it exist?
- If it does, select a Login record that matches its ClientId.

Activity 19

What are the Goals of the Workout with the Name 'This Is Parkour'? You need three queries to answer this.

1. Select the WorkoutId from Workout where Name equals 'This Is Parkour' (1 row).
2. Select GoalId from WorkoutGoal where the WorkoutId matches the WorkoutId from your first query (three rows).
3. Select the goal name from Goal where the GoalId is one of the GoalIds from your second query (three rows).

Your results should be as follows:

- Endurance
- Muscle Bulk
- Focus: Shoulders

Lesson 11
Adding JOIN Queries

Relational databases model both data and relationships within the data. Their approach to relationships is clever.

- Related things don't have to be stored together.

- You can ignore related data when you don't need it.

- When you need related data, it's quick to retrieve.

Up to this point, the SELECT queries you've created ignore related data. They retrieve data from one table at a time. A single table SELECT is powerful, but it doesn't take advantage of SQL's full potential. With one small tweak, adding a bit of JOIN syntax, SELECT queries can read from multiple tables and express relationships between data explicitly.

Learning Objectives

By the end of this lesson, you will be able to:

- See the relationship between tables in a database relationship diagram, also called an entity-relationship diagram
- Understand the purpose of the JOIN keyword
- Use the JOIN keyword to retrieve data from two or more tables in a single query
- Differentiate between an INNER JOIN, an OUTER JOIN, a CROSS JOIN, and a SELF JOIN
- Use SQL aliases

STARTING WITH A SCHEMA

For this lesson, the TrackIt schema will be used. You can create this schema by running the `trackit-schema-and-data.sql` script that can be found in the Lesson 11 folder on the downloadable files for this book.

> **NOTE** If you haven't downloaded the files for this book, you can find them at `www.wiley.com/go/JobReadySQL`. For this lesson, you should use the script file in the Lesson 11 folder.

The script contains a predefined set of data required for this lesson. The data is for a video game company, GameIt. Their workers (employees) contribute to software projects. Some of the terms used with this database include the following:

- **Project** is a large chunk of work that usually results in a deliverable. Projects take months or even years to complete. In the sample data, Projects are software projects, mostly video games.
- **Worker** is a person available to work on a Project.
- **Task** is a discrete chunk of work that can be completed within several hours. A Project is completed one Task at a time.
- **TaskType** is a Task category. Each task can have one and only one type, so TaskType has a one-to-many relationship with Task.
- **TaskStatus** is a Task status. Each Task can have one and only one status, so TaskStatus has a one-to-many relationship with Task.

Some of the additional relationships and rules for TrackIt include the following:

- Project has a one-to-many relationship with Task.
- Project has a many-to-many relationship with Worker.
- Worker has a one-to-many relationship with Task.

A Task has an optional relationship with itself. How does that make sense? If a Task is large, it can be divided into smaller Tasks. A relationship is created between parent and child by including the parent's identifier in each child row. There's nothing in the schema preventing multiple levels of parents and children, but the sample data provided for this lesson is only two levels deep.

The tables and relationships for the TrackIt database can be represented visually with an entity-relation diagram (ERD) as shown in Figure 11.1. You should look at the relationships described in the previous bulleted lists and see how each is represented in the ERD.

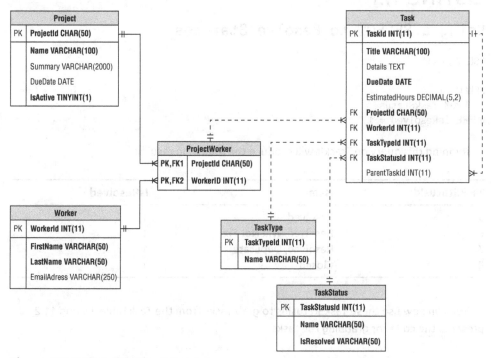

Figure 11.1 ERD for the TrackIt database

This ERD represents the database schema. You may find it useful to refer to this diagram when creating JOIN queries on the database throughout this lesson, because it shows you where each field lives and how the tables are related to each other.

GET DATA FROM MULTIPLE TABLES

Imagine you work at GameIt. Your manager asks for a list of Tasks that are in resolved status. It's not possible to generate the list from one table. To find resolved statuses, you need to look in the TaskStatus table. To find Tasks with resolved statuses, you need to look in the Task table for records with a resolved TaskStatusId.

To accomplish this, you first SELECT resolved statuses, as shown in Listing 11.1.

LISTING 11.1

Using a SELECT to Resolve Statuses

```
USE TrackIt;

SELECT *
    FROM TaskStatus
WHERE IsResolved = 1;
```

Running this query on TrackIt will produce the following results:

TaskStatusId	Name	IsResolved
5	Resolved	1
6	Resolved, Will Not Fix	1
7	Resolved, Duplicate	1
8	Closed	1

You can now use these TaskStatusIds to grab Tasks from the Task table. Listing 11.2 presents the code for grabbing the tasks.

LISTING 11.2

Selecting the Tasks

```
-- TaskStatusIds happen to be in a sequential order, so we can use BETWEEN.
-- If they were out of sequence, we might use an IN (id1, id2, idN).
SELECT *
  FROM Task
WHERE TaskStatusId BETWEEN 5 AND 8;
```

Because TaskStatusIds happen to be in a sequential order from 5 to 8, you can use BETWEEN to select the ones we want, in this case between 5 and 8. If the results were not in sequential order (such as 1, 3, 7 and 8), then you would use a WHERE clause with the IN operator, like the following:

```
WHERE TaskStatusId IN (1, 3, 7, 8);
```

When this query is executed, 276 resolved Tasks should be listed. The following is a partial set of the results:

TaskId	Title	EstimatedHours	ProjectId	TaskStatusId
3	Refactor service layer and classes	4.75	payroll	6
5	Refactor interface	7.75	payroll	6
6	Log out	26.25	payroll	8
8	Construct service layer and classes	2.25	payroll	7

You found the resolved Tasks, but the results are fragile. Consider why:

- If you want both the Task title and status name displayed together, then you must combine results from the two queries manually. With 276 tasks, that's a lot of copying and pasting.

- The second query may change each time it is executed. If the resolved statuses change, where statuses are added, removed, or edited, then the task query has to be modified. The queries can't be written once and then run whenever they are needed.

- Worst of all, the approach is error prone. It's easy to make a mistake. What happens if a status ID is missed while copying or an ID is included that doesn't belong?

USE THE JOIN CLAUSE

The JOIN clause is an optional clause in a SELECT statement. It expands a SELECT so it can retrieve results from more than one table and express relationships between rows. Rows from one table are **joined** to rows from another table and their values are combined in a single result.

A JOIN clause follows the FROM clause and precedes the WHERE in a SELECT. The basic structure is as follows:

```
SELECT
    Table1.Column1,
    Table1.Column2,
    Table2.Column1,
    Table2.ColumnN
FROM Table1
[Join Type] JOIN Table2 ON [Relationship Condition]
WHERE [Filter Condition];
```

JOIN [Table2] adds the table, Table2, to the query and makes its rows available for retrieval and filtering.

ON [Relationship Condition] defines how rows in one table relate to rows in another.

[Join Type] modifies the JOIN. It determines how unmatched rows are handled. Valid values include the following:

- INNER
- LEFT OUTER
- RIGHT OUTER
- FULL OUTER
- CROSS

Each of these will be covered in the remainder of this lesson.

INNER JOIN

An INNER JOIN returns a result *only* when rows from both tables match on their relationship condition. Visually, if you have tables A and B, the query results are the intersection of rows that satisfy the join condition, as shown in Figure 11.2. If a row from A doesn't match a row from B, it isn't included, and vice versa.

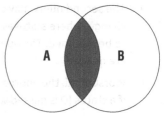

Figure 11.2 An INNER JOIN

Returning to the resolved tasks, an INNER JOIN addresses the shortcomings of the original approach. The result combines the Task title and status name, *and* it is done with a single query that can be written once yet will work again and again. There's never a need to change it.

Consider each keyword, table name, and column name in Listing 11.3. Map each to the basic JOIN structure. Pay special attention to the ON condition.

LISTING 11.3

Using a JOIN

```
SELECT
    Task.TaskId,
    Task.Title,
    TaskStatus.Name
FROM TaskStatus
INNER JOIN Task ON TaskStatus.TaskStatusId = Task.TaskStatusId
WHERE TaskStatus.IsResolved = 1;
```

In this code you can see that a TaskId and Title are being selected along with a Name from the TaskStatus table. An INNER JOIN is being used to connect the Task table to the TaskStatus table. Records will be selected when a TaskStatus record and a Task record match as a result of having the same TaskStatusId. Finally, the results are filtered based on the IsResolved status being equal to 1.

When you execute this script, you should see 276 rows of data. The following is an example of what your first four rows might look like:

TaskId	Title	Status (Name)
3	Refactor service layer and classes	Resolved, Will Not Fix
5	Refactor interface	Resolved, Will Not Fix
6	Log out	Closed
8	Construct service layer and classes	Resolved, Duplicate

Of course, it is likely your first four rows will differ. This example purposefully repeats the four Tasks from our two-query approach. You will soon see how to control the order of results.

Optional Syntax Elements

It's valid, though not necessarily recommended, to omit some of the JOIN basic structure. This includes table names, the INNER keyword, and more.

Omitting Table Names

If you look closely at the query in Listing 11.3 and compare it to single-table SELECT queries, you will notice that each of the field names is **qualified** with the name of the table that contains that field.

```
SELECT
    Task.TaskId,
    Task.Title,
    TaskStatus.Name
...
```

When dealing with a single table, it's obvious where each field lives, so qualifying each field name is redundant. When creating queries that reference two or more tables, the table names can *usually* be left out of the SELECT clause. Compare the queries in Listings 11.4 and 11.5.

LISTING 11.4

Query 1

```
-- (no table names):
SELECT
    TaskId,
    Title,
    `Name`
FROM TaskStatus
INNER JOIN Task ON TaskStatus.TaskStatusId = Task.TaskStatusId
WHERE TaskStatus.IsResolved = 1;
```

LISTING 11.5

Query 2

```
-- (includes table names).
SELECT
    Task.TaskId,
```

```
    Task.Title,
    TaskStatus.Name
FROM TaskStatus
INNER JOIN Task ON TaskStatus.TaskStatusId = Task.TaskStatusId
WHERE TaskStatus.IsResolved = 1;
```

These queries are equivalent other than the use of table names in the SELECT area of the statement. Their results and performance are identical. To the SQL engine, they are the same query.

Be aware that it is not *always* possible to omit table names. Execute the query in Listing 11.6.

LISTING 11.6

Omitting Table Names

```
SELECT
    TaskId,
    Title,
    `Name`,
    TaskStatusId -- This will cause problems.
FROM TaskStatus
INNER JOIN Task ON TaskStatus.TaskStatusId = Task.TaskStatusId
WHERE TaskStatus.IsResolved = 1;
```

When you execute this query, it returns an error.

```
Error Code: 1052. Column 'TaskStatusId' in field list is ambiguous
```

TaskStatusId is a column in both TaskStatus and Task. If it is included without a table name, the SQL engine doesn't know which one to use. In this case, it doesn't matter. The values are identical. But the SQL engine can't know that ahead of time, so it stops and warns us.

As a general rule of thumb, if your query includes two or more tables, you should qualify each field name with the appropriate table name. In cases where the same field exists in both tables *and* those fields represent a primary key and its related foreign key, you can technically use either table name. However, the convention is to use the name of the primary table rather than the name of the related table.

Similarly, in the INNER JOIN clause, the fields can be put in either order. However, because the fields have the same name, you must qualify both of them.

Omitting the INNER Keyword

The INNER keyword is also optional. If it is omitted, the SQL engine assumes an INNER JOIN. INNER JOIN is the default, as shown by running Listing 11.7.

LISTING 11.7

Omitting the INNER Keyword

```
SELECT
    Task.TaskId,
    Task.Title,
    TaskStatus.Name
FROM TaskStatus
-- INNER omitted in the following
JOIN Task ON TaskStatus.TaskStatusId = Task.TaskStatusId
WHERE TaskStatus.IsResolved = 1;
```

You can see that the INNER keyword is omitted in this listing; however, it runs without issue. Regardless, you should always include the INNER keyword. When INNER is explicit, your intentions are clear. There's no possibility that you forgot it and intended a different join type.

Multiple JOINs

On the job, you will work with databases containing hundreds or even thousands of tables. It is common to join many tables in one statement, and SQL makes this easy. Once you understand how to build one JOIN clause, adding additional JOINs is simple—the JOIN syntax is repeated for each new relationship.

In a many-to-many relationship, there are at least three tables in a SELECT statement: one many, a bridge table, and the other many. Projects and Workers have a many-to-many relationship in the TrackIt schema. Let's use that relationship to determine who's working on the "Who's a GOOD boy!?" game Project.

Start by using Project in the FROM clause. Add the INNER JOIN for the ProjectWorker bridge. Finally, add the INNER JOIN to Worker, as shown in Listing 11.8.

LISTING 11.8

Omitting the INNER Keyword

```
SELECT
    Project.Name,
    Worker.FirstName,
    Worker.LastName
FROM Project
INNER JOIN ProjectWorker ON Project.ProjectId = ProjectWorker.ProjectId
INNER JOIN Worker ON ProjectWorker.WorkerId = Worker.WorkerId
WHERE Project.ProjectId = 'game-goodboy';
```

You can see from the code that this script is selecting three fields from the tables: the project name and the first and last names of the workers. You can see that Project is being joined with ProjectWorker in the first INNER JOIN by using their ProjectId fields. In the second INNER JOIN you can see that ProjectWorker is being connected to Worker using the WorkerId. Finally, you can see that the results will only contain records where the ProjectId is equal to 'game-goodboy'.

When you run this script, you should see a list containing the project name, along with the first and last names, as shown here:

Name	FirstName	LastName
Who's a GOOD boy!?	Vlad	Anfusso
Who's a GOOD boy!?	Ealasaid	Blinco
Who's a GOOD boy!?	Ardyce	Lewins
Who's a GOOD boy!?	Evita	Shepeard
Who's a GOOD boy!?	Philis	Marion
Who's a GOOD boy!?	Dannie	Bradly
Who's a GOOD boy!?	Winny	Lawles

There are a couple of things to note about this script. After the first INNER JOIN clause, you can see that the second INNER JOIN clause was added. Note that there are no commas or separators between clauses.

Additionally, you should note that you are not required to use fields in the FROM or JOIN tables. FROM and JOIN make a table's fields available for retrieval or filtering, but you don't have to use them. In this case, ProjectWorker's fields are used only in the `ON` conditions. They're ignored in the `SELECT` value list and in `WHERE`.

To add a fourth table, add another `JOIN` and determine whether field retrieval or filtering is required. For example, if we want to see who's working on each Task in the "Who's a GOOD boy!?" project, connect the Task table with an `INNER JOIN` and retrieve the Task title, as shown in Listing 11.9.

LISTING 11.9

Joining Another Table (the Task Table)

```
SELECT
    Project.Name,
    Worker.FirstName,
    Worker.LastName,
    Task.Title
FROM Project
INNER JOIN ProjectWorker ON Project.ProjectId = ProjectWorker.ProjectId
INNER JOIN Worker ON ProjectWorker.WorkerId = Worker.WorkerId
INNER JOIN Task ON ProjectWorker.ProjectId = Task.ProjectId
    AND ProjectWorker.WorkerId = Task.WorkerId
WHERE Project.ProjectId = 'game-goodboy';
```

You can see that in Listing 11.9, an additional `INNER JOIN` is added to connect the Task table. In this case, two fields are used to make the connection, `ProjectWorker.ProjectId` is connected to `Task.ProjectId`, and `ProjectWorker.WorkerId` is used to connect to the `Task.WorkerId`. Any Task records that have the two fields match the two in the ProjectWorker table will be joined. The results are that 21 records should be displayed. The following shows five of those records:

Name	FirstName	LastName	Title
Who's a GOOD boy!?	Vlad	Anfusso	Model scene rules and structure
Who's a GOOD boy!?	Vlad	Anfusso	Prototype front-end components
Who's a GOOD boy!?	Ealasaid	Blinco	Build Level 1
Who's a GOOD boy!?	Ealasaid	Blinco	Model UI
Who's a GOOD boy!?	Ealasaid	Blinco	Add front-end components

Look closely at the `INNER JOIN` *Task ON* condition in Listing 11.9. The condition used can be any Boolean expression, as complex as required. In this case, the `ON` matches two different field values using an AND operator. The overall expression can use any of the Boolean operator including OR, AND, IS NULL, BETWEEN, etc. The expression can also match on field values or literal values. What you will find is that the use of ON is just as flexible as WHERE.

RULE OF THUMB A SELECT statement that includes N tables should have N-1 JOIN statements. For example, when two tables are used, only one JOIN is needed. A SELECT statement with four tables requires three JOINs to work correctly. Each JOIN should represent a different pair of tables.

A number of common questions come up with using multiple joins. First, can you JOIN only on foreign key constraints? The answer is no. The ON condition can include anything that evaluates to a Boolean.

A second common question is does the order of JOINs matter? In this case, the answer is yes and no, but mostly no. As long as you define your relationships correctly, the SQL engine will come up with a strategy, or *query plan*, that optimizes your query's performance. The JOIN order is most important in expressing meaning to other developers. Start with the most important concepts and link related tables in the most meaningful way. Occasionally, the SQL engine gets confused and doesn't optimize your query correctly. In those rare cases, a DBA will work with you to rewrite your query. It's not a task for a junior developer.

To be successful with JOIN queries, you must first map out tables and conditions for the ON statements. A few minutes of research will save countless minutes of debugging.

INNER JOIN Limitations

INNER JOIN returns a record for each row match between joined tables. What happens when a row exists in one table but doesn't match a row in the other? For example, grab all TrackIt Tasks with this:

```
SELECT * FROM Task;
```

This query returns 543 rows. Now, JOIN each Task to its status.

```
SELECT *
    FROM Task
INNER JOIN TaskStatus ON Task.TaskStatusId = TaskStatus.TaskStatusId;
```

The asterisk effectively includes all fields from both tables (including the duplicated TaskStatusID), but this second query returns only 532 rows. What's going on?

To clarify, do one final query.

```
SELECT *
FROM Task
WHERE TaskStatusId IS NULL;
```

The query returns 11 rows. There are our missing rows! The 532 results of the second query with the 11 results of this third query equal the total 543 shown in the first query.

532 + 11 = 543

In the Task status query, the JOIN condition Task.TaskStatusId = TaskStatus.Task-StatusId fails for the 11 tasks without a TaskStatusId. An INNER JOIN requires a match, so those tasks are eliminated from the result.

Sometimes that's what is wanted, but sometimes it's not. There are scenarios where every task is absolutely required regardless of its status. To accomplish that, a new JOIN type is needed.

OUTER JOIN: LEFT, RIGHT, AND FULL

OUTER JOINs are forgiving. They return a record even when rows don't match in joined tables. There are three types.

- LEFT OUTER JOIN
- RIGHT OUTER JOIN
- FULL OUTER JOIN

The left or right designation indicates where a table is mentioned in relation to the JOIN clause. If a table is mentioned before a JOIN (e.g., in the FROM clause), it is "left" of the JOIN. If it is mentioned after, it is "right" of the JOIN.

Consider the following:

```
SELECT *
FROM A
[Join Type] OUTER JOIN B ON [Condition];
```

When the [Join Type] is LEFT, the results include "everything from table A and whatever matches from table B." RIGHT results include "everything from table B and whatever matches from table A." FULL OUTER JOIN results are "everything from both tables regardless of match." Table 11.1 presents a visual representation of the three OUTER JOIN statements.

Just like INNER, the OUTER keyword is optional. The LEFT, RIGHT, and FULL keywords are not optional. (If you omit both LEFT and OUTER, the SQL engine would assume an INNER JOIN.)

> **NOTE** MySQL does not support FULL OUTER JOIN. The FULL OUTER is included here so you are aware of option. Many other database engines support it.

Table 11.1 Visual Representation of OUTER JOINs

JOIN Type	Diagram
	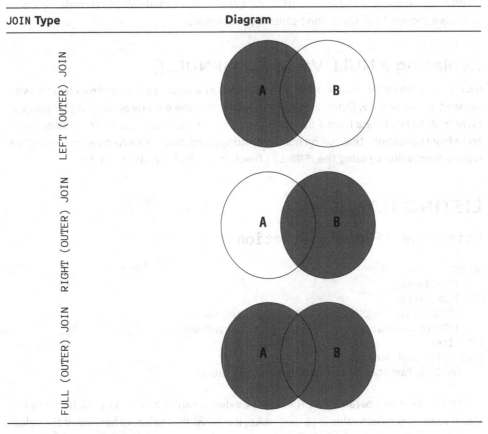

To fix the Task query, add a LEFT OUTER JOIN, as shown in Listing 11.10. Because a LEFT OUTER JOIN is being used, all records in the table mentioned before the JOIN, in this case the Task table, will be included.

LISTING 11.10

Adding the LEFT OUTER JOIN

```
SELECT *
  FROM Task
LEFT OUTER JOIN TaskStatus
    ON Task.TaskStatusId = TaskStatus.TaskStatusId;
```

With the addition of the LEFT OUTER JOIN, the results include all 543 records. This is true even though 11 of them don't contain status values.

Replacing a NULL Value with IFNULL()

NULL values can cause trouble. NULL is the absence of a value, so it's unsafe to treat it as a number, string, or date. Depending on how you receive the data (programming languages offer tools to fetch data from a database), you'll be forced to account for NULL values separate from validations that run on numbers, strings, and dates. It's often easier to specify a replacement value by using the IFNULL() function, as shown in Listing 11.11.

LISTING 11.11

Using the IFNULL() Function

```
SELECT
    Task.TaskId,
    Task.Title,
    IFNULL(Task.TaskStatusId, 0) AS TaskStatusId,
    IFNULL(TaskStatus.Name, '[None]') AS StatusName
FROM Task
LEFT OUTER JOIN TaskStatus
    ON Task.TaskStatusId = TaskStatus.TaskStatusId;
```

IFNULL takes two parameters. The first is a value. It can be a field, a calculation, or a literal value. If the field value is IS NOT NULL, it returns that value. Otherwise, if the value is IS NULL, it returns the second parameter. The second parameter can be any value from a field, a calculation, or a literal value.

IFNULL(Task.TaskStatusId, 0) is an expression, not a column, so the AS keyword is used to label it. Without AS, the column is labeled by the expression, something like IFNULL(Task.TaskStatusId, 0). That's not as clear as something like TaskStatusId.

The AS keyword is optional. A name can be assigned without using it.

```
IFNULL(TaskStatus.Name, '[None]') StatusName
```

Explicitly labeling a column is called *aliasing*. Aliases are discussed in-depth later in this lesson.

Projects Without Workers

Consider another example. In the TrackIt schema, Workers are assigned to Projects (or vice versa). Are there Projects without Workers or Workers without Projects? How would this be determined?

To start, investigate Projects without Workers. You need a JOIN that will include Project rows even if there are no matched Worker rows. To make matters more complicated, Workers are associated with Projects via a bridge table. That means a minimum of two JOINs are needed.

If Project is put into the FROM clause, a LEFT OUTER can be used to ensure each Project row is included. The LEFT OUTER connects to ProjectWorker. From there, you can connect to Worker. Again, a LEFT OUTER is needed. If you connect ProjectWorker to Worker via an INNER JOIN, it will undo the plan for the LEFT OUTER from Project to ProjectWorker. The INNER JOIN *requires* a Worker, so the whole query would behave like an INNER JOIN. Listing 11.12 presents the code for these joins.

RULE OF THUMB As you walk from related table to related table via JOINs, once you need an OUTER JOIN, you likely always need an OUTER JOIN.

LISTING 11.12

Finding Projects Without Workers

```
SELECT
    Project.Name ProjectName, -- An alias makes this clearer.
    Worker.FirstName,
    Worker.LastName
FROM Project
LEFT OUTER JOIN ProjectWorker ON Project.ProjectId = ProjectWorker.ProjectId
LEFT OUTER JOIN Worker ON ProjectWorker.WorkerId = Worker.WorkerId;
```

In this listing you can see that the project name is being selected and used with an alias. Also selected are the worker's first and last names. These are pulled from Project with the OUTER JOINs. The result is that 166 records are displayed including the ones without workers. The following are five of the records you should see:

ProjectName	FirstName	LastName
GameIt Accounts Payable	Halli	Vel
GameIt Accounts Payable	Kenon	Kirkham
GameIt Accounts Payable	Ealasaid	Blinco
GameIt Accounts Payable	Zea	Irving
GameIt Accounts Payable	Cherri	Binden

That works, but it's not great. There *is* a Project without Workers, but you have to scroll through 166 records to find it. Did you find it?

If all you care about are the Projects without Workers, then you can add a WHERE clause that throws out Projects *with* Workers. In a way, it's the inverse of an INNER JOIN. It's an INNER's negative space. From this, you can see that the following are true:

- INNER JOIN: Relationship *must* exist

- OUTER JOIN: Relationship is optional

- OUTER JOIN with filter: Relationship *must not* exist

We filter missing relationships by detecting NULL. This is shown in Listing 11.13.

LISTING 11.13

Removing Projects with Workers

```
SELECT
    Project.Name ProjectName,
    Worker.FirstName,
    Worker.LastName
FROM Project
LEFT OUTER JOIN ProjectWorker ON Project.ProjectId = ProjectWorker.ProjectId
LEFT OUTER JOIN Worker ON ProjectWorker.WorkerId = Worker.WorkerId
WHERE ProjectWorker.WorkerId IS NULL; -- Throws out projects with workers.
```

With the addition of the WHERE statement, you can see that the output has now changed. There's only one Project without Workers, which is now displayed. This is for ProjectId equal to **game-smell** with the Name **Do you smell that?**

Because you don't care about Workers, you can simplify the query by omitting the Worker table, as shown in Listing 11.14. There is no reason to include Workers if you're only checking that they don't exist.

LISTING 11.14

Omitting the Worker Table

```
-- Projects without workers, you only need the bridge table to confirm.
SELECT
    Project.Name ProjectName
FROM Project
LEFT OUTER JOIN ProjectWorker ON Project.ProjectId = ProjectWorker.ProjectId
WHERE ProjectWorker.WorkerId IS NULL;
```

This listing operates exactly like the previous one; however, it is more efficient because it no longer includes the unneeded LEFT OUTER JOIN for the Worker table.

Workers Without a Project

It's also possible to find all Workers who are not assigned to a Project without changing the order of your query. If you change all LEFTs to RIGHTs, it's the last joined table, Worker, that is always included regardless of what's on the "left." Add a NULL ProjectId filter, and you will get Workers without Projects. Listing 11.15 shows these changes.

LISTING 11.15

Getting Workers Without a Project

```
SELECT
    Project.Name ProjectName,
    Worker.FirstName,
    Worker.LastName
FROM Project
RIGHT OUTER JOIN ProjectWorker ON Project.ProjectId = ProjectWorker.ProjectId
RIGHT OUTER JOIN Worker ON ProjectWorker.WorkerId = Worker.WorkerId
WHERE ProjectWorker.ProjectId IS NULL;
-- WHERE ProjectWorker.WorkerId IS NULL; // This works as well. Why?
```

This code contains the changes that were described. The result is 12 records of workers who don't have a project. The following are 5 of the 12 records:

ProjectName	FirstName	LastName
	Nora	Riha
	Carny	Atton
	Renell	Cathel
	Viviana	Seabridge
	Tabbie	Toothill

Because you know these workers are not associated with a project, you know the project name is going to be blank. Thus, again, you can simplify the listing by omitting Project, as shown in Listing 11.16.

LISTING 11.16

Simplifying the Workers Without a Project to Drop Project Name

```
-- Workers without a project
SELECT
    Worker.FirstName,
    Worker.LastName
FROM ProjectWorker
RIGHT OUTER JOIN Worker ON ProjectWorker.WorkerId = Worker.WorkerId
WHERE ProjectWorker.ProjectId IS NULL;
```

Better yet, rewrite the query to put the important concept, Worker, first. Change the RIGHT to LEFT OUTER JOIN and reorder the tables.

LISTING 11.17

Workers Without Projects, from the Left

```
SELECT
    Worker.FirstName,
    Worker.LastName
FROM Worker
LEFT OUTER JOIN ProjectWorker ON Worker.WorkerId = ProjectWorker.WorkerId
WHERE ProjectWorker.WorkerId IS NULL;
```

The results and performance characteristics of these queries in Listing 11.16 and Listing 11.17 are identical. It is simply two ways to get to the same results.

RULE OF THUMB Any `RIGHT OUTER JOIN` can be rewritten as a `LEFT`, and it's often easier to visualize relationships when they all go in the same, single direction. Consider transforming `RIGHT`s to `LEFT`s for consistency.

SELF-JOIN AND ALIASES

Look closely at the foreign key, ParentTaskId, in the Task table in Figure 11.1 presented earlier in the lesson. ParentTaskId is nullable and references Task's primary key, TaskId. The Task table has a self-referential relationship. Any single Task can be a parent to another Task by setting the parent's TaskId as the value of the child's ParentTaskId. The parent-child relationship is optional because ParentTaskId is nullable.

Self-referential relationships are unusual, but not *that* unusual. They're useful for homogeneous data organized in a hierarchy. Examples include the following:

- **File system folders:** Each folder lives inside another, root folder excluded.
- **Comment threads:** Comments may be a response to another comment, which in turn may be a response to a comment.
- **Software UI menus:** The File menu opens a list of menu options; select one and it opens a list of menu options, etc.

Can you `JOIN` a table to itself? You can try to do this as shown in Listing 11.18.

LISTING 11.18

Joining a Table to Itself

```
SELECT *
FROM Task
INNER JOIN Task ON Task.TaskId = Task.ParentTaskId;
```

In this listing, you can see that all fields are being selected in the Task table. An `INNER JOIN` is being used to connect the `TaskId` to the `ParentTaskID`.

If you execute this query, you'll find that it won't work. You will get the following error:

```
Error Code: 1066. Not unique table/alias: 'Task'
```

The SQL engine can't tell how one Task table is different from the other. There needs to be a way to differentiate between parent and child. Earlier you learned about using a column alias. It's also possible to create a *table alias*. The syntax is similar: label the table with a name immediately following it and replace the table name with the label everywhere else it is used. Listing 11.19 shows table aliases in use.

LISTING 11.19

Table Aliases to Differentiate Parent vs. Child Tasks

```
SELECT
    parent.TaskId ParentTaskId,
    child.TaskId ChildTaskId,
    CONCAT(parent.Title, ': ', child.Title) Title
FROM Task parent
INNER JOIN Task child ON parent.TaskId = child.ParentTaskId;
```

In this listing, you can see that table aliases are being added for the Task table. Data is being selected from a Task table aliased as parent, which is then being joined to another Task table being aliased as child. The appropriate fields from the two aliased tables are then used to connect the tables. The result is that 416 records are displayed in the format shown here with four of the records:

ParentTaskId	ChildTaskId	Title
1	2	Log in: Refactor data store
1	3	Log in: Refactor service layer and classes
1	4	Log in: Create network architecture
1	5	Log in: Refactor interface

This listing prints three values for each record. The first two are the parent TaskId and the child record TaskId. The third, however, is a created value that uses the parent and child Titles. You can see that the CONCAT function is used to concatenate the two values along with a colon and space. The result is much more legible output.

SQL EXPRESSIONS SQL is a rich programming language. You are not limited to field values and value literals in your SELECT value list, WHERE condition, or ON condition. You can use functions like ISNULL or CONCAT in combination with values and operators. The only restriction is that your final expression must evaluate to a value.

Aliases aren't just for self-referential joins. They are commonly used to tidy up queries and make them less verbose. Listing 11.20 is similar to the multitable project and task query shown earlier in Listing 11.9.

LISTING 11.20

Multitable Project and Task Query

```
SELECT
    p.Name ProjectName,
    w.FirstName,
    w.LastName,
    t.Title
FROM Project p
INNER JOIN ProjectWorker pw ON p.ProjectId = pw.ProjectId
INNER JOIN Worker w ON pw.WorkerId = w.WorkerId
INNER JOIN Task t ON pw.ProjectId = t.ProjectId
    AND pw.WorkerId = t.WorkerId
WHERE p.ProjectId = 'game-goodboy';
```

In this example, the field names are qualified, but an alias is used for each table name. The aliases themselves are defined after the name of each table.

```
FROM Project p
INNER JOIN ProjectWorker pw ON p.ProjectId = pw.ProjectId
INNER JOIN Worker w ON pw.WorkerId = w.WorkerId
INNER JOIN Task t ON pw.ProjectId = t.ProjectId
    AND pw.WorkerId = t.WorkerId
```

In some ways, these aliases feel like variables you might use in Java or another programming language, and in those languages, you have to define a variable before you can assign a value to it. The database engine executes the entire query as a unit, however, so it allows the aliases to be assigned *after* they have been used. When the database engine sees a qualifier it doesn't recognize, it simply reads the rest of the query to figure it out. Aliases also don't persist outside of the current query, even when they are in the same script. As soon as the database engine finishes running the query, the aliases are forgotten.

For many teams, this is less "chatty" than the version with explicit table names, but using individual letters as aliases can be tricky if you have multiple tables whose name starts with the same letter. Check on your team's coding standard. If it doesn't exist, collaborate and create one. Consistent layout and aliases make code easier to read.

CROSS JOIN

CROSS JOIN does not use an ON clause because it does not match on a condition. Instead, CROSS JOIN creates a **Cartesian product**, with every possible combination of rows between the joined tables included in the results.

Let's say you want to see Inez Fanthome, WorkerId 1, combined with every nongame Project. The results don't show actual relationships; they just show every possible combination. Listing 11.21 shows the query for this.

LISTING 11.21

CROSS JOIN

```
SELECT
    CONCAT(w.FirstName, ' ', w.LastName) WorkerName,
    p.Name ProjectName
FROM Worker w
CROSS JOIN Project p
WHERE w.WorkerId = 1
AND p.ProjectId NOT LIKE 'game-%';
```

There are six nongame Projects and 1 Worker, so the Cartesian product consists of the six combinations shown here:

WorkerName	ProjectName
Inez Fanthome	GameIt Accounts Payable
Inez Fanthome	GameIt Accounts Receivable
Inez Fanthome	GameIt Enterprise
Inez Fanthome	GameIt Human Resource Intranet
Inez Fanthome	GameIt HR Intranet V2
Inez Fanthome	GameIt Payroll

Another way to imagine a CROSS JOIN is to think of cards. If one table holds suits (hearts, clubs, diamonds, spades) and another table holds values (2–10, J, Q, K, A), the CROSS JOIN of suits and values would be a full deck of cards.

CROSS JOINs are rare in database processes, but they can appear in more advanced scenarios.

SUMMARY

The JOIN clause extends the SELECT statement. It allows data to be fetched from multiple tables and express relationships between rows in separate tables. JOIN combines values from multiple tables into a single record.

There are several JOIN types. They differ in the way they handle missing rows in related tables.

- **INNER JOIN:** Returns a record only when rows from each side of the relationship match.
- **LEFT OUTER JOIN:** Always returns rows from the table named before the JOIN. Returns matching rows from the table named after the JOIN if they exist.
- **RIGHT OUTER JOIN:** Always returns rows from the table named after the JOIN. Returns matching rows from the table named before the JOIN if they exist.
- **FULL OUTER JOIN:** Returns rows from both joined tables, regardless of a matching row on the other side of the relationship. MySQL does not support FULL OUTER JOIN.
- **CROSS JOIN:** Returns a Cartesian product of rows from two tables.

This lesson also mentioned that a self-join is any JOIN that relates a table to itself. Additionally, you learned that an alias is an explicit label for result columns and tables. Aliases are useful to remove ambiguity and make queries less verbose.

EXERCISES

The following exercises are provided to allow you to experiment with concepts presented in this lesson:

Exercise 11.1: User Stories

Exercise 11.2: Personal Trainer Activities

> **NOTE** The exercises are for your benefit. They help you apply what you learn in the lessons.

Exercise 11.1: User Stories

Write a single SELECT statement that will allow you to present all the User Story tasks within the TrackIt database. Include the TaskType name along with the Project Names where the task has been included as well as the First and Last Name of the workers on that project.

Exercise 11.2: Personal Trainer Activities

Complete a series of JOIN queries in each of the following activities by using the PersonalTrainer schema. If you already have the PersonalTrainer database, you are welcome to use it. If not, you can use find and run the personaltrainer-schema-and-data.sql script within the downloaded files for this book. This is the same database used in the previous lesson.

After running the script, use MySQL Workbench or a MySQL Command Line to review the tables in the database and the fields in each table. You may also want to reference the ERD in Figure 11.3 to identify the relationships between tables.

Use the following information to write queries shown in the following activities:

- Run each query and check your results against the expected row count.
- Remember to include an appropriate USE statement with each query.
- You may use aliases if you want, but you are not required to do so unless the instructions specify it.
- Verify that the results include only the columns requested in the instructions.

Each activity indicates the number of expected rows that the results should include.

Activity 1 (64 Rows)

Select all columns from the ExerciseCategory and Exercise tables. The tables should be joined on ExerciseCategoryId. This query should return all Exercises and their associated ExerciseCategory.

Activity 2 (9 Rows)

Select ExerciseCategory.Name and Exercise.Name where the ExerciseCategory does not have a ParentCategoryId (it is null). Again, join the tables on their shared key (ExerciseCategoryId).

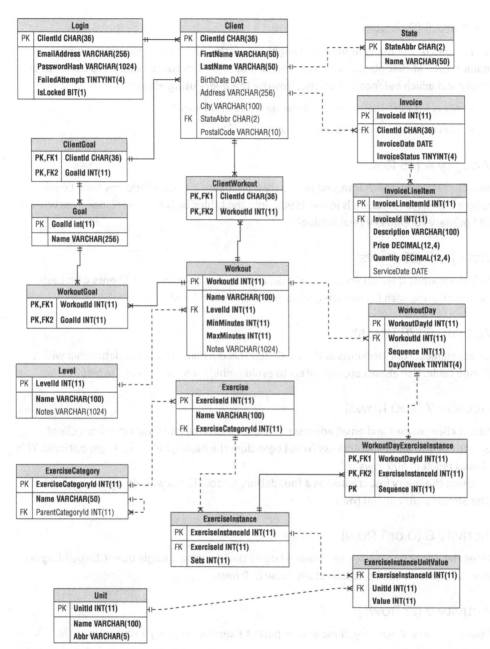

Figure 11.3 The Personal Trainer schema

Activity 3 (9 Rows)

The results of the query in Activity 2 might be a little confusing. If you used the field names, then at first glance, it is probably hard to tell which Name belongs to ExerciseCategory and which belongs to Exercise. Rewrite the query using aliases:

- Alias `ExerciseCategory.Name as 'CategoryName'`.
- Alias `Exercise.Name as 'ExerciseName'`.

Activity 4 (35 Rows)

Select FirstName, LastName, and BirthDate from Client and EmailAddress from Login where `Client.BirthDate` is in the 1990s. Join the tables by their key relationship. What is the primary-foreign key relationship?

Activity 5 (25 Rows)

Select `Workout.Name`, `Client.FirstName`, and `Client.LastName` for Clients with Last-Names starting with C. How are Clients and Workouts related?

Activity 6 (78 Rows)

Select Names from Workouts and their Goals. This is a many-to-many relationship with a bridge table. Use aliases appropriately to avoid ambiguous columns in the result.

Activity 7 (200 Rows)

Select client names and email addresses. Select FirstName and LastName from Client. Select ClientId and EmailAddress from Login. Join the tables, but make Login optional. This should result in 500 rows.

Using the query just created as a foundation, select Clients who do *not* have a Login. This should result in 200 rows.

Activity 8 (0 or 1 Row)

Does the Client Romeo Seaward have a Login? Decide using a single query. Depending on how this query is set up, it will return 1 row or 0 rows.

Activity 9 (12 Rows)

Select `ExerciseCategory.Name` and its parent ExerciseCategory's Name. Hint: This requires a self-join.

Activity 10 (16 Rows)

Rewrite the query from Activity 9 so that every ExerciseCategory.Name is included, even if it doesn't have a parent.

Activity 11 (50 Rows)

Are there Clients who are not signed up for a Workout? Write the query to determine the answer.

Activity 12 (6 Rows, 4 Unique Rows)

Which Beginner-Level Workouts satisfy at least one of Shell Creane's Goals? Note that Goals are associated to Clients through ClientGoal. Additionally, Goals are associated to Workouts through WorkoutGoal.

Activity 13 (26 Workouts, 3 Goals)

Select all Workouts. Join to the Goal 'Core Strength', but make it optional. Note that you might need to look up the GoalId before writing the main query.

If you filter on Goal.Name in a WHERE clause, Workouts will be excluded. Why?

Activity 14 (744 Rows)

The relationship between Workouts and Exercises is…complicated. Workout links to WorkoutDay (one day in a Workout routine), which links to WorkoutDayExerciseInstance (Exercises can be repeated in a day so a bridge table is required), which links to ExerciseInstance (Exercises can be done with different weights, repetitions, laps, etc.), which finally links to Exercise.

Select Workout.Name and Exercise.Name for related Workouts and Exercises.

Lesson 12
Sorting and Limiting Query Results

As row counts increase, it becomes increasingly important to control the order in which results are returned. If results include hundreds, thousands, or even millions of records, the most relevant records should be first. Users do not have the patience to scroll through records to find what they need, nor should they have to.

It is also important to limit results when they get too big. There's no sense fetching 10,000 records from a database when a user looks at only the first 10. Restricting the results prevents the user from being overwhelmed and conserves resources. Limited results cut down on network bandwidth and server processing.

Learning Objectives

By the end of this lesson, you will be able to:

- Use the ORDER BY clause to sort query results
- Use LIMIT to control the number of records returned
- Use DISTINCT to return only unique records

The TrackIt schema from the Lesson 11, "Adding JOIN Queries" will be used again for this lesson. If you already have a copy from an earlier lesson, you are welcome to use that copy. Otherwise, you can run the `TrackIt.sql` script found in the downloadable files for this book. This will allow you to run the queries provided in this lesson to see the results.

USING ORDER BY

You have the ability to sort the output from a SQL query. You can do this by using ORDER BY. The ORDER BY clause is an optional extension to the SELECT statement. The ORDER BY keywords are followed by one or more columns, and the results of the query will be sorted by the columns' values. An ORDER BY clause also has the option to include the sort direction, either in ascending or descending order. The default direction is ascending.

Results can be sorted by any column, not just columns retrieved in the SELECT value list. Sorting occurs before SELECT values are evaluated, so the SQL engine has access to all columns.

Sort by a Single Column

Let's look at sorting by a single column. As an example, start with TrackIt's Workers. Select all the columns from the Worker table.

```
SELECT * FROM Worker;
```

Using this standard SELECT statement, the results are sorted in *natural order*. In this case, it's by a Worker's primary key, WorkerId, ascending. There are 100 Workers, so spotting one particular Worker isn't easy.

To explicitly sort the results, you can add the ORDER BY clause mentioned previously. ORDER BY follows the WHERE clause if it's present. This query doesn't have a WHERE, so you add the ORDER BY after FROM, as shown in Listing 12.1.

LISTING 12.1

Using ORDER BY

```
SELECT *
   FROM Worker
ORDER BY LastName;
```

The default sort direction is ascending, so the Workers are sorted from last name Achromov to Zorzi. To reverse the direction, you must be more explicit. The keyword ASC sorts ascending, while DESC sorts descending. In Listing 12.2, the sort order is set to be ascending by LastName.

LISTING 12.2

Using ASC

```
SELECT *
   FROM Worker
ORDER BY LastName ASC;
```

In this listing, ASC isn't strictly required since it is the default sort direction. As such, the results of Listing 12.2 should be identical to those of Listing 12.1. To change the sort direction to descending by LastName, you would use the DESC keyword, as shown in Listing 12.3.

LISTING 12.3

Sorting in Descending Order

```
SELECT *
   FROM Worker
ORDER BY LastName DESC;
```

Sorting is no different for JOIN queries. When you do a sort within JOINed tables, you should qualify your sort column with its table name or alias. Listing 12.4 shows information on Workers sorted by LastName using a qualifier.

LISTING 12.4

Sorting Joined Tables

```
SELECT
    w.FirstName,
    w.LastName,
    p.Name ProjectName
FROM Worker w
INNER JOIN ProjectWorker pw ON w.WorkerId = pw.WorkerId
INNER JOIN Project p ON pw.ProjectId = p.ProjectId
ORDER BY w.LastName ASC;
```

With this query, the first and last names are displayed along with the project name. To get both the worker and project name, the Worker, ProjectWorker, and Project tables need to be joined. You can see that each of the joined tables is given a qualifier name to make it easy to keep track of what columns and tables are being used. In this case, the Worker table is qualified as w, and the sort then uses w.LastName.

With the results sorted, it is relatively easy to scan through the Workers and see which Projects they're working on.

Sort by Multiple Columns

Sometimes you need to sort by multiple columns. Sorting by one column creates groups of data with the same value in that column. Adding a second sort column organizes the data within each group. This is similar to the sort order in a phone book or contact list, where each person's name may be sorted first by last name to create groups of people with the same last name (like Smith or Jones). You can then sort by first name so that Bob Jones appears before Robert Jones, but both of them appear before anyone with the last name Smith.

In the TrackIt database, some Workers are assigned to many Projects. The Projects are in natural order within the sorted results, so spotting a particular Project is hard because their order is jumbled. It would be easier if the Projects' order was explicit.

To make the order more usable and explicit, first sort by a Worker's last name and *then* sort by the Project's name, as shown in Listing 12.5.

LISTING 12.5

Sorting by LastName, Then the project Name

```
SELECT
    w.FirstName,
    w.LastName,
    p.Name ProjectName
FROM Worker w
INNER JOIN ProjectWorker pw ON w.WorkerId = pw.WorkerId
INNER JOIN Project p ON pw.ProjectId = p.ProjectId
ORDER BY w.LastName ASC, p.Name ASC;
```

You can see in this listing that the sort now includes both the LastName from the Worker table followed by the Name from the Project table. These are separated by a comma. Thus, the results are grouped by Worker, and Projects are listed alphabetically within each Worker group. The following are the first 11 rows of the output:

FirstName	LastName	ProjectName
Thorin	Achromov	It's the Economy, Stupid!
Ephrayim	Aleswell	It's the Economy, Stupid!
Dionisio	Allnatt	Midge
Vlad	Anfusso	GameIt Enterprise
Vlad	Anfusso	It's the Economy, Stupid!
Vlad	Anfusso	Who's a GOOD boy!?
Roshelle	Antoniades	Middle School Breakout
August	Arthurs	GameIt Human Resource Intranet
Dianemarie	Atley	CookerMaker
Dianemarie	Atley	Midge
Dianemarie	Atley	Midge II

Each column in an ORDER BY has an independent sort direction. If you want Workers by last name descending and Projects by project name ascending, it's an easy change, as shown in Listing 12.6.

LISTING 12.6

Changing Sort Order for Individual Sort Items

```
SELECT
    w.FirstName,
    w.LastName,
    p.Name ProjectName
FROM Worker w
INNER JOIN ProjectWorker pw ON w.WorkerId = pw.WorkerId
INNER JOIN Project p ON pw.ProjectId = p.ProjectId
ORDER BY w.LastName DESC, p.Name ASC;
```

When you run this, you can see that the last names are in descending order. The following are the first 11 rows from the output. You can see that the first row has Zorzi as the last name:

FirstName	LastName	ProjectName
Tally	Zorzi	GameIt HR Intranet V2
Tally	Zorzi	Grumps
Tally	Zorzi	Tic-Tac-Toga
Remington	Youell	Midge II
Inglis	Wilne	Horror in Iowa
Inglis	Wilne	Midge
Courtney	Wichard	CookerMaker
Courtney	Wichard	Postmodern Love Letter
Neddy	Wethered	Churlish Curling
Halli	Vel	GameIt Accounts Payable
Mari	Tootell	Horror in Iowa

> **NOTE** Remember, the default sort direction is ascending. If you omit ASC or DESC, your results will be sorted in ascending order.

Changing the Order of the Columns

The results from Listing 12.5 listed each Worker and then the Projects each Worker is working on. What if we wanted to see a list of Projects and then the Workers who are working on each project? Can you make a couple of simple changes to the previous query to get that result? Try to make the changes before continuing. The following are the first 11 rows of output with the data sorted by the Project followed by the worker's last name:

ProjectName	FirstName	LastName
Churlish Curling	Andrej	Fernao
Churlish Curling	Xavier	Gheorghescu
Churlish Curling	Cassandry	Hendin
Churlish Curling	Minna	Jonk
Churlish Curling	Rickie	Osgodby
Churlish Curling	Luci	Reeves
Churlish Curling	Alia	Rozycki
Churlish Curling	Neddy	Wethered
CookerMaker	Dianemarie	Atley
CookerMaker	Cherri	Binden
CookerMaker	Julia	Creenan

Listing 12.7 contains the query to generate the changes.

LISTING 12.7

Projects Before Workers

```
SELECT
    p.Name ProjectName,
    w.FirstName,
    w.LastName
FROM Worker w
INNER JOIN ProjectWorker pw ON w.WorkerId = pw.WorkerId
INNER JOIN Project p ON pw.ProjectId = p.ProjectId
ORDER BY p.Name ASC, w.LastName ASC;
```

There are two basic changes that were made. First the order of the fields listed in the SELECT were changed to put the project name first. This means the project name will display first. The other change was to the order of the two sort items following ORDER BY. Again, the project name was moved to be first, so it will be the first grouping that the SQL query will perform.

Handling NULL

Try the query in Listing 12.8. This query will print all task titles along with the name of their status.

LISTING 12.8

Printing Tasks with Their Status

```
SELECT
    t.Title,
    s.Name StatusName
FROM Task t
LEFT OUTER JOIN TaskStatus s ON t.TaskStatusId = s.TaskStatusId
ORDER BY s.Name ASC;
```

The following is the first 15 rows of output of the 543 rows returned:

Title	StatusName
Design domain services	null
Create physics engine	null
Construct user interface	null
Check service layer and classes	null
Model front-end components	null
Add vehicle, clothing, and building assets	null
Create service layer and classes	null
Extend service layer and classes	null
Profile domain rules and structure	null
Check front-end components	null
Implement character assets	null
Build 2D game models	Closed
Check level and scene services	Closed
Add an employee	Closed
Build UI	Closed
Prototype user interface	Closed
Design UI	Closed
Log out	Closed

Notice that the first 11 records have a NULL StatusName. That's a bit weird. Should NULL, a nonvalue, come before the first alphabetically sorted string value? That is hard to say.

To think about it another way, should NULL come *after* the last alphabetically sorted string value? That's a bit weird too.

The MySQL engine had to make a choice. They chose to put NULL first. If you dislike NULLs first, you can force their order by adding an ORDER BY condition. The query in Listing 11.9 sorts NULLs last.

LISTING 12.9

Sorting NULL Values to the End

```
SELECT
    t.Title,
    s.Name StatusName
FROM Task t
LEFT OUTER JOIN TaskStatus s ON t.TaskStatusId = s.TaskStatusId
ORDER BY ISNULL(s.Name), s.Name ASC;
```

You can see that a call to ISNULL is added to the sort phrase. This means that the first group sorted will be whether the name of the status is NULL. The results will be sorted in non-null to null order. Once the nulls are sorted, then the names are sorted in ascending order. This puts the nulls at the end of the output.

As demonstrated, ORDER BY is not limited to columns. You can sort by any value. An ORDER BY can include expressions built from functions, operators, field values, and literal values.

USING LIMIT

In many of the queries that you have created and executed in the lessons in this book, there have been hundreds of results. Sometimes you just want to see a few of the results. The LIMIT clause is an optional extension to the SELECT statement. It restricts (or limits) the records returned from a query. Its base form is as follows:

```
LIMIT [Row offset], [Number of rows]
```

LIMIT is the last syntax element in a SELECT statement. [*Row offset*] refers to the row the database engine should start counting from, while [*Number of rows*] specifies the number of rows to include in the results. LIMIT can be used in all SELECT queries, regardless of their complexity.

Consider, again, Workers. There are 100 Workers in the TrackIt database. If you want just the first 10 Workers, ordered by last name in descending order, then you could use the code in Listing 12.10.

LISTING 12.10

Selecting a Limited Number of Workers

```
SELECT *
FROM Worker
ORDER BY LastName DESC
LIMIT 0, 10;
```

This returns workers Zorzi through Strivens. Zero is the first item listed for the LIMIT, so there is no offset (remember that programmers start counting from zero). This is followed by 10, so 10 rows are grabbed and returned.

Row offset is optional and uses the default value 0. The query in Listing 12.10 could also be written as shown in Listing 12.11.

LISTING 12.11

Selecting Without the Row Offset

```
SELECT *
FROM Worker
ORDER BY LastName DESC
LIMIT 10;
```

In this case, you can see that the zero was dropped and 10 rows are simply grabbed and returned based on the ORDER BY clause.

You can also choose to select records starting from a specified offset. In Listing 12.12 an offset of 10 rows is defined as well as instructions to grab 10 rows.

LISTING 12.12

Using an Offset

```
SELECT *
FROM Worker
```

```
ORDER BY LastName DESC
LIMIT 10, 10;
```

With this code, the selected records are no longer starting from the first record, but rather the 10th. As such, the results show Workers Steinhammer through Romayn.

We know that the Workers table has 100 rows or records. What happens if you set an offset that is past (higher than) the available number of records? Take a look at Listing 12.13.

LISTING 12.13

Using an offset beyond the data

```
SELECT *
FROM Worker
ORDER BY LastName DESC
LIMIT 200, 10;
```

When this query is executed, there's no error. The result is empty. No records are returned.

NOTE It is worth noting again that LIMIT works in all SELECT queries, regardless of their complexity.

USING DISTINCT

There are times when you don't need to see duplicate records but rather want to simply see a distinct list of results. For example, with the TrackIt database, you might want to see all projects that have a task. Consider Listing 12.14.

LISTING 12.14

List All Projects That Have a Task

```
SELECT
    p.Name ProjectName,
    p.ProjectId
FROM Project p
INNER JOIN Task t ON p.ProjectId = t.ProjectId
ORDER BY p.Name;
```

This query does an INNER JOIN to connect all projects to their tasks. When the query is executed, it returns 543 records. The ProjectId and ProjectName values are repeated, once for each Task linked to the Project, but those are not really the desired results. Rather, it would be better to see each distinct project once.

DISTINCT is an optional keyword that may appear in the SELECT value list. If present, it removes duplicate records from the query result. To remove the duplicates shown in Listing 12.14, you add DISTINCT, as shown in Listing 12.15.

LISTING 12.15

List All Projects Once That Have a Task

```
SELECT DISTINCT
    p.Name ProjectName,
    p.ProjectId
FROM Project p
INNER JOIN Task t ON p.ProjectId = t.ProjectId
ORDER BY p.Name;
```

You can see that the new query returns only 26 records, one for each Project with a Task. The following are the first few rows:

ProjectName	ProjectId
Churlish Curling	game-churlish
CookerMaker	game-cooker
Diva Diva Diva	game-diva
Don't Eat The Cheese!	game-cheese

SUMMARY

From this lesson, you've seen that you can present the data returned from your queries in sorted order. You learned about ORDER BY as well as LIMIT and DISTINCT.

The ORDER BY clause is an optional element of a SELECT statement. It sorts results on one or more field values or expressions. LIMIT is an optional clause in a SELECT statement. It restricts resulting records to a subset of the original query. DISTINCT allows the retrieval of only unique records that match a request, without duplicate records.

EXERCISES

The following exercises are provided to allow you to experiment with concepts presented in this lesson:

Exercise 12.1: What's in the World Database?

Exercise 12.2: Small Cities

Exercise 12.3: Cities by Region

Exercise 12.4: Speaking French

Exercise 12.5: No Independence

Exercise 12.6: Country Languages

Exercise 12.7: No Language

Exercise 12.8: City Population

Exercise 12.9: Average City Population

Exercise 12.10: GNP

Exercise 12.11: Capital Cities

Exercise 12.12: Country Capital Cities

> **NOTE** The exercises are for your benefit. The exercises help you apply what you learn in the lessons.

Getting Started: World Database

For the exercises in this lesson, the world sample database that is included with a full installation of MySQL Server will be used. You can check that you have this database in MySQL Server using either of the following steps:

- If you are using MySQL Workbench, connect to the server and look for the *world* schema in the Navigator pane on the left, as shown in Figure 12.1.

- If you are using a command-line interface, connect to MySQL Server and run the show databases; command at a mysql prompt. Look for *world* in the list of databases.

Check that the schema includes these three tables:

- city
- country
- countrylanguage

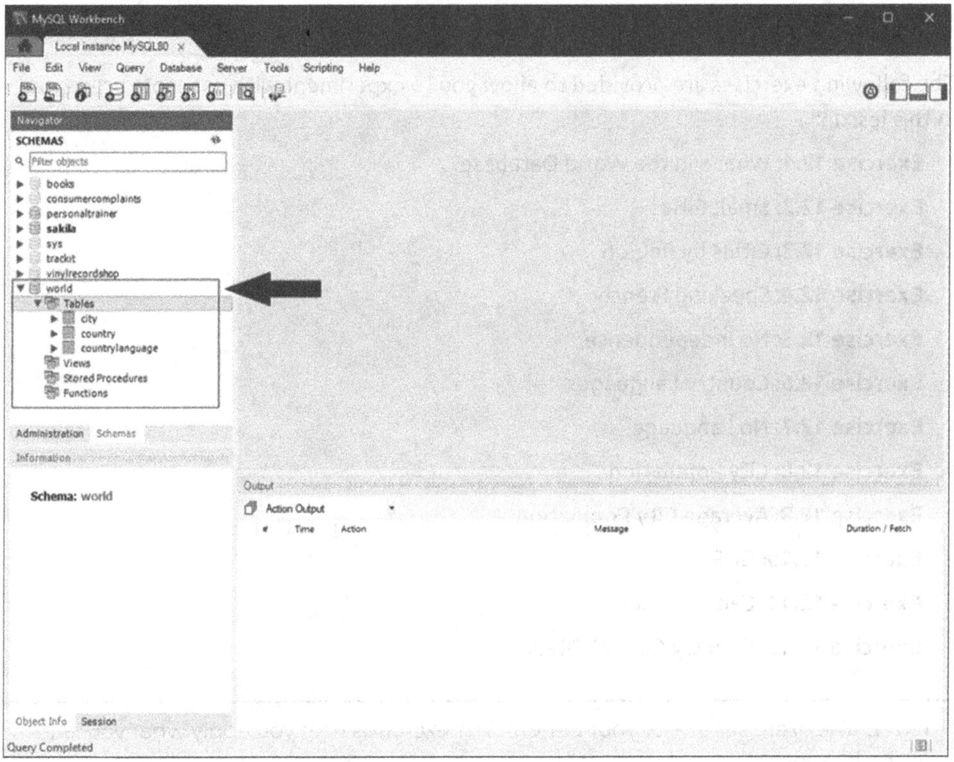

Figure 12.1 The world database schema

If your MySQL Server installation does not include this database or if any of the tables are missing, you can download and run a SQL script to create it. Use the link under Example Databases on MySQL's page, "MySQL Documentation: Other MySQL Documentation" at download.nust.na/pub6/mysql/doc/index-other.html.

Generating an ERD for World

You may also find it useful to reference the ERD for this website as you create the queries in this exercise. After verifying that the database is set up in MySQL Workbench, you can use the following steps to generate the ERD:

1. Open the Database menu and click **Reverse Engineer** (or use the shortcut Ctrl+R).

2. Follow the prompts to connect to the database and select the world schema.

3. Accept default options for all the remaining steps.

MySQL Workbench will create an ERD that shows all tables, the fields in each table, and the relationships between the tables. You can use this as a guide when writing the requested queries in the exercises.

Guidelines

The following exercises indicate how many records you should expect to see in the results, except in exercises in which you are retrieving a specific number of rows or you are retrieving all rows. Note that MySQL Workbench includes a default limit of 1,000 rows per query. You can change this setting in the SQL Editor toolbar, but you should be aware that you may not see all the results for queries with more than 1,000 records.

Exercise 12.1: What's in the World Database?

For the first exercise, start by simply looking at the data in each table. Use SELECT queries to view the first 10 rows of data and all columns in each of the three tables. Note the columns included in the table and what the data in each column looks like.

Exercise 12.2: Small Cities (42 rows)

Generate a list of all cities with a population less than 10,000.

- Include all fields in the city table in the results.
- Sort the results with the largest population at the top of the list and the lowest population at the end of the list.

Exercise 12.3: Cities by Region (4,079 rows)

Generate a list of all cities grouped by region and country.

- Include only the name of the region, the name of the country, and the name of the city.
- Sort the results in alphabetical order by region, country, and city.

Exercise 12.4: Speaking French (22 rows)

Generate a list of all countries where any form of French is spoken.

- Include the name of the country, the language, and the percentage of people who speak that language.
- Sort the data by percentage, with the largest value at the top of the list.
- Use a single WHERE statement without OR.

Exercise 12.5: No Independence (47 rows)

Generate a list of countries for which no year of independence is provided.

- Include only the country name, continent, and population for each country in the list.

- Sort in alphabetical order by the country names.

Exercise 12.6: Country Languages (990 rows)

Generate a list of countries and the languages that are spoken in each country.

- Include only the country name, continent, language, and percentage spoken for each country.

- Include all countries, even those for which no language is specified.

- Sort by country name in alphabetical order and then by percentage, with the highest percentage first.

Exercise 12.7: No Language (6 rows)

Generate a list of countries for which no language is specified.

- Include only the country name and continent.

- Sort alphabetically by continent and country name.

Exercise 12.8: City Population (232 rows)

Calculate the total city population for each country.

- Include the country name and total population in the results.

- Sort the results by total population, starting with the smallest value.

Exercise 12.9: Average City Population (7 rows)

Calculate the average city population for each continent.

- Include all continent names and average population in the results.

- Sort the results by average population, starting with the largest value.

Exercise 12.10: GNP

Generate a list of the 10 countries with the highest GNP.

- Include the country name and GNP columns.

Exercise 12.11: Capital Cities (4,079 rows)

Generate a list of the capital cities with the population and the official language(s) for that country.

- Include the name of the city, the country where the city is located, the city's population, and the country's official languages.
- Use meaningful names to distinguish the column headings.
- Sort by city name alphabetically.

Exercise 12.12: Country Capital Cities (239 rows)

Generate a list of countries and their capital cities.

- Include the name of the country and the name of the city in the results, using a meaningful name for each column.
- Include countries with no capital city.
- Sort alphabetically by country name.

Lesson 13
Grouping and Aggregates

SQL can compute **aggregate** values. Aggregates are single values calculated from many values. If you have a table of students with GPAs, you could calculate the average GPA. The average value is an aggregate. The minimum or maximum GPA could also be calculated. Both are aggregates. Regardless of the number of students, an aggregate "rolls up" or "cooks down" to one value.

The GROUP BY clause allows for the further partitioning of a result and for the calculation of aggregates per partition. Using GROUP BY, there is the ability to calculate the average GPA per home state, the minimum GPA per major, or the number of classes each student completed.

Learning Objectives

By the end of this lesson, you will be able to:

- Use the aggregate functions: COUNT, SUM, AVG, MIN, and MAX

- Group data using GROUP BY

- Filter groups with the HAVING clause

- Use multiple aggregates in the same query

The lesson will once again use the TrackIt database and schema. You will need to have it installed to run the queries provided in this lesson to see the results.

AGGREGATE FUNCTIONS

There are a dozen or more SQL aggregate functions, depending on what SQL database system you use. The following are the most common and universally supported:

- **COUNT:** Counts the number of non-NULL values in a set; works on any non-NULL value

- **SUM:** Sums values in a set; values must be numeric

- **AVG:** Calculates the average of values in a set; values must be numeric

- **MIN:** Determines the minimum value in a set; values must be comparable

- **MAX:** Determines the maximum value in a set; values must be comparable

An aggregate function commonly appears in the SELECT value list. Listing 13.1 presents a simple query against the TrackIt database that counts the number of TaskIds.

LISTING 13.1

Using an Aggregate Function to Count

```
USE TrackIt;

-- Count TaskIds, 543 values
SELECT COUNT(TaskId)
FROM Task;

-- Count everything, 543 values
SELECT COUNT(*)
FROM Task;
```

The previous listing queries the TrackIt database and counts the number of TaskIds and then counts the number of Tasks. The output will be a count of 543 values for both queries.

Each of the five aggregate functions requires one argument: the source of values to be aggregated. It can be a field or any value expression. The * argument in COUNT(*) is special. It tells the SQL engine to count records, not values. In the queries in Listing 13.1, the result is identical, but that's not always the case. Consider TaskStatusIds, as shown in Listing 13.2.

LISTING 13.2

Counting TaskStatusIds

```
SELECT COUNT(TaskStatusId)
FROM Task;
```

This query returns 532 values. The number of tasks was 543, so the number of TaskStatusIds doesn't match the number of Tasks. This is because NULLs are omitted. Task.TaskStatusId can be NULL and is NULL 11 times out of 543.

You can aggregate any value. The value can come from a joined table or from a result filtered with WHERE. Listing 13.3 counts resolved Tasks.

LISTING 13.3

Counting Resolved Tasks

```
SELECT
    COUNT(t.TaskId)
FROM Task t
INNER JOIN TaskStatus s ON t.TaskStatusId = s.TaskStatusId
WHERE s.IsResolved = 1;
```

In this listing, the Task table has been joined with the TaskStatus table. The TaskIds are then counted, but only where the IsResolved status is equal to 1. The results show that there are 276 resolved Tasks. (Your result may be different if you have previously added, updated, or deleted Tasks.)

USING GROUP BY

As you've seen, GROUP BY is an optional clause in a SELECT statement. It partitions a result into groups. GROUP BY can be used with aggregate functions to compute a value per group instead of computing across the entire result.

While you can write SELECT statements that do not include GROUP BY, you must include a GROUP BY statement if the SELECT clause includes both aggregate and nonaggregate fields.

If you do not provide a GROUP BY statement in these cases, your query will not group the results appropriately. The GROUP BY clause is placed after WHERE, if it's present, and before ORDER BY.

In Listing 13.4, Tasks are counted per status. In this case, the results will be grouped by status, and the number of tasks that are associated with each status will be counted.

LISTING 13.4

Counting Tasks per Status

```
SELECT
    IFNULL(s.Name, '[None]') StatusName,
    COUNT(t.TaskId) TaskCount
FROM Task t
LEFT OUTER JOIN TaskStatus s ON t.TaskStatusId = s.TaskStatusId
GROUP BY s.Name
ORDER BY s.Name;
```

You can see in this listing that the name of the status is being selected along with the count of TaskIds. If the status name is NULL, then it will be categorized under the name [None]. A LEFT OUTER JOIN is used to connect the Task table to the TaskStatus table before grouping by the Task Name and also ordering by the task name. The final output when this query is executed is as follows:

StatusName	TaskCount
[None]	11
Closed	80
In Progress	64
Parked	64
Pending Release	65
Resolved	53
Resolved, Duplicate	62
Resolved, Will Not Fix	81
Testing/Validation	63

There are a few nuances in the query, as listed here:

- Note that the GROUP BY statement references the nonaggregated field in the SELECT statement (s.Name). As shown in Listing 13.5, if GROUP BY is not included, the database engine will calculate the total TaskCount across all records and display it with the first Task.Name value.

LISTING 13.5

Dropping GROUP BY

```
SELECT
    IFNULL(s.Name, '[None]') StatusName,
    COUNT(t.TaskId) TaskCount
FROM Task t
LEFT OUTER JOIN TaskStatus s ON t.TaskStatusId = s.TaskStatusId
ORDER BY s.Name;
```

The following is the output for this modified query:

StatusName	TaskCount
[None]	543

- A LEFT OUTER JOIN is used to get all Tasks. An INNER JOIN would eliminate NULL TaskStatusIds.

- The sort is by s.Name because it's the value that drives IFNULL(s.Name, '[None]'). You could instead sort by COUNT(s.TaskId).

- Because s.Name can be NULL, a replacement value is provided so it's easy to display the NULL status.

- Aliases provide meaningful names for aggregate values.

Grouping and Multiple Columns

What happens if you want to know if a status is resolved as well as know its name? What happens when the TaskStatus.IsResolved column is added, as shown in Listing 13.6?

LISTING 13.6

Adding IsResolved

```
-- This script should not work.
SELECT
    IFNULL(s.Name, '[None]') StatusName,
    s.IsResolved,
    COUNT(t.TaskId) TaskCount
FROM Task t
```

```
LEFT OUTER JOIN TaskStatus s ON t.TaskStatusId = s.TaskStatusId
GROUP BY s.Name
ORDER BY s.Name;
```

This listing should not work; however, this should create the following results when using MySQL:

StatusName	IsResolved	TaskCount
[None]	Null	11
Closed	1	80
In Progress	0	64
Parked	0	64
Pending Release	0	65
Resolved	1	53
Resolved, Duplicate	1	62
Resolved, Will Not Fix	1	81
Testing/Validation	0	63

You should note that not all relational database management systems (RDBMSs) are this forgiving. For example, in Oracle or SQL Server, you may receive a message like the following:

```
Error Code: 1055. Expression #2 of SELECT list is not in GROUP BY clause and
contains nonaggregated column 'trackit.s.IsResolved' which is not functionally
dependent on columns in GROUP BY clause; this is incompatible with
sql_mode=only_full_group_by
```

This error can happen because in core SQL, SELECT...GROUP BY can't select a value that's not an aggregate or part of the group. That makes sense. If the value would create new groups, what happens to the original groups, and how should the aggregate behave?

As an example, what should happen if Task.TaskId is added to the SELECT list? Are results now grouped by TaskId? If so, the Task count would be pretty boring. Each TaskId has one and only one Task. If results are not grouped by TaskId, what then?

No worries. Even though this query works in MySQL, it's good practice to write queries deliberately and correctly, especially if the same queries might be used in a different system.

To add TaskStatus.IsResolved, make it part of the GROUP BY clause when it is added to the SELECT list. This is shown in Listing 13.7. Conceptually, this groups the results by TaskStatus.Name *and* TaskStatus.IsResolved. Practically, it doesn't change the original groups. Can you see why this is true?

LISTING 13.7

Adding TaskStatus.IsResolved to the Groupings

```
SELECT
    IFNULL(s.Name, '[None]') StatusName,
    IFNULL(s.IsResolved, 0) IsResolved,
    COUNT(t.TaskId) TaskCount
FROM Task t
LEFT OUTER JOIN TaskStatus s ON t.TaskStatusId = s.TaskStatusId
GROUP BY s.Name, s.IsResolved -- IsResolved is now part of the GROUP.
ORDER BY s.Name;
```

You can see in this listing that IsResolved is being added to the SELECT but is including a check to see if it is null. If IsResolved is null, then it is included in a group identified as 0. You can also see that IsResolved is also part of what is being grouped within the GROUP BY clause. The output from this is the same as the previous listing, except for the first row showing a value of 0 for IsResovled instead of null.

StatusName	IsResolved	TaskCount
[None]	0	11
Closed	1	80
In Progress	0	64
Parked	0	64
Pending Release	0	65
Resolved	1	53
Resolved, Duplicate	1	62
Resolved, Will Not Fix	1	81
Testing/Validation	0	63

Adding DISTINCT

Most uses of DISTINCT can be accomplished by grouping data with GROUP BY. In fact, MySQL uses GROUP BY optimizations to optimize DISTINCT queries. Consider using a GROUP BY if it's more appropriate, and it's usually more appropriate.

For example, the code in Listing 13.8 can be used to get a list of unique project names.

LISTING 13.8

Getting a List of Distrinct Project Names

```
SELECT DISTINCT
    p.Name ProjectName,
    p.ProjectId
FROM Project p
INNER JOIN Task t ON p.ProjectId = t.ProjectId
ORDER BY p.Name;
```

This query produces a list of the 26 unique project names. The following are the first few entries of the output:

ProjectName	ProjectId
Churlish Curling	game-churlish
CookerMaker	game-cooker
Diva Diva Diva	game-diva
Don't Eat The Cheese!	game-cheese
GameIt Accounts Payable	accounts-payable

While this list presents a list of distinct project names, you could do the same by using GROUP BY Project.Name instead. This is shown in Listing 13.9.

LISTING 13.9

Getting Unique Project Names Using GROUP BY

```
SELECT
    p.Name ProjectName,
    p.ProjectId
FROM Project p
INNER JOIN Task t ON p.ProjectId = t.ProjectId
GROUP BY p.Name, p.ProjectId
ORDER BY p.Name;
```

The results from Listing 13.8 and Listing 13.9 are the same. The GROUP BY in Listing 13.9 provides the same results as if you had used DISTINCT.

USING HAVING

There is another clause that can be used with SELECT called HAVING. The HAVING clause works with GROUP BY and allows data to be filtered based on defined criteria. It will specify the condition or conditions that make up a group or aggregation.

For the TrackIt database, the next goal is to fetch the estimated hours in Tasks assigned to Workers, calculate a total per Worker, and find all Workers with more than 100 total hours. Three tables are needed: Worker, ProjectWorker, and Task. INNER JOINs can be used in all relationships. There are no optional rows.

Determine groups and selected values. We're interested in total hours per Worker, so you should select the Workers' names. Just to be careful, the WorkerId can be added to the group. That ensures two or more Workers are not treated as one if they share the same names, because each Worker has a unique WorkerId. Listing 13.10 shows what a first draft of a query might be.

LISTING 13.10

First Draft of Filtering

```
SELECT
    CONCAT(w.FirstName, ' ', w.LastName) WorkerName,
    SUM(t.EstimatedHours) TotalHours
FROM Worker w
INNER JOIN ProjectWorker pw ON w.WorkerId = pw.WorkerId
INNER JOIN Task t ON pw.WorkerId = t.WorkerId
    AND pw.ProjectId = t.ProjectId
GROUP BY w.WorkerId, w.FirstName, w.LastName;
```

This query is selecting the name of the worker, which is displayed as a concatenation of the first and last names with a space between them. It also displays the aggregate sum of sum of the estimated hours. This is done for each worker based on project hours. These are then grouped by the WorkerID followed with the first and last names also being part of the GROUP BY.

Executing this query will show 88 records. The first five could look like this:

WorkerName	TotalHours
Inez Fanthome	65.50
Lindy Chattoe	67.75
Thorin Achromov	45.50
Rickie Osgodby	24.25
Andriette Dimsdale	168.50

Aggregate values can't be filtered using the WHERE clause. The WHERE clause is evaluated before aggregate functions, so it happens too late. Instead, the HAVING clause can be used. As mentioned, HAVING is an optional clause in a SELECT statement, and it can be included only when a GROUP BY clause exists. HAVING is followed by an expression that evaluates to a Boolean value, just like a WHERE clause, but the expression includes comparisons against aggregate values.

To exclude totals less than 100 hours, add a HAVING clause to Listing 13.10. The HAVING clause is placed after GROUP BY and before ORDER BY, as shown in Listing 13.11.

LISTING 13.11

Adding HAVING

```
SELECT
    CONCAT(w.FirstName, ' ', w.LastName) WorkerName,
    SUM(t.EstimatedHours) TotalHours
FROM Worker w
INNER JOIN ProjectWorker pw ON w.WorkerId = pw.WorkerId
INNER JOIN Task t ON pw.WorkerId = t.WorkerId
    AND pw.ProjectId = t.ProjectId
GROUP BY w.WorkerId, w.FirstName, w.LastName
HAVING SUM(t.EstimatedHours) >= 100;
```

You can see in this listing that the HAVING statement has been added. It uses the SUM aggregate function to determine which totals of EstimateHours are greater than or equal to 100 and includes only those results. With the addition of the HAVING statement, the new results now show only nine records.

WorkerName	TotalHours
Andriette Dimsdale	168.50
Vlad Anfusso	153.50
Karlen Egalton	116.75
Kenon Kirkham	218.00
Luci Reeves	132.25
Ealasaid Blinco	136.50
Juliet Strivens	114.25
Winston Marien	105.50
Danyelle O'Hanley	125.50

NOTE Note that you could add an ORDER BY statement to Listing 13.11 with a call to the aggregate function SUM to sort the workers by hours worked. The statement to add as the last line of code would look like this:

```
ORDER BY SUM(t.EstimatedHours) DESC;
```

SELECT EVALUATION ORDER

There is an order to how a SELECT statement is evaluated. Specifically, the key words in a SELECT statement are evaluated in the following order:

1. **FROM:** Determine where to start
2. **JOIN ON:** Link other tables and formalize row relationships
3. **WHERE:** Filter table rows
4. **GROUP BY:** Partition the data and calculate aggregates
5. **HAVING:** Filter by aggregate
6. **SELECT:** Decide what is part of the final result
7. **DISTINCT:** Remove duplicates from the result
8. **ORDER BY:** Sort the final result
9. **LIMIT:** Return a subset of the final result

This order shows why you can't filter aggregates in a WHERE clause but you can ORDER BY aggregate values.

OTHER EXAMPLES

Consider Tasks from the Project perspective. You could get a sense of when each Project truly started by grabbing its Tasks and finding the minimum due date. That would tell when the first concrete Task is due, and concrete assigned Tasks might be more reliable than an idealized schedule.

Strictly speaking, only two tables are needed: Project and Task. In the worker queries, ProjectWorker is included, but it's not really necessary. Can you see why? Task includes ProjectWorker's primary key ProjectId and WorkerId as a foreign key. That ensures an invalid combination can't be created of ProjectId and WorkerId in Task; for example, a Project's Task can't be assigned to a Worker who isn't assigned to the project. That's pretty nice. With that insurance in place, the ProjectWorker table can be safely ignored. The JOIN will work just fine without it, as shown in Listing 13.12.

LISTING 13.12

Query for Tasks Minimum Due Dates

```
SELECT
    p.Name ProjectName,
    MIN(t.DueDate) MinTaskDueDate
FROM Project p
INNER JOIN Task t ON p.ProjectId = t.ProjectId
WHERE p.ProjectId LIKE 'game-%'
    AND t.ParentTaskId IS NOT NULL
GROUP BY p.ProjectId, p.Name
ORDER BY p.Name;
```

This query returns 20 rows. The following are the first five records:

ProjectName	MinTaskDueDate
Churlish Curling	2000-09-13
CookerMaker	2000-05-05
Diva Diva Diva	2002-08-16
Don't Eat The Cheese!	2000-03-24
Grumps	2000-01-15

This listing uses the MIN function with DueDate. It is worth noting that MIN and MAX work on any data type that can be compared and ranked. They definitely work for numbers, but they also work with dates, times, and strings.

What if an overview of each Project is wanted: first and last Task due date, total estimated hours, total number of Tasks, and average Task hours estimate? This can be done in one query, as shown in Listing 13.13.

Once a group has been defined, you can run any number of aggregate calculations on it. To make things a bit more interesting, Listing 13.13 eliminates Projects with fewer than 10 Tasks.

LISTING 13.13

An Overview of Each Project with 10 or More Tasks

```
SELECT
    p.Name ProjectName,
    MIN(t.DueDate) MinTaskDueDate,
    MAX(t.DueDate) MaxTaskDueDate,
    SUM(t.EstimatedHours) TotalHours,
    AVG(t.EstimatedHours) AverageTaskHours,
    COUNT(t.TaskId) TaskCount
```

```
FROM Project p
INNER JOIN Task t ON p.ProjectId = t.ProjectId
WHERE t.ParentTaskId IS NOT NULL
GROUP BY p.ProjectId, p.Name
HAVING COUNT(t.TaskId) >= 10
ORDER BY COUNT(t.TaskId) DESC, p.Name;
```

You should be able to follow each line of this query, which uses the aggregate functions mentioned at the beginning of this lesson. As you go through the query, pay close attention to where each clause is declared in the SELECT. As you can see, the query is using everything available to it. The following are 4 of the 21 records returned:

ProjectName	MinTaskDue-Date	MaxTaskDue-Date	Total-Hours	AverageTask-Hours	Task-Count
Gametic Enterprise	2000-01-06	2019-11-22	205.75	5.143750	40
GameIt Accounts Receivable	2001-03-23	2018-11-02	129.00	5.375000	24
GameIt HR Intranet V2	2000-08-10	2018-12-26	122.25	5.093750	24
GameIt Payroll	2000-03-23	2019-07-03	137.25	5.718750	24

In looking at the results, when nongame Projects are allowed, it's clear they dominate total hours and number of Tasks (in our fake data).

SUMMARY

Aggregate functions compute a single value from many values. The source values come from fields and calculations. On their own, aggregates compute one value per query result. Common aggregates include COUNT, SUM, MIN, MAX, and AVG.

The GROUP BY clause is an optional extension to the SELECT statement. It partitions results into distinct groups. Aggregate functions can operate on groups and provide a single computed value per group.

The HAVING clause is an optional extension to the SELECT statement. It is valid only if a SELECT contains a GROUP BY. HAVING evaluates a Boolean expression using aggregate values. As with WHERE, a record is included if the expression evaluates to true; otherwise, the record is excluded. You cannot filter aggregate values in the WHERE clause. Aggregates are not computed until *after* the WHERE is evaluated.

EXERCISES

The following exercises are provided to allow you to experiment with concepts presented in this lesson:

Exercise 13.1: Number of Clients

Exercise 13.2: Counting Client Birth Dates

Exercise 13.3: Clients by City

Exercise 13.4: Invoice Totals

Exercise 13.5: Invoices More Than $500

Exercise 13.6: Average Line Item Totals

Exercise 13.7: More Than $1,000 Paid

Exercise 13.8: Counts by Category

Exercise 13.9: Exercises

Exercise 13.10: Client Birth Dates

Exercise 13.11: Client Goals

Exercise 13.12: Exercise Unit Value

Exercise 13.13: Categorized Exercise Unit Value

Exercise 13.14: Level Ages

> **NOTE** The exercises are for your benefit. They help you apply what you learn in the lessons.

The Personal Trainer Database

For the exercises in this lesson, you will use the PersonalTrainer database and schema that you've seen in previous lessons. If you already have the PersonalTrainer database, you are welcome to use it. If not, you can use the `personaltrainer-schema-and-data.sql` script from the downloadable files for this book. The downloadable files are at www.wiley.com/go/jobreadysql.

After running the script, use MySQL Workbench or a MySQL command line to review the tables in the database and the fields in each table. You may also want to reference the ERD in Figure 13.1 to identify the relationships between tables.

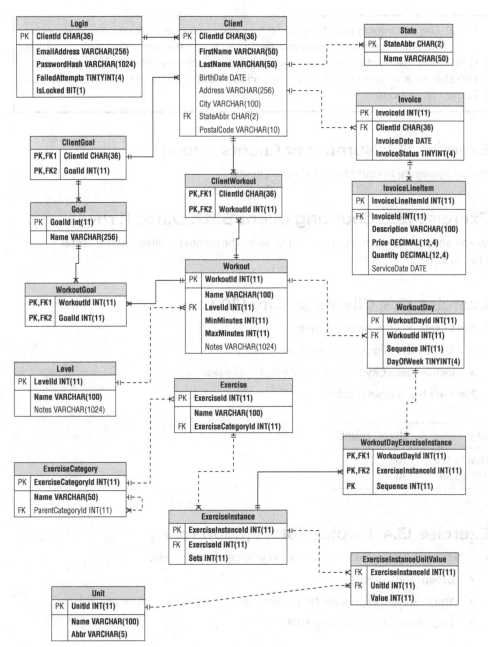

Figure 13.1 The PersonalTrainer database schema

Exercise 13.1: Number of Clients (1 row)

Use an aggregate to count the number of Clients.

Exercise 13.2: Counting Client Birth Dates (1 row)

Use an aggregate to count Client.BirthDate. The number is different from total Clients. Why?

Exercise 13.3: Clients by City (20 rows)

Group Clients by City and count them.

- Sort by the number of Clients descending.
- Include both City and the client count in the results.

Here are the sample results:

city	client_count
New Orleans	105
Jefferson	30

Exercise 13.4: Invoice Totals (1,000 rows)

Calculate a total per invoice using only the InvoiceLineItem table.

- Group by InvoiceId.
- You'll need an expression for the line item total: Price * Quantity.
- Aggregate per group using SUM.

Here are the sample results:

invoiceid	invoice_total
1	283.12500000
2	105.00000000

Exercise 13.5: Invoices More Than $500 (234 rows)

Modify the query in Exercise 13.4 for the following:

- Only include totals greater than $500.00.
- Sort from lowest total to highest.

Here are the sample results:

invoiceid	invoice_total
368	502.50000000
557	502.50000000

Exercise 13.6: Average Line Item Totals (3 rows)

Calculate the average line item total, grouped by InvoiceLineItem.Description. The following are sample results:

description	invoice_average
Individual Instruction	160.502717391304
Group Instruction	25.482495511670

Exercise 13.7: More Than $1,000 Paid (146 rows)

Select ClientId, FirstName, and LastName from Client for clients who have *paid* more than $1,000 total.

- Paid is Invoice.InvoiceStatus = 2.
- Sort by LastName, then FirstName.

Here are the sample results:

ClientId	FirstName	LastName	Total
bcf40948-b93b-4c1f-b1c7-ee10c05b9faf	Randal	Aberkirdo	1540.99500000
d0a2212e-6332-4541-9e00-116ddf88fe45	Phyllys	Acome	1115.62500000

Exercise 13.8: Counts by Category (13 rows)

Count exercises by category.

- Group by ExerciseCategory.Name.
- Sort by exercise count descending.

Here are the sample results:

CategoryName	ExerciseCount
Bodyweight	11
Flexibility	9

Exercise 13.9: Exercises (64 rows)

Select Exercise.Name along with the minimum, maximum, and average ExerciseInstance.Sets. Sort the results by Exercise.Name.

Here are the sample results:

ExerciseName	MinSets	MaxSets	AvgSets
Air squats	1	2	1.2500
Ananda Balasana	1	10	3.5000

Exercise 13.10: Client Birth Dates (26 rows)

Find the minimum and maximum Client.BirthDate per Workout. Sort the results by the workout name.

Here are the sample results:

WorkoutName	EarliestBirthDate	LatestBirthDate
3, 2, 1... Yoga!	1928-04-28	1993-02-07
Agility Training	1935-05-11	2004-02-28

Exercise 13.11: Client Goal Count (500 rows, 50 rows with no goal)

Count the client goals. Be careful not to exclude rows for clients without goals. Your sample results should include the following:

ClientId	GoalCount
00268ec4-cdb6-4643-8e94-3aa467419af6	0
04971685-17d8-4973-bf35-42e8a2d4810c	0

Exercise 13.12: Exercise Unit Value (82 rows)

Select Exercise.Name, Unit.Name, and minimum and maximum ExerciseInstanceUnitValue.Value for all exercises with a configured ExerciseInstanceUnitValue. Sort the results by Exercise.Name and then Unit.Name.
Here are the sample results:

ExerciseName	UnitName	MinValue	MaxValue
Air squats	Repetitions	25	150
Ananda Balasana	Minutes	5	25

Exercise 13.13: Categorized Exercise Unit Value (82 rows)

Modify the query in Exercise 13.12 to include ExerciseCategory.Name. Order the output by ExerciseCategory.Name, then Exercise.Name, and then Unit.Name.

Here are the sample results:

CategoryName	ExerciseName	UnitName	MinValue	MaxValue
Biking	Street ride	Miles	5	40
Biking	Trail ride	Miles	5	40

Exercise 13.14: Level Ages (4 rows)

Select the minimum and maximum age in years for each Level. To calculate age in years, use the MySQL function DATEDIFF. (Do online research to see how this function works. One location online you can review is dev.mysql.com/doc/refman/8.0/en/date-and-time-functions.html.)

Here are the sample results:

LevelName	MinAge	MaxAge
Beginner	15.0466	94.2110
Intermediate	14.0329	95.2575

Lesson 14

Pulling It All Together: Adding Data to the Vinyl Record Shop Database

In this lesson, you will pull together what you've learned into an application. Specifically, you will return to the record shop database that you saw in past lessons. This time, you will add and manage data in the database for the shop.

Learning Objectives

By the end of this lesson, you will be able to:

- Add data to the vinyl record shop database

- Describe a flat file and a CSV file

- Manually add data to a database using INSERT

- Explain what needs to be done prior to importing data from a CSV file

- Import data into a database from an existing file

- Create a script to load data into a database

Before starting, execute the `vinylerecordshop-schema.sql` script, which can be found in the downloaded files for this book, which can be downloaded from `wiley.com/go/jobreadysql`. This will provide you with the tables that will store the data. These are the tables and fields required for this lesson.

You should run this script even if you built the database earlier in the book. You may run the script again if you want to start this lesson over again for any reason. Note that running the script will overwrite the database named *vinylrecordshop*.

You will also use data files that can be found with the download files for this book. The data files are included in the zipped folder called `vinylrecordshop-data`. Save this file to your computer and extract the `.csv` files it contains.

IMPORTANT! This script will delete the database named *vinylrecordshop* if it already exists on your system. If you have your own version of this database and you want to keep it for other purposes, you should either rename the database in MySQL or verify that you have a script to rebuild it before running the new script.

Organize the Tables

Using the script, you will create a normalized database that is represented in the entity-relationship diagram (ERD) shown in Figure 14.1.

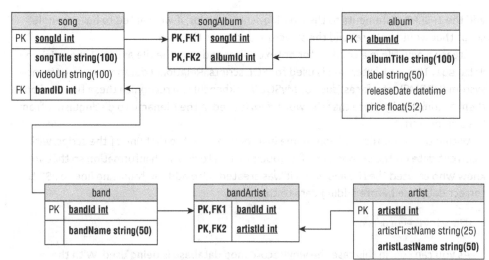

Figure 14.1 ERD for the VinylRecordShop database

Referential integrity requires that any value added to a foreign key field must first exist in the related primary key field. This means that when data is added to a database, that data must first be added to the primary tables (tables that do not depend on other tables) before it can be added to the related tables.

Looking at the ERD for the database, you can see that the following are primary tables:

- band
- album
- artist

The other three tables include at least one foreign key field:

- song references band
- bandArtist references band and artist
- songAlbum references song and album

For the primary tables, the order in which the tables are created doesn't really matter. The most important thing is to make sure that any primary keys that are related to foreign keys have data in them before the same values are used as foreign keys. To that end, you must create the song table before the songAlbum table is created.

Create a Script File

We will create a SQL script that can be reused as necessary to reset the data in the database. It is assumed that anyone using this script already has the schema itself and would create a separate data-only script in this code-along. Another option would be to add the INSERT statements to the existing schema script, if we wanted to have a single script that would both rebuild the structure and reset the data.

Create a new file in a code editor or text editor and save the file as vinylrecordshop-data.sql. The .sql extension is used for SQL scripts. Relational database management system (RDBMS) interfaces (such as MySQL Workbench) can recognize these files and open them automatically. Note that the word *data* is used in the filename to distinguish it from the schema script.

Within the script file, add your name in a comment on the first line of the script, with a current date on the second line. It is good practice to add such information so that you know who created the file and when it was created. Also add the following line to USE the correct database before adding data to the tables:

```
USE vinylrecordshop;
```

As you can see, in this case the vinylrecordshop database is being used. With the database set, you are now ready to add data.

INSERTING DATA

There are generally two options for adding data to a database. The first is to manually key in each record. We will add a few records this way to show you how it works, but this approach is relatively slow and can introduce many errors into the database in the form of typos.

Fortunately, most data we might want to add to a database already exists in an electronic format, such as copying data from a web page, downloading a dataset from a server, or importing data from a flat file, such as an Excel worksheet or .csv file. When data is already in an electronic format, it can usually be imported more quickly, with less risk of introducing errors into the data.

What Is a Flat File?

By definition, relational databases are three-dimensional. Data is stored in two-dimensional tables, but the relationships between tables adds a third dimension that allows us to streamline the data and minimize data redundancy.

However, there are petabytes of existing data on all kinds of topics stored in so-called *flat files*. They are called *flat* because they are only two-dimensional. An Excel worksheet, for example, includes only columns and rows. Data can also be stored in text-delimited formats, where records are stored as individual lines and individual values within each record are separated by a defined character, such as a comma or a pipe (|).

Comma-delimited files (which use commas to separate individual values) are extremely common and well-supported by all DBMSs. These files normally use the extension .csv, which stands for "comma-separated values."

Flat files typically include a lot of redundant data, but they allow users to store large amounts of data in a single file. They are also more user-friendly than RDBMSs, so businesses often rely on Excel or similar worksheet applications even where a relational database might make more sense.

In this lesson you will get the chance to use flat files. More important, you'll get a chance to work directly with CSV files. For now, however, let's look at adding data directly to the vinylrecordshop database.

SQL INSERT

You learned in Lesson 6, "Diving into SQL," that when data is added directly to a table using SQL, the INSERT statement is used. For the vinylrecordshop database, start with the album table. Table 14.1 shows how the columns in the album table are defined in SQL. Table 14.2 contains a sample dataset that can be added.

Table 14.1 The Album Table Definition

Field	Type	Null	Key	Default	Extra
albumId	int	NO	PRI	NULL	auto_increment
albumTitle	varchar(100)	NO		NULL	
Label	varchar(50)	YES		NULL	
releaseDate	date	YES		NULL	
Price	decimal(5,2)	YES		NULL	

Table 14.2 Sample Dataset for the Album Table

albumId	albumTitle	releaseDate	price	label
1	Imagine	9/9/1971	9.99	Apple
2	2525 (Exordium & Terminus)	7/1/1969	25.99	RCA
3	No One's Gonna Change Our World	12/12/1969	39.35	Regal Starline
4	Moondance Studio Album	8/1/1969	14.99	Warner Bros
5	Clouds	5/1/1969	9.99	Reprise
6	Sounds of Silence Studio Album	1/17/1966	9.99	Columbia
7	Abbey Road	1/10/1969	12.99	Apple
9	Smiley Smile	9/18/1967	5.99	Capitol

There are a couple of things to note with these tables.

- The fields do not appear in the same order in the dataset as they do in the table. This needs to be taken into account when data is added from the dataset to the table.

- The date in the dataset in Table 14.2 is in the format m/d/yyyy. MySQL's default date format is yyyy-mm-dd.

Neither of these is a problem, but you do need to be aware before trying to add the data to the table.

Inserting by Table Order

When an `INSERT INTO` statement is used, you have the option to simply add data in the same left-to-right order as the columns appear in the table. For the first record, this looks like the following:

```
INSERT INTO album
VALUES (1,'Imagine','Apple','1971-9-9',9.99);
```

There are several things to notice within this `INSERT` statement. You should notice that even though the albumId column is set up to automatically number records as they are added to the table, you must include a value in this statement because you did not use any column names. If you leave out the value for the albumId, MySQL will assume that the album title ('`Imagine`') should go in the first field and throw an error.

You should also notice that the String values that are being added to the database are enclosed in quotes. This is a requirement: Strings must be enclosed in quotation marks. You can use either double quotes or single quotes, as long as you are consistent for each value.

Finally, you should notice that the date must be presented in the expected format of '`yyyy-mm-dd`'. If you don't use this format, then MySQL will not recognize it as a date. Note, too, that the date must be in quotation marks, like a string value. MySQL will recognize it as a date and convert it internally.

> **NOTE** Note that MySQL uses a format of '`yyyy-mm-dd`'; however, it will generally accept single digit months and days as well as those with a leading zero. All of the following should work: '`2023-01-09`', '`2023-01-9`', '`2023-1-09`', and '`2023-1-9`'. Regardless of which you use, MySQL will treat it as '`2023-01-09`'.

Adding by Field Name

As an alternative to inserting fields in the order they are listed in the table, the INSERT statement can be modified to name the fields the data should be added to. For example, the following adds data from the second row of Table 14.2:

```
INSERT INTO album (albumTitle, releaseDate, price, label)
VALUES ('2525 (Exordium & Terminus)', '1969-7-1', 25.99, 'RCA');
```

In this statement, you can see that the INSERT statement includes the list of fields that will be added (albumTitle, releaseDate, price, and label). This is followed by the values to be added to each field. The value list must match the list of columns from left to right, but neither list has to match the order in which the columns are defined in the table. This gives more flexibility for situations where the columns in the original dataset might not be in the same order as the MySQL table. It is also worth noticing that albumId is not included in the list of columns. Because the albumId is the primary key and not included, MySQL will automatically number it.

After adding the new records, you can verify that the correct values for things like the date and albumId have been added by using the following statement:

```
SELECT * FROM album;
```

The results of this command should be as follows:

albumId	albumTitle	label	releaseDate	price
1	Imagine	Apple	1971-09-09	9.99
2	2525 (Exordium & Terminus)	RCA	1969-07-01	25.99

We can add multiple records in a single statement by defining individual rows. The following statement uses the same syntax as the previous INSERT statement, but it includes two separate rows of data:

```
INSERT INTO album (albumTitle, releaseDate, price, label)
VALUES
    ROW ("No One's Gonna Change Our World", '1969-12-12', 39.95,'Regal Starline'),
    ROW ('Moondance Studio Album', '1969-8-1',14.99,'Warner Bros');
```

Note the following:

- Values for albumID are not provided, thus allowing the database engine to automatically number the records.

- Each row is identified with the ROW keyword, separated by a comma. You can include as many rows as you want using the same pattern.

- The album title "No One's Gonna Change Our World" includes a single quote as a possessive marker. This means that the value itself must be inside double quotes. This is something you might need to take into account when importing data.

After running the new INSERT statement, use a SELECT query to check that all values were added to the table. The results should look like the following:

albumId	albumTitle	label	releaseDate	price
1	Imagine	Apple	1971-09-09	9.99
2	2525 (Exordium & Terminus)	RCA	1969-07-01	25.99
3	No One's Gonna Change Our World	Regal Starline	1969-12-12	39.95
4	Moondance Studio Album	Warner Bros	1969-08-01	14.99

On Your Own

Use the patterns provided so far to write an INSERT statement to add the remaining four records from Table 14.2 to the album table. Those records are as follows:

albumTitle	releaseDate	price	label
Clouds	5/1/1969	9.99	Reprise
Sounds of Silence Studio Album	1/17/1966	9.99	Columbia
Abbey Road	1/10/1969	12.99	Apple
Smiley Smile	9/18/1967	5.99	Capitol

Once you've added the remaining records, once again use a SELECT statement to verify that the album table includes all eight sample data records. Your album table should contain the following:

albumId	albumTitle	label	releaseDate	price
1	Imagine	Apple	1971-09-09	9.99
2	2525 (Exordium & Terminus)	RCA	1969-07-01	25.99
3	No One's Gonna Change Our World	Regal Starline	1969-12-12	39.95
4	Moondance Studio Album	Warner Bros	1969-08-01	14.99
5	Clouds	Reprise	1969-05-01	9.99
6	Sounds of Silence Studio Album	Columbia	1966-01-17	9.99
7	Abbey Road	Apple	1969-01-10	12.99
8	Smiley Smile	Capitol	1967-09-18	5.99

Update Records

If you had problems adding records, then you may notice that the albumId values are no longer sequential from 1 to 8. Because this is an auto-increment field, the database engine will not reuse values that have been deleted or skipped. Instead, it will always look at the highest existing value in that column and increment that value by 1 for each new record.

You can see how this works by deleting one of the records using the following statement:

```
DELETE FROM album
WHERE albumID = 5;
```

This statement simply deletes the record with an albumId of 5. After deleting the record, you can add it back into the database by using an INSERT statement such as the following:

```
INSERT INTO album (albumTitle, releaseDate, price, label)
VALUES ("Clouds", '1969-5-1', 9.99,'Reprise');
```

If you execute a SELECT statement using the album table, you will see that the record was added, but with an albumId of 9 rather than with the missing value 5.

albumId	albumTitle	label	releaseDate	price
1	Imagine	Apple	1971-09-09	9.99
2	2525 (Exordium & Terminus)	RCA	1969-07-01	25.99
3	No One's Gonna Change Our World	Regal Starline	1969-12-12	39.95
4	Moondance Studio Album	Warner Bros	1969-08-01	14.99
6	Sounds of Silence Studio Album	Columbia	1966-01-17	9.99
7	Abbey Road	Apple	1969-01-10	12.99
8	Smiley Smile	Capitol	1967-09-18	5.99
9	Clouds	Reprise	1969-05-01	9.99

Because the primary key values will be used as foreign key values in the songAlbum table, you must make sure that each record uses the correct primary key value. Use an UPDATE statement as shown in Listing 14.1 to change the albumID for *Clouds* back to 5.

LISTING 14.1

Updating the albumID

```
USE vinylrecordshop;
UPDATE album
   SET albumId = 5
WHERE albumTitle = 'Clouds';
```

You might also have noticed that in the original dataset in Table 14.2, the last album, *Smiley Smile*, has the value 9 assigned to albumId. Use an UPDATE statement to correct that value as well, as shown in Listing 14.2.

LISTING 14.2

Updating the Smiley Smile albumId

```
USE vinylrecordshop;
UPDATE album
   SET albumId = 9
WHERE albumTitle = 'Smiley Smile';
```

Review the records in your table and make sure that each record is assigned the correct primary key. You can reference Table 14.2 or the album.csv file included in the data files for this lesson.

IMPORT CSV DATA

As you completed the previous section, you were essentially keying the data into the database by hand, and you likely encountered several errors related to typos. In fact, even if your final INSERT statements work to add all eight records, there could well be typos in the data itself.

While it is important to know how to enter data manually (and you can use these processes to your advantage if you are using a SQL database as a back end for a Java or C# application), in many cases, you will already have a copy of the data in another format, such as an Excel file or a document table. As a general rule, it is much better to import existing data that is already in a digital format than it is to rekey the data by hand.

In the next step, you will add data to another primary table: the artist table. Table 14.3 contains information on the column definitions for the artist table in MySQL based on the schema script provided for this lesson. Table 14.4 contains the first few rows of data.

Table 14.3 The artist Table in MySQL

Field	Type	Null	Key	Default	Extra
artistId	int	NO	PRI	NULL	auto_increment
fname	varchar(25)	NO		NULL	
lname	varchar(50)	NO		NULL	
isHallOfFame	tinyint(1)	NO		NULL	

Table 14.4 First Few Rows of Data for artist Table

artistId	Fname	lname	isHallOfFame
1	Lennon	John	TRUE
2	McCartney	Paul	TRUE
3	Harrison	George	TRUE
4	Starr	Ringo	TRUE
5	Zager	Denny	FALSE

Before you can import the data from the .csv file into MySQL, you must use the following checklist and update the .csv data as necessary:

- Remove the heading row from the .csv file, if it exists. This row will be easy to recognize if it exists because it will contain names for the columns instead of data.
- Verify that the source file (in this case, the .csv file) includes the same fields as the target MySQL table.
- Verify that the fields in the source file are in the same order as the fields in the table.
- Verify that all fields in the .csv file are compatible with the data types defined in MySQL. For example, numbers should not have quotes around them and strings should.

Set Up MySQL

By default, MySQL is set up to prevent users from importing data from external files, as a security measure. In normal database use, only administrators would perform these tasks, but here, you are working with a local server. Regardless, it's good to know that these steps are possible, even if you are not likely to use them often.

MySQL has an external configuration file that includes startup options for the server. This is a plain-text file that can be edited as necessary to change the configuration. You will edit this file to change the startup options.

First, close and stop MySQL Server. Close any windows or clients that are connected to MySQL and use the MySQL Notifier icon in the notifications panel (in the lower-right corner of Windows 10 or 11 desktop) to stop the server. This can be done with the following three steps:

1. Expand the notifications panel and find the MySQL icon.

2. Right-click the icon and point to MySQL80 - Running.

3. Click the Stop option in the submenu, as shown in Figure 14.2.

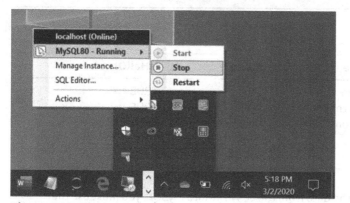

Figure 14.2 The Stop option

> **NOTE** Installing the MySQL Notifier was covered in Lesson 5, "Working with MySQL Server," if you have trouble finding or using it.

After stopping the service, use File Explorer to find MySQL's configuration file. In Windows, this file is named my.ini, and it should be located in C:\ProgramData\MySQL\ MySQL Server 8.0. Making changes to this file might prevent MySQL from running correctly. You should make a backup copy that you can use to restore the existing settings if you run into problems.

Open the file using any text editor and search for the entry [mysql]. If it exists, add the following code at the bottom of any existing settings for that entry:

```
local-infile
```

For example, you may find the following:

```
[mysql]
no-beep
```

Add the new setting under the no–beep option, as shown here:

```
[mysql]
no–beep
local–infile
```

If you cannot find [mysql] at all, add it along with the local–infile setting at the bottom of the file.

Repeat these steps for the entry [mysqld]. Search for it and update it if it exists or create a new entry if you cannot find it. When done, you should have both of the following settings somewhere in the revised file, although they may not follow each other, and each entry may have additional settings not shown here:

```
[mysqld]
local–infile
```

```
[mysql]
local–infile
```

Save the changes, close the file, and restart MySQL using steps similar to those you used to close the server. When you restart the server, the local–infile option will be available, allowing you to import external files into an existing database.

Prepare the CSV File

With the configuration file now updated, it's time to take a look at the .csv file itself. The artist.csv file is included in the data files mentioned at the start of this lesson.

We can use many different types of applications to open a CSV file to view its contents. It is really just a text file, where each row is on a separate line of text and the individual values are separated by commas.

If you open the artist.csv file in Notepad or a similar text editor, you will see the plain-text version of the file, as shown in Figure 14.3.

```
artist.csv - Notepad
File  Edit  Format  View  Help
artistId,artist.lname,artist.fname,hallOfFame
1,Lennon,John,TRUE
2,McCartney,Paul,TRUE
3,Harrison,George,TRUE
4,Starr,Ringo,TRUE
5,Zager,Denny,FALSE
6,Evans,Rick,FALSE
10,Morrison,Van,TRUE
11,Collins,Judy,FALSE
12,Simon,Paul,TRUE
```

Figure 14.3 The artist.csv file in Notepad

While this can be a useful way to see what the data looks like, opening the file in a spreadsheet application such as Excel, Numbers, or Google Sheets will also provide you with tools that allow you to manipulate the data. In fact, if you have a spreadsheet application already installed on your computer, it is likely to be the default application for CSV files.

The following steps use Microsoft Excel, but the steps would be similar in any spreadsheet application. You may see a warning about possible data loss, which Excel displays because the data is in CSV format, rather than an Excel XLSX format. You can ignore or close this warning if you see it.

If you opened the artist.csv file in your text editor, then close it now. You should then reopen it using a spreadsheet application, as shown in Figure 14.4. In this view, you can see and manipulate the columns more easily.

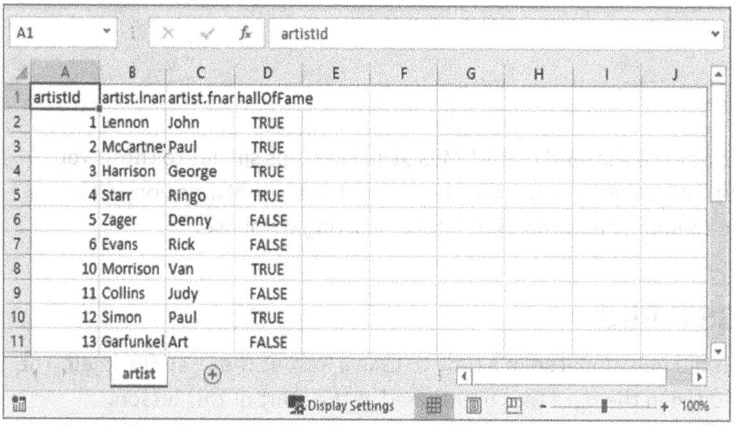

Figure 14.4 Opening the artist.csv file in Excel

When data is imported into MySQL, everything in the CSV file will be treated as data, so the first thing that needs to be done is to remove the heading row that contains the column names. Delete the entire row, not just the values in the cells, using the following steps:

1. Right-click the number 1 on the left edge of the table, to the left of artistId.

2. Click Delete in the context menu to delete the entire row.

3. Verify that John Lennon's record appears on row 1 of the worksheet, as shown in Figure 14.5.

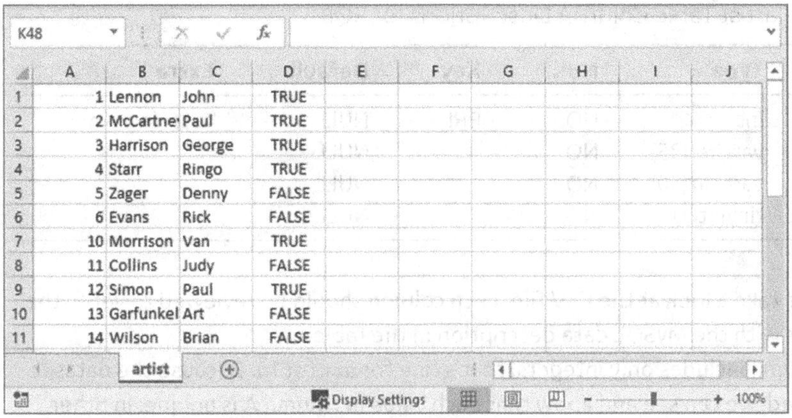

Figure 14.5 `artist.csv` file with header row removed

Next, you need to make sure that the columns in the CSV file are in the same order as the columns in the MySQL table. In this case, the first name and last name columns are reversed, so that needs to be fixed. The following steps walk through making this change in Excel:

1. Right-click the letter *C* above the first name column.

2. Click Cut in the context menu.

3. Right-click the letter *B* above the last name column.

4. Click Insert Cut Cells in the context menu.

These steps will effectively reverse the two columns in the dataset. Figure 14.6 shows the current state of the data in the Excel spreadsheet.

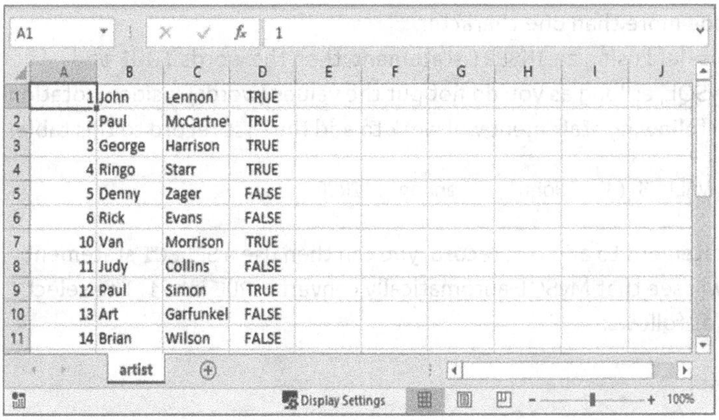

Figure 14.6 The `artist.csv` file with the names reversed

The last thing to check is whether the data in each column is appropriate for the data type defined in MySQL. The artist table has the description shown in Table 14.5.

Table 14.5 The artist Table Column Descriptions for SQL

Field	Type	Null	Key	Default	Extra
artistId	int	NO	PRI	NULL	auto_increment
fname	varchar(25)	NO		NULL	
lname	varchar(50)	NO		NULL	
isHallOfFame	tinyint(1)	NO		NULL	

At this point, take a look at the CSV file. Each column should be reviewed to verify the data type aligns with the MySQL data description in the table.

The first column includes only integers, so it's fine for `artistId`. Because the dataset is already created, we can see and know that each value in column A is unique. In other cases, you would want to either remove the column from the data (and allow the database engine to add auto-increment values as the data is imported) or verify that there are no duplicate values in the column(s) that you plan to use as the primary key.

The next two columns include the first and last names as string values. These are both presented as text, so no additional changes are needed.

The `isHallOfFame` column uses TRUE/FALSE in the CSV file, but it is defined as `TINYINT(1)` in the MySQL table. Because these are different, a closer look is needed.

This last field is a Boolean field in that it can include one of two possible values. However, Boolean values can be represented in a variety of ways, including TRUE/FALSE, YES/NO, and ON/OFF. The most basic option, however, is to use 1 or 0, where 1 is equivalent to TRUE and 0 represents FALSE.

In MySQL, a 1-digit integer can be used to represent a Boolean value, hence the data type tinyint(1) for this field. The words TRUE and FALSE seem more like string values than numbers, and they include more than one character.

If data is added to this field using an `INSERT` statement, then the words TRUE and FALSE can be used in MySQL, as long as you do not put the values (words) inside quotation marks. For example, the following statement will work to add the first record to this table:

```
INSERT INTO artist VALUES (1, 'John', 'Lennon', TRUE);
```

If you execute this statement to add this record, you can then use a `SELECT` statement to see the results. You will see that MySQL automatically converts `TRUE` into 1. The select statement to see this is as follows:

```
SELECT * FROM artist;
```

This produces the following output:

artistId	fname	lname	isHallOfFame
1	John	Lennon	1

Importing from an external file is trickier because each field is treated as a string or a number. For this reason, before you can import the data from a CSV file, all of the TRUE values should be replaced with 1 and all of the FALSE values should be replaced with 0.

With the file open in Excel, click the column letter D to select the contents of that column. You should see the entire column highlighted, as shown in Figure 14.7.

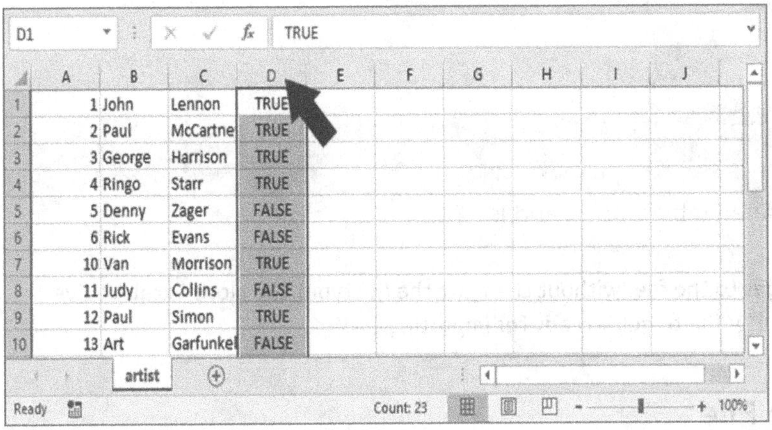

Figure 14.7 Selecting a column in Excel

Open the Find and Replace dialog by selecting Find & Select and then Replace in the Editing group on the Home ribbon or using the shortcut Ctrl+H. Enter TRUE as the Find What option, and enter 1 as the Replace With value, as shown in Figure 14.8. Click Replace All.

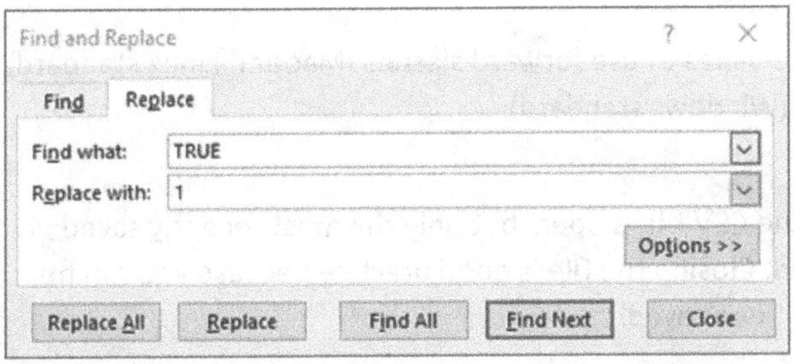

Figure 14.8 The Find and Replace dialog in Excel

This will replace all the TRUE values with the number 1. Repeat the process to replace all the FALSE values with the number 0. When you finish, you should see only 1s and 0s in the fourth column, as shown in Figure 14.9.

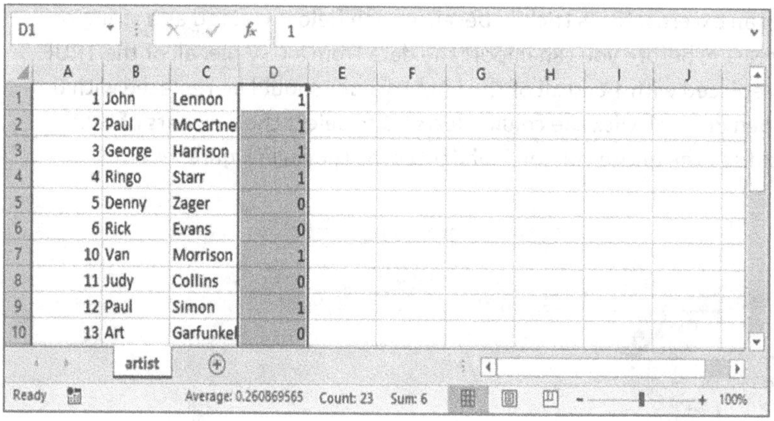

Figure 14.9 Updated table with 0s and 1s

Save the changes to the file (without changing the file type) and close Excel. You've now updated the CSV file to get it ready for importing.

Import the File

At this point, you should check the following again:

- The columns in the CSV file are in the same order as the columns in the MySQL table.
- You have the path (including the filename) for the CSV file.
    - In the examples here, the file is located in the Windows Documents library for a user named *user*. You will need to update the path as appropriate for your file.
    - If necessary, update the slashes to use forward slashes (Mac and Linux standard) rather than backslashes (Windows standard).
- The CSV file is closed.

You can import the file even if the CSV file is open, but only the most recently saved version of the data will be imported. Closing the file is good practice because you can be more certain that all changes have been saved.

Command-Line Import

To import from the command line, start by opening the MySQL command window and then connecting to MySQL. If you added the record for John Lennon earlier in this lesson, then you will want to delete it from the artist table of your database. This needs to be done because the record for John Lennon is also in the CSV file. Run the script in Listing 14.3 to remove the record.

LISTING 14.3

Deleting Artist Records

```
USE vinylrecordshop;
DELETE FROM artist WHERE artistId < 30;
```

This script will delete ALL data from the table. It does assume that the records all have an artistID less than 30. If you had added your own records or had added a record with an artistID equal to 30 or greater, then you might need to adjust the code.

With the artist table cleared, you are ready to load the CSV file. At the MySQL prompt, enter the command in Listing 14.4.

LISTING 14.4

Loading the artist.csv File

```
LOAD DATA LOCAL INFILE 'C:/Users/user/Documents/artist.csv'
INTO TABLE vinylrecordshop.artist
FIELDS TERMINATED BY ',';
```

This command will load the CSV file. It is worth looking at the details of what this script is doing.

- LOCAL INFILE tells MySQL to look for data in a local file. This will not work if you have not set up MySQL to allow local-infile for both mysqld (the database server) and mysql (the client interface).

- The table name is qualified to include the database name: vinylrecordshop.artist. This is more reliable than the USE command to be certain that the data is loaded into the correct table.

- The command specifies that the file uses commas to separate the data values on each row. A comma-separated file is being used here, but it is also possible to use other characters such as tabs or pipes for the same purpose.

After running this command, you should see a response like this:

```
Query OK, 23 rows affected (0.00 sec)
Records: 23  Deleted: 0  Skipped: 0  Warnings: 0
```

Use the following command to confirm that all records were successfully added to the table:

```
SELECT * FROM artist;
```

This should yield results that look like the following:

artistId	fname	lname	isHallOfFame
1	John	Lennon	1
2	Paul	McCartney	1
3	George	Harrison	1
4	Ringo	Starr	1
5	Denny	Zager	0
6	Rick	Evans	0
10	Van	Morrison	1
11	Judy	Collins	0
12	Paul	Simon	1
13	Art	Garfunkel	0
14	Brian	Wilson	0
15	Dennis	Wilson	0
16	Carl	Wilson	0
17	Ricky	Fataar	0
18	Blondie	Chaplin	0
19	Jimmy	Page	0
20	Robert	Plant	0
21	John Paul	Jones	0
22	John	Bonham	0
23	Mike	Love	0
24	Al	Jardine	0
25	David	Marks	0
26	Bruce	Johnston	0

MySQL Workbench

The previous command should work in a SQL editing window in MySQL Workbench, but SQL Workbench also includes an import wizard. Use the wizard to import the third primary table, band.

When you import data using LOAD DATA, you must make sure that there is no heading row in the data and that the columns in the CSV file are in the same order as the columns in the corresponding MySQL table. MySQL Workbench's data import wizard is more flexible, in that it will recognize and skip column headings, as well as allow you to map columns from the dataset to the table, meaning that the columns do not have to be in the same order. You can even choose to skip columns that exist in the CSV file but that you do not want to include in your database table.

If you open the band.csv file included in the data files, you will see (as shown in Figure 14.10) that it includes a column named *year_founded* that does not exist in the schema.

▲	A	B	C	D
1	id	band_name	year_founded	
2	1	The Beatles	1957	
3	2	Zager and Evans	1969	
4	3	Van Morrison	1958	
5	4	Judy Collins		
6	5	Simon and Garfunkel	1963	
7	7	Beach Boys	1961	
8	8	Led Zeppelin	1968	
9				

Figure 14.10 The band.csv file

If you wanted to use LOAD DATA to import this data, you would have to remove the column heading row and the extra year_founded column before importing. You do not need to make changes to the file to use MySQL Workbench instead.

To use MySQL Workbench to import the band data, use the following steps:

1. Open MySQL Workbench and connect to MySQL.

2. Right-click the vinylrecordshop database and click Table Data Import Wizard, as shown in Figure 14.11.

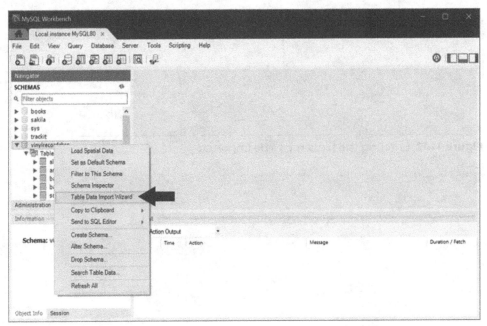

Figure 14.11 Starting the Table Data Import Wizard in MySQL Workbench

3. Enter the path or browse to find the band.csv file, as shown in Figure 14.12, and then click Next.

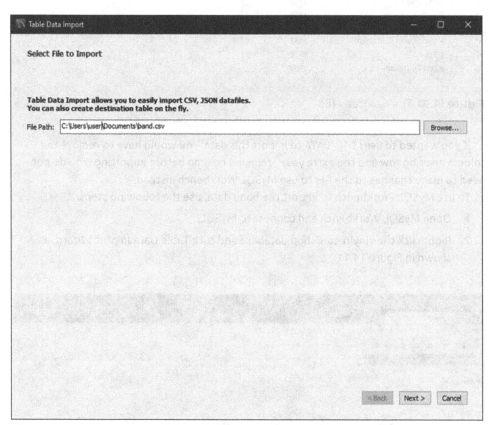

Figure 14.12 Entering the filename to be imported

4. Set the option to use the existing vinylrecordshop.band table, as shown in Figure 14.13, and click Next.

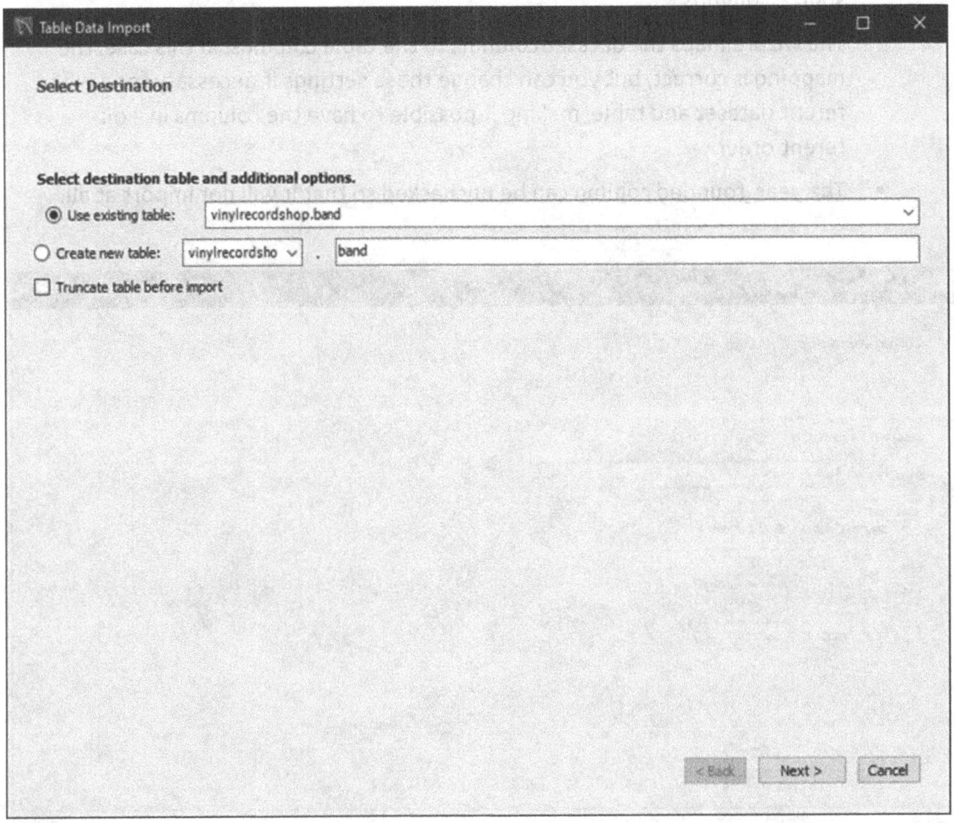

Figure 14.13 Selecting the table to use

5. The next window will show the import settings, as shown in Figure 14.14. Note the following and then click Next:

- The wizard identifies the column headings in the CSV file and lists them as the source columns.

- The wizard maps the dataset columns to the table columns. In this case, the mapping is correct, but you can change these settings if necessary for a different dataset and table, making it possible to have the columns in a different order.

- The year_founded column can be unchecked so that it will not import at all.

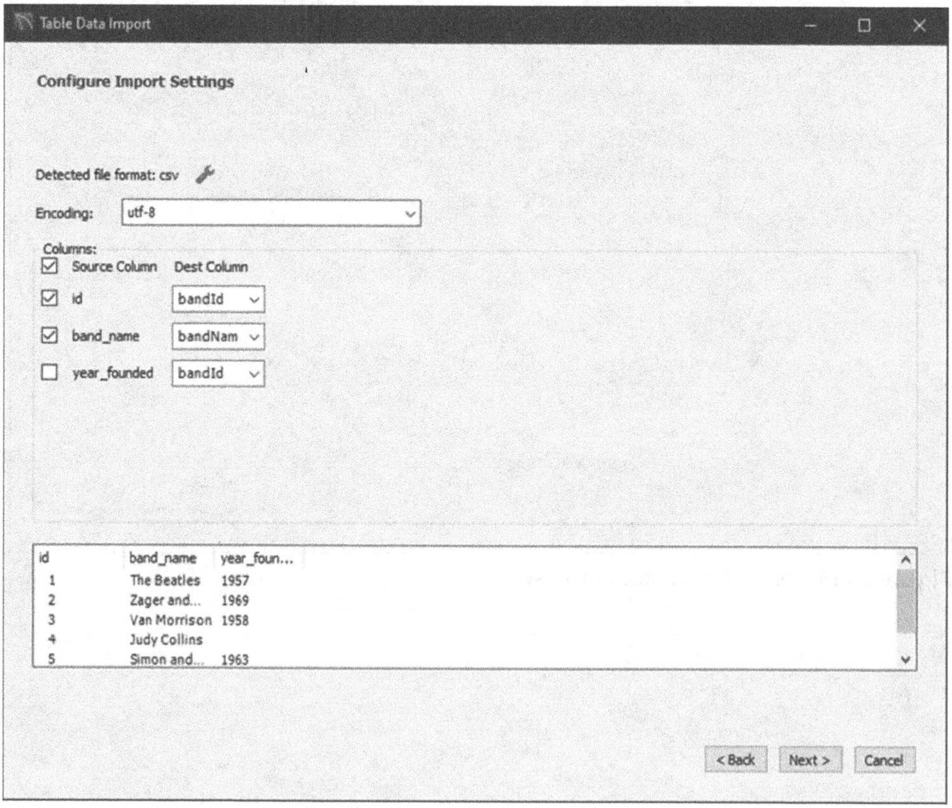

Figure 14.14 The import settings

6. The final window shown in Figure 14.15 asks you to confirm the import. Click Next.

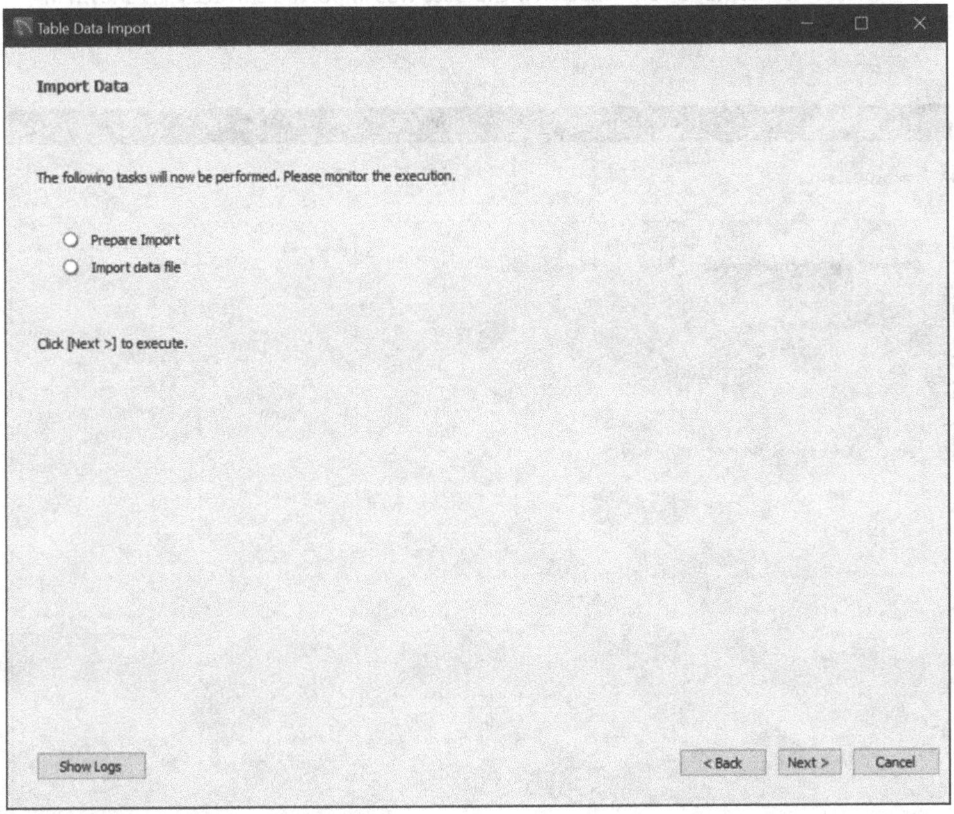

Figure 14.15 Confirming the import

7. The import should proceed without error, and each step will be checked off. The wizard will display a confirmation if the data was imported correctly, as shown in Figure 14.16. You will need to click Next to continue.

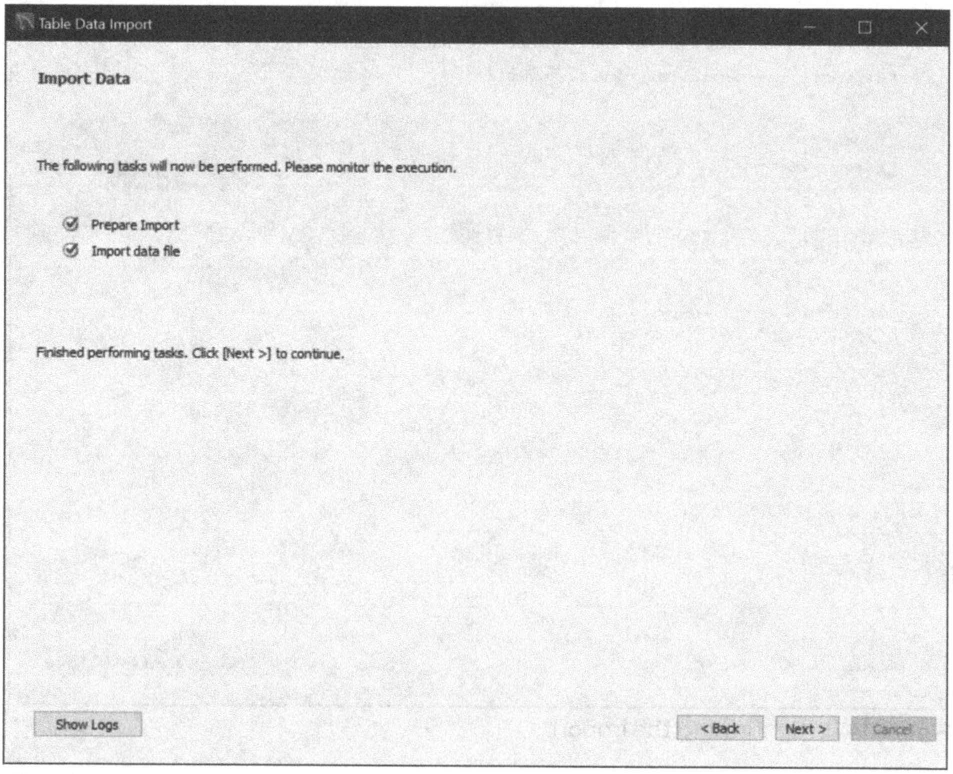

Figure 14.16 Confirmation that the import occurred

8. The final window will confirm that seven records were imported. Click Finish to close the wizard.

You can verify that the data was imported correctly by running a SELECT command such as the following in a SQL editor window:

```
USE vinylrecordshop;
SELECT * FROM band;
```

Figure 14.17 shows the results of running this in MySQL Workbench.

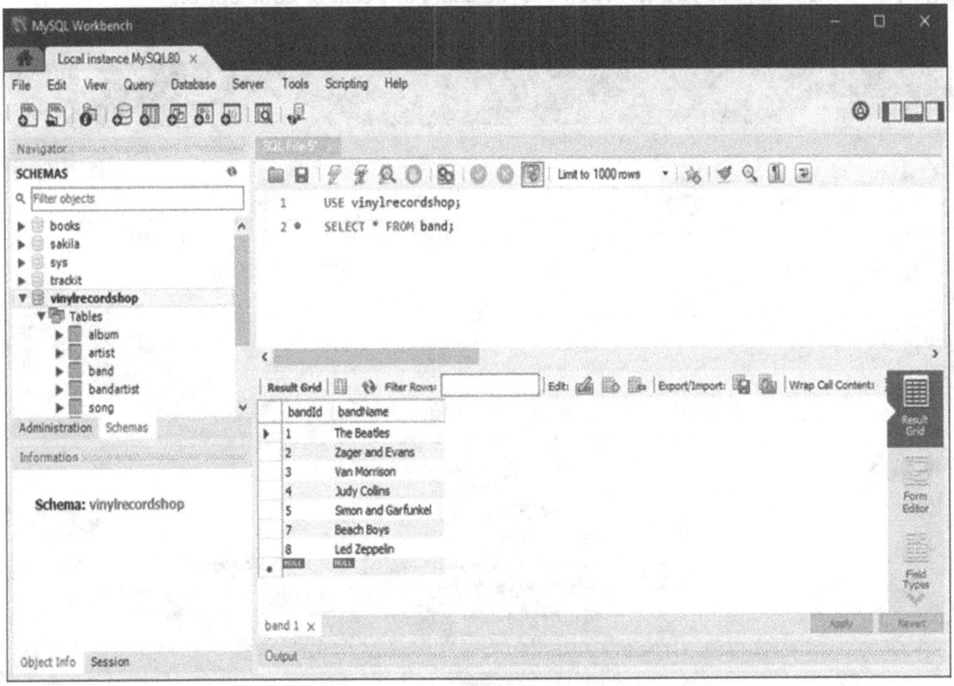

Figure 14.17 Using SELECT to verify band data is imported

ADD DATA TO THE SCRIPT

If you want a script that can rebuild the database, then you need to create IMPORT statements that can be added to the script. You can use mysqldump for this purpose.

Open your command-line interface and use the cd command to open the bin subdirectory for your MySQL installation. On most Windows computers, this will be as follows:

```
cd C:\Program Files\MySQL\MySQL Server 8.0\bin
```

Run mysqldump from the command line in this subdirectory. The syntax looks like this:

```
mysqldump -p --user=root database table > destination_filepath
```

In this example, the .sql file is sent to a new file in the user's Documents folder. Note that you will have to change the path appropriately for your own computer.

```
mysqldump -p --user=root vinylrecordshop artist > C:/Users/user/Documents/
artist.sql
```

After running the command, find and open the exported .sql file. Figure 14.18 shows MySQL Workbench, but you can open the file using any text or code editor.

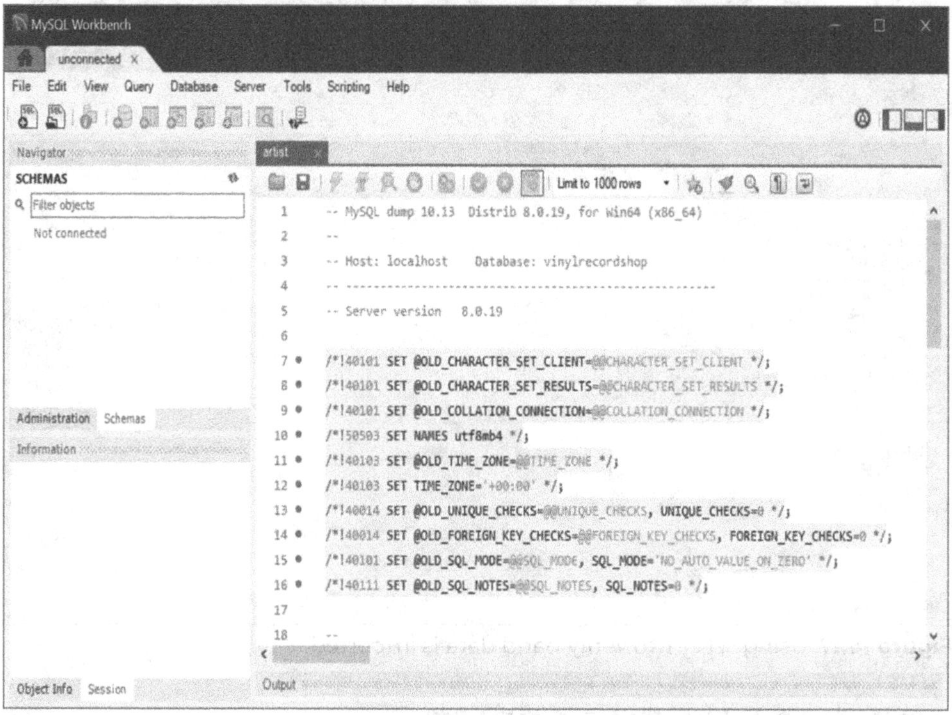

Figure 14.18 Viewing the .sql file from the mysqldump process

The file will contain many more lines of code than you really need for your script, including a statement to re-create the table. All you really need is the data itself.

Scan through the file until you see the INSERT INTO statement.

```
INSERT INTO `artist` VALUES (1,'John','Lennon',1),(2,'Paul','McCartney',1),
(3,'George','Harrison',1),(4,'Ringo','Starr',1),(5,'Denny','Zager',0),
(6,'Rick','Evans',0),(10,'Van','Morrison',1),(11,'Judy','Collins',0),(12,
'Paul','Simon',1),(13,'Art','Garfunkel',0),(14,'Brian','Wilson',0),(15,'Dennis',
'Wilson',0),(16,'Carl','Wilson',0),(17,'Ricky','Fataar',0),(18,'Blondie',
'Chaplin',0),(19,'Jimmy','Page',0),(20,'Robert','Plant',0),(21,'John Paul',
'Jones',0),(22,'John','Bonham',0),(23,'Mike ','Love',0),(24,'Al ','Jardine',0),
(25,'David','Marks',0),(26,'Bruce ','Johnston',0);
```

Copy that statement from the SQL file and paste it at the end of your existing vinylrecordshop-data.sql file.

TEST THE SCRIPT

At this point, you should be able to run your vinylrecordshop scripts to drop the database, rebuild it with the tables, and then add data to both the album and the artist tables. If the scripts do not work as expected, troubleshoot them, and fix the problems before continuing.

WRAP UP THE VINYL MUSIC SHOP SCRIPT

On your own, you should go ahead and add the data to the remaining tables, using the data in the CSV files provided. Remember that you must add data to the primary tables before adding data to the related tables.

Check the new data against the data in the CSV files to ensure that the data in each table is correct. As a quick check, you can verify that each table has the correct number of records.

- band: 7 records
- album: 8 records
- artist: 23 records
- song: 11 records
- bandArtist: 23 records
- songAlbum: 11 records

After you are sure that the data imported correctly for each table, save the IMPORT statement for that table to your data script.

> **NOTE** If you run into problems, remember that you can reset the database structure by running the schema script provided for this lesson and then adding data you have already set up using your data script.

SUMMARY

In this lesson, you added data to existing tables, first by keying the data in manually using an INSERT INTO statement and then by using two different import methods. Whenever possible, it is best to import existing data into a database rather than expecting someone to key the data in by hand, both because it is significantly faster to import data and because there is less risk of introducing new errors into the data.

The script to rebuild the database is currently in two parts: the first part creates the schema by dropping the database and rebuilding all of the tables, and the second part adds data to those tables. You could also have a single script that includes both the database schema and the data itself. When creating a script to rebuild a database, you must follow these rules:

- You must create the structure to hold the data before you can add the data. It would be fine to create a table and then add data to that table before creating the next table, for example.

- You must create primary tables before you can create related tables. Referential integrity will prevent you from creating foreign key fields if the associated primary key field does not yet exist.

- You must add data to primary tables before you can add data to related tables. Referential integrity will also prevent you from using a value as a foreign key if the value does not already exist in the associated primary key field.

Lesson 15
Diving into Advanced SQL Topics

You've covered creating, reading, updating, and deleting tables and fields. You've also covered various aspects of selecting and manipulating the data within those databases and tables. There are a number of other actions and features you can tap into when working with SQL.

In this lesson a variety of topics will be touched upon that add to the foundation that you've already established. These topics are considered more advanced, but each is important in its own way.

Learning Objectives

By the end of this lesson, you will be able to:

- Use a simple subquery

- Explain the pros and cons of views

- Explain the requirements of a database transaction

- Use optimization techniques to improve the performance of a MySQL database

- Describe the use of indexes to improve database performance

ADDING SUBQUERIES

SQL is a specialized language that executes only in the context of a relational database. You can't create a video game with it. Despite that, SQL is incredibly powerful, flexible, and expressive. To get a sense of its flexibility, consider this: any value, table, or set of values can be replaced by a second, separate query.

A **subquery** is a syntactically correct, complete query that is embedded in another query to produce a value or tabular result set. Removed from its parent, a subquery is still valid, though it may use values from its parent to establish context. Three main areas where subqueries are often used include the IN clause, where a table can be used, and where a value can be used.

To better understand subqueries, the TrackIt schema will be used in this lesson. If you already have this database set up in your MySQL Server instance, you are welcome to use it. If you do not have it or if you want to rebuild it for this lesson, you can run the trackit-schema-and-data.sql script that can be found with the downloadable files for this book.

Subqueries in the IN Operator

Values in an IN operator can come from a query. What if you wanted to find all Workers who are assigned to a Project? All the ProjectWorker.WorkerId values could be grabbed with a query that is within an IN clause, and the resulting values from that query would be used for the IN clause. This is shown in Listing 15.1.

LISTING 15.1

Grabbing All the Workers Assigned to a Project

```
USE TrackIt;

SELECT *
FROM Worker
WHERE WorkerId IN (
    SELECT WorkerId FROM ProjectWorker
);
```

In this query, the identifier, `WorkerId`, means two different things depending on where it's mentioned. In the main query, it refers to `Worker.WorkerId`. Inside the `IN`, it refers to `ProjectWorker.WorkerId`. It's easy to get confused.

An alternative approach might be to use `JOIN Worker` with `ProjectWorker`. That's a good idea, but it would return duplicate Workers because Workers can be assigned to more than one Project. The `IN` approach, on the other hand, does not duplicate Workers. If a value occurs more than once in an `IN`, it is ignored.

> **Warning!** `IN(subquery)` does not perform well when the subquery returns a large result. In that case, it is much faster to `JOIN` tables and use `GROUP`. Do not use `IN(subquery)` if your subquery returns much more than 100 values.

Subqueries for Tables

Any table named in a query can be replaced by a subquery. A secondary `SELECT` can be built on top of a subquery, or a subquery can be `JOIN`ed to a table. A subquery can even be `JOIN`ed to another subquery.

Some queries are impossible without a subquery. Consider grabbing both a Project and the first Task added to it. You could use `GROUP BY ProjectId` and `SELECT MIN(TaskId)`, as shown in Listing 15.2.

LISTING 15.2

A Query with an Issue

```
-- This doesn't do what we want.
SELECT
    p.Name ProjectName,
    MIN(t.TaskId) MinTaskId
    -- t.Title is what we want, but the SQL Engine
    -- doesn't know which Task we're talking about.
    -- t.Title is not part of a group and there's
    -- no aggregate guaranteed to grab the Title from the MinTaskId.
FROM Project p
INNER JOIN Task t ON p.ProjectId = t.ProjectId
GROUP BY p.ProjectId, p.Name;
```

The solution in this listing identifies the first Task added, but then we're stuck. There's no way to fetch the first Task's fields. The only values that can be selected are grouped Project fields and Task aggregates. There's no aggregate function that grabs a field from a specific record.

A subquery solves the problem, as shown in Listing 15.3.

LISTING 15.3

Solving the Problem with a Subquery

```
SELECT
    g.ProjectName,
    g.MinTaskId,
    t.Title MinTaskTitle
FROM Task t
INNER JOIN (
    SELECT
        p.Name ProjectName,
        MIN(t.TaskId) MinTaskId
    FROM Project p
    INNER JOIN Task t ON p.ProjectId = t.ProjectId
    GROUP BY p.ProjectId, p.Name) g ON t.TaskId = g.MinTaskId;
```

The original query becomes the subquery. It's joined to Task and given the alias g. Because a subquery doesn't have a name, an alias is required. Fields from the subquery are available for ON conditions and WHERE conditions and to be selected in the SELECT value list. They retain their aliased name. It's a lot to look at, but if you loosen up your expectations, you start to see the table/tabular data hiding in the subquery.

Subqueries for Values

Any field or calculated value can be replaced by a subquery. In effect, the subquery becomes the calculation. As an example, the query in Listing 15.4 fetches Workers and counts their assigned Projects.

LISTING 15.4

Fetching Workers with Project Counts

```
SELECT
    w.FirstName,
    w.LastName,
    (SELECT COUNT(*) FROM ProjectWorker
    WHERE WorkerId = w.WorkerId) ProjectCount
FROM Worker w;
```

The subquery is embedded directly in the SELECT value list. Be careful with identifiers. Here, WorkerId refers to ProjectWorker.WorkerId, and w.WorkerId aliases back to Worker.WorkerId. If you missed the alias (WHERE WorkerId = WorkerId), every Worker would have a ProjectCount of 165 (all ProjectWorker records). Listing 15.5 presents another way to solve this Project/MIN Task problem.

LISTING 15.5

Sovling the Project/MIN Task Problem

```
SELECT
    p.Name ProjectName,
    MIN(t.TaskId) MinTaskId,
    (SELECT Title FROM Task
    WHERE TaskId = MIN(t.TaskId)) MinTaskTitle
FROM Project p
INNER JOIN Task t ON p.ProjectId = t.ProjectId
GROUP BY p.ProjectId, p.Name;
```

This solution is probably a bad idea, though, because value subqueries don't perform well. If a query is defined in the SELECT list, it is run once for every record in the result. If you have 1,000 records, your subquery runs 1,000 times. If you have one million records, your subquery runs one million times. Generally, that's bad.

You can always achieve the same result with other techniques. You should always be a good database citizen and avoid executing a subquery for each record.

> **NOTE** Don't expect to master subqueries immediately! The purpose here is to show what's possible. Entire books have been dedicated to advanced query techniques. If you enjoy database work, it's a topic you should explore in more detail after completing this book.

WORKING WITH VIEWS

A view is a named query that's stored in a database. Once it's stored, other queries can build on it. A view can be treated like a table anywhere in a SELECT statement. You can also think of it as a named subquery.

A bit of DDL is needed to create a view. It follows the DDL pattern shown here:

```
CREATE objectType objectName
```

The view's query follows the AS keyword, as shown in Listing 15.6.

LISTING 15.6

Creating a View

```
CREATE VIEW ProjectNameWithMinTaskId
AS
SELECT
    p.Name ProjectName,
    MIN(t.TaskId) MinTaskId
FROM Project p
INNER JOIN Task t ON p.ProjectId = t.ProjectId
GROUP BY p.ProjectId, p.Name;
```

You can see in this listing that a view is created called ProjectNameWithMinTaskId. The definition of the view follows the AS clause. The code after the SELECT should look familiar as it is simply a standard SELECT statement.

With the view created, it can now be used as a data source.

```
SELECT * FROM ProjectNameWithMinTaskId;
```

You can also build more complex queries on top of it, as shown in Listing 15.7.

LISTING 15.7

A More Complex Query Using a View

```
SELECT
    pt.ProjectName,
    pt.MinTaskId TaskId,
    t.Title
FROM Task t
INNER JOIN ProjectNameWithMinTaskId pt -- Aliased just like a table.
    ON t.TaskId = pt.MinTaskId;
```

Like any technology, views have advantages and disadvantages. The advantages of using views include the following:

- Encapsulating complex joins can reduce code complexity and increase code reuse.
- Views can be secured separately from a table, for example, to grant user access to a view without granting access to the tables underneath.
- Views can limit columns and rows shown to some users.

There are, however, also disadvantages to views.

- Within MySQL, views are not a permanent structure. While the view's definition is always available, the subset of the table it creates is temporary. In other words, the table created by the view is generated each time the view is accessed.
- Just because a view appears simple doesn't mean the underlying data model is. A view with simple results may be very expensive to run.
- Developers can be tempted to build more and more on top of views because views are easy to understand. As views are joined to views that are joined to other views, performance issues may arise.
- If you are using a database other than MySQL, you'll want to confirm whether the tables generated by views remain or are re-created each time as well.

UNDERSTANDING TRANSACTIONS

Because database processes can involve several individual steps that rely on each other, good database design must support the concept of a transaction: an operation that includes multiple individual steps, all of which must complete successfully for the transaction itself to be successful.

Transaction Example

A transaction is a set of operations that together form one indivisible operation. This means that a transaction must succeed or fail as a single operation.

Consider an example of a flat transaction where money is transferred between two accounts. This involves performing two different operations: taking money from one account and adding money to another account. These two operations must be completed together and either succeed or fail together.

Before starting the transfer, the system will check the available balance in the source account to ensure that the balance is higher than the amount to be transferred. Next, the system will perform two operations: deduct the transfer amount from the source account and add the same amount to the target account. Because these two operations must happen together, it is considered to be a single transaction. If the second step fails for any reason, then both operations must be reversed.

To understand this, consider the following example. Assume a customer has a balance of $400 in Account A and wants to transfer $200 to Account B. First, the amount is removed from Account A. The remaining balance in Account A is now $200. The next step is to add the $200 to Account B. Now imagine that during the second step, a computer glitch occurs, and the system cannot finish adding the $200 to Account B. In this scenario, the customer just lost $200 from Account A that did not transfer to Account B.

This is problematic and can be avoided by using transactions. In this case, the transaction includes both operations: the first one deducts the amount from Account A, and the second one adds the amount to Account B. A transaction is defined as a single indivisible operation, which means that if one of the two operations fails, then the other step will fail as well, and the transaction will abort. Aborting the transaction will cancel whatever processing happened during the transaction. In this example, the second operation fails, so the transaction will cancel the first operation that deducted the amount from Account A. We thus ensure that the transaction succeeds only if each operation in the transaction succeeds.

Let's consider a more complicated example that uses a transaction with more than two operations. When you purchase an item from an online retailer, the purchase transaction must include each of the following steps:

1. Check the available quantity of the item to ensure that there are enough to fulfill the purchase request.

2. Deduct 1 from the available quantity.

3. Check that the customer has valid credit card information in the database.

4. Receive authorization from the credit card merchant account to transfer the purchase amount to the retailer.

5. Generate an order number in the database to keep track of the purchase.

These steps are considered a single transaction, and for the transaction to complete successfully, each of the steps must be successful. If the merchant account declines the customer's credit card in step 4, step 2 is also rejected, and the available quantity of that item will be reset to the original value. Similarly, if there is a glitch in the database and the system cannot generate an order number, the entire sale is canceled. Not only will the available quantity of the item reset, but the payment through the merchant account will also be canceled.

In a robust system, the code may include gates that will give the user the opportunity to fix errors as they occur, rather than blindly canceling everything as soon as an error is detected. For example, if the customer's credit card information is invalid, the system could prompt the user for another form of payment.

Transactions are widely used in databases and software development, and they represent an important concept that guarantees consistency and recovery of data in case of an error. A transaction can succeed, which means that the operations within the transaction all executed successfully. A transaction can also fail, which means that one or more operations within the transaction failed.

The execution of a transaction typically works as follows:

1. Initialize the transaction.
2. Perform operations.
3. Do either a commit or an abort.
   - **Commit**: The operations are successfully executed, and the data is submitted.
   - **Abort**: If one of the operations in the transaction fails, then all the operations are rolled back, and the data goes back to its original state.

ACID

The acronym ACID was covered in Lesson 1, "Exploring Relation Databases and SQL." You learned that ACID is an acronym for atomicity, consistency, isolation, and durability. A transaction must satisfy these same four properties. You can refer to Lesson 1 for more details, but here is a summary of the four properties:

- **Atomicity:** Either all operations in the transaction succeed or all of them fail. When the transaction fails, the state of the data that the operation was being applied on will remain unaffected by the transaction.
- **Consistency:** A transaction should not have any adverse effect on the data. If the data is consistent prior to the transaction, then it should remain consistent after the transaction.
- **Isolation:** Transactions occur independently of each other, but they cannot interfere with each other. This means that two transactions cannot operate on the same data at the same time.
- **Durability:** The changes made by the individual operations are permanent if the transaction is successful.

In the case where the operating system is needed to execute several transactions concurrently, the transactions must be scheduled appropriately to avoid problems. One option is to use serialization, which is the process of executing several transactions one after the other so transactions occur sequentially. The first transaction is executed, then the second one is executed, and so on. In other words, the transactions are executed one after the other without any interleaving of the instructions from different transactions. Serialization allows each transaction to execute safely, without interference from other transactions. However, this approach can be inefficient because it can leave resources in a waiting state, doing nothing while the system executes other operations in the transaction.

To avoid this inefficiency, it is common to interleave instructions from one transaction with instructions from other transactions. Thus, the execution of several transactions will occur concurrently. However, when we interleave the execution of different transactions that are working on the same data, we could have two operations that work on the same data. This could be problematic if it breaks the consistency rule. This means that mechanisms must also be defined that allow the operations to be interleaved from multiple transactions while also ensuring the consistency of the data.

A transaction can have several states, and the different states form a finite state machine. A finite state machine is a system that can have a finite number of states. Figure 15.1 shows the different states of a transaction.

The states shown in Figure 15.1 include the following:

- **Active:** A transaction is active during its execution. This is the initial state of any transaction.

- **Partially committed:** Once a transaction executes its final operation, it is considered partially committed.

- **Committed:** Once a transaction has successfully executed all its operations, if there are no conflicts with other active transactions, the operations are permanently committed.

- **Failed:** A transaction fails when one of its operations cannot complete successfully.

- **Aborted:** If the transaction fails, then the transaction manager rolls back the data to its original state, and the operations are aborted.

In MySQL, a transaction can be built using the START TRANSACTION statement. Listing 15.8 shows how to perform three operations as one transaction. This mimics a typical transfer of money between checking and saving accounts.

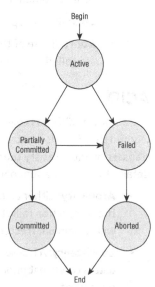

Figure 15.1 Flowchart showing possible transaction states

LISTING 15.8

Performing a Transaction

```
START TRANSACTION;
SELECT balance FROM checking WHERE customer_id=10233276;
UPDATE checking SET balance = balance - 200.00 WHERE customer_id=10233276;
UPDATE savings SET balance = balance + 200.00 WHERE customer_id=10233276;
COMMIT;
```

In other situations, MySQL automatically saves new data as it is added to a table or when existing data is modified or deleted, and you do not need to formally commit those changes. In a transaction, however, you must use the COMMIT keyword to save the changes defined by the SELECT and UPDATE statements. If any of those statements fails, the COMMIT also fails, and none of the changes is saved to the database.

SCHEMA OPTIMIZATION

During the design and development of data engineering solutions, the main constraint is scalability. Companies are constantly acquiring new data that must be organized, processed, and used to improve business intelligence. Data engineers must always think about scaling when designing any data solution. In the case of MySQL databases, there are design considerations that can dramatically optimize the performance of the databases and, consequently, any data routines that use databases.

There are different strategies to optimize the schema of MySQL tables that include choosing the optimal data types as well as using proper indexing to improve the performance of read and write operations. These techniques can be used to design databases that can be used in extract-transform-load (ETL) processes as well as data-intensive applications.

> **NOTE** Optimizing schema and indexing requires both attention to detail and being able to see the big picture. A data engineer must know how the system will work in order to optimize MySQL databases to fit the needs of the system.

Choosing Optimal Data Types

MySQL has an extensive list of data types that can be used to represent data. For a complete list of the data types available in MySQL, please see MySQL's page on Data Types at dev.mysql.com/doc/refman/5.7/en/data-types.html.

Choosing the appropriate data type for a column can improve the performance dramatically. In general, a few guidelines can be used to choose the appropriate data type.

- **Use the smallest reasonable data type:** If the age of a customer is being stored, there is no need to use a 32-bit integer. Using bigger data types requires more space on the disk, memory, and the CPU cache. Moreover, smaller data types require fewer CPU cycles to be processed, which makes them faster. When choosing a data type, always go with the smallest data type that can hold your information. However, make sure that you account for future issues with the range of the data type chosen. Underestimating the range could result in a time-consuming process to alter the table to change the range of the data type.

- **Keep it simple:** When choosing a data type, always go with the simplest possible. For instance, it is better to store an IP address in an integer field than a varchar field because comparing numbers requires fewer CPU cycles than comparing characters. Dates and times should also be stored in the MySQL built-in date type because it is optimized to compare dates.

- **Consider nulls:** When designing tables, a not null column should always be favored over a null column. Queries with nullable columns are harder for MySQL to optimize. Moreover, a nullable column requires more storage space and extra processing by MySQL. Instead of using null values, other data types can be used to refer to a nonexisting value. For instance, an impossible or meaningless value like 0 could be used for cases where the age of a customer is not defined, because this is easier to process and optimize than using a null value. Columns that are used for indexing should always be NOT NULL to avoid the extra processing by MySQL to index null values.

When choosing a data type, start by identifying the class of data that is appropriate to represent the data. The classes on MySQL are numeric, string, date, etc. This choice is typically obvious. A customer's name should be represented by a string, and age should be represented by a numeric type. Once you have identified the appropriate class, you can choose the specific data type that will be used to represent the data. There are several types of integers on MySQL, and each type has a specific range, precision, and storage space needed to store the data.

For integers, there are types TINYINT, SMALLINT, MEDIUMINT, INT, and BIGINT, which require respectively 8, 16, 24, 32, and 64 bits of storage. Moreover, integer types can have an unsigned attribute, which limits the integer to be only positive. A data engineer needs to envision the data to be stored and then decide if the data will be positive or negative and use the appropriate data type.

MySQL also includes numeric types for floating numbers: FLOAT, DOUBLE, and DECIMAL.

- DECIMAL stores exact fractional numbers. (It is ideal for financial applications or when exact math is needed.)

- Floating-point types use less space than DECIMAL to store the same range of values.

For strings, MySQL offers the VARCHAR and CHAR types.

- **VARCHAR is used for variable-length strings:** VARCHAR uses only as much storage as needed for specific values, which in many situations takes less storage than the CHAR type, especially for short strings and empty strings. The VARCHAR type helps performance by reducing disk space waste. However, because of the dynamic size of the VARCHAR type, increasing the length of a string stored in VARCHAR type can cause the data to be moved to another location on the disk so it can fit the new size. This causes some performance issues.

- **CHAR is used for fixed-length strings:** CHAR is ideal to store short strings. For instance, CHAR can be used to store MD5 hash values of user passwords because they have the same length (128 bits). The CHAR type is also faster for updates because the size of the string is always known in advance, and thus data does not need to be moved around if the new value does not fit in the original location in the disk.

Choosing the appropriate data type for a column requires knowledge of the different data types offered by MySQL as well as how these data types are stored and processed by MySQL. A data engineer must choose the right data type that provides the best performance of information processing.

Indexing

Indexes are an important factor in MySQL performance. Indexes, also known as *keys*, are data structures used within MySQL to speed up data lookups and improve the performance of read operations. For big data, it is important to index the data so that data can be retrieved quickly. For example, the user database of Facebook contains more than two billion users. Looking up their information requires indexing the table to allow data retrieval to be done in a reasonable time.

MySQL uses different types of indexes, which are appropriate for different situations. Indexes are implemented in the storage engine of MySQL. There are different storage engines available on MySQL. If no storage engine is specified, MySQL uses the default

InnoDB storage engine, which supports primary and foreign keys. For more complex databases, it might be better to designate a different storage engine that will handle the data and relationships a little differently.

For this lesson, two types of indexes will be covered. The first is B-tree indexes. The second is hash indexes.

B-Tree Indexes

B-tree indexes use a B-tree data structure to store data. This creates a hierarchical structure of data where the root nodes point to the next child nodes. The storage engine follows those pointers until it reaches the data needed. Each node in the tree has a key along with a pointer to the child page and the next leaf in the tree.

B-tree indexes speed up data access because an entire table does not need to be scanned to find the data needed. Instead, searching starts at the root of the B-tree and uses the right pointer to access the data needed. The node pages keep track of the range of each index, which is used to locate the needed data.

B-tree indexes work well with data lookups by a full key value, a key range, or a key prefix. For instance, if first and last names are used as a key such as in the case in Listing 15.9, then all people with the same first and last names can be easily located. All people who have the same first name or the same last name can also be found quickly.

LISTING 15.9

Creating an Index

```
CREATE TABLE person(
    lastname VARCHAR(50) NOT NULL,
    firstname VARCHAR(50) NOT NULL,
    dob DATE NOT NULL,
    KEY(firstname,lastname,dob)
);
```

In the example shown in Listing 15.9, an index is created in the final KEY clause based on the first name, last name, and date of birth. The order of the attributes in the key is important. Using this key, lookups for first names can be sped up, but not dates of birth because the key is built using the first name first.

> **NOTE** A good article introducing B-Tree indexing is at www.geeksforgeeks.org/ introduction-of-b-tree-2.

Hash Indexes

A hash index uses a hash table to perform fast data lookups. However, unlike the B-tree indexes, hash indexes are used to perform an exact lookup of the key. This means that every column of the key is used. In hash indexes, the value of the columns used in the key are hashed together to produce a unique value for each row, and this hash value can then be used to look up data. If you want to search for a person with a specific first name, last name, and date of birth, you first compute the hashed value of the three columns and then look up the hash table to search the row that has the same hash value.

In Listing 15.9, the key could be used to look up people with specific first names because the index starts with the first name column. In the hash index, the three columns could be needed in the lookup; see Listing 15.10.

LISTING 15.10
Using a Hash Index

```
CREATE TABLE person(
    firstname VARCHAR(50) NOT NULL,
    lastname VARCHAR(50) NOT NULL,
    KEY USING HASH(firstname)
)Engine=MEMORY;
```

In this example, the first name is used as an index using hash indexes. MEMORY is used as the storage engine because hash indexing is the default type of indexing in the MEMORY engine. Moreover, MEMORY is the only storage engine that supports explicit hash indexing in MySQL. However, hash indexes can be used on other storage engines implicitly using some hacks or workarounds.

Because the first name is defined as a hash index, the MEMORY storage engine will generate a hash table where each row in the person table has a hash value based on the first name. This hash value is used to look up data quickly. For instance, if you want to search for all people with the first name John, MySQL will first compute the hash value of John and then compare it to the hash table. The hash table is comprised of key-value pairs, where the key is the hash, and the value is the row that has the same hash. By doing this, rows can be quickly found that have a known hash value.

Hash indexes are extremely fast for data lookups, but they do have some limitations. For instance, hash indexes cannot be used in sorting because the hash function doesn't preserve the order of the rows. Moreover, hash indexes can be used only for equality (=), and they cannot be used for other SQL operators such as IN or LIKE. On other storage engines, hash indexes can be implemented using MySQL built-in functions that allow hash values to be computed for any column; an example is the CRC32 function.

For a more in-depth look at indexing in MySQL and a comparison of the options, see Krzysztof Ksiazek's article "An Overview of MySQL Database Indexing" found at severalnines.com/blog/overview-mysql-database-indexing.

SUMMARY

In this lesson, a number of advanced topics were covered. First was coverage of subqueries, which are complete queries embedded inside another. Subqueries can stand alone with few modifications. A subquery can provide values for an IN operator, behave like a table in a join, or evaluate to a single value in a SELECT list. Some query results are not possible without a subquery.

Views are named queries stored in the database. They operate like tables. Views can hide the complexity of a data model and provide an easy-to-use abstraction. Like any abstraction, they can also hide decisions that cause performance issues.

Transactions are sets of operations that together form one indivisible operation. This set of actions must succeed or fail as a single operation. Transactions are often described using the acronym ACID, which stands for atomicity, consistency, isolation, and durability. Transactions need to satisfy these four properties to be valid.

Two ways to help optimize your MySQL databases were presented. The first was to use the appropriate data type for columns. A data engineer must choose the right data type that provides the best performance of information processing. The second way to optimize that was presented was to optimize queries into your data through the use of indexing. You learned two types of indexing in this lesson. First was B-tree, which uses a B-tree data structure to store data. The second was hash indexing that uses a hash table.

In addition to optimizing data, as your systems get larger, you might need to apply replication and/or scaling. Within the lesson you learned about two types of replication, statement-based replication and row-based replication, before seeing a three-step process for replicating data from the primary to the secondary server on MySQL.

The lesson concluded by covering the concept of high availably of data. As mentioned, high availability is a characteristic of a system that can continue to operate even in the event of an error or failure. High availability depends on the application, and the constraints and thresholds for availability vary from one scenario to another.

EXERCISES

The following exercises are provided to allow you to experiment with concepts presented in this lesson:

Exercise 15.1: Recent Tasks

Exercise 15.2: Before Grumps

Exercise 15.3: Project Due Dates

Exercise 15.4: The Work of Ealasaid Blinco

Exercise 15.5: Other Databases

Use the TrackIt schema from Lesson 11, "Adding JOIN Queries" to complete the following exercises using subqueries.

> **NOTE** The exercises are for your benefit. They help you apply what you learn in the lessons. Note that these exercises are provided for you to do on your own, so solutions are not provided.

Exercise 15.1: Recent Tasks

Retrieve a list of all project names from the TrackIt database that includes the most recent task assigned to each project. The results should display the TaskId and the Task Title.

For your solution, no project should appear in the results more than once. Your query results should include 26 rows, including the following sample output:

ProjectName	MaxTaskID	MaxTaskTitle
GameIt Accounts Payable	132	Construct user interface
GameIt Accounts Receivable	107	Construct front-end components
GameIt Enterprise	182	Profile UI

> **TIP** The TaskID is an autoincremented field, which means that higher values are more recent than lower values.

Exercise 15.2: Before Grumps

Generate a list of tasks whose due date is on or before the due date for the project named Grumps. By using a subquery, you do not need to know the project due date to generate the results. Write the query without including a specific date. The query results will include 513 results, including the following sample output:

Title	DueDate
Log in	2007-02-19
Refactor data store	2015-04-04
Refactor service layer and classes	2018-09-03

Exercise 15.3: Project Due Dates

A view is a saved query that can be selected by other queries in the same way that a query can select a table. Note that the results of a view are dynamic, just like the results of a query, so a view will always retrieve the most recent version of the data. However, if you find yourself writing the same query over and over, you can save the query as a view and then run just the view. Views are especially useful for queries that include multiple joins across tables.

Create a view that displays a list of all project names and due dates, the title of each task associated with each project, and the first name and last name of each work assigned to the tasks. Assign the view any name that makes sense to you.

The results will include 543 records, including the following sample output:

Name
GameIt Accounts Receivable
GameIt Accounts Receivable
GameIt Accounts Receivable

TIP Create a regular SELECT query to verify the syntax required to create the view and then use the SELECT query to generate the view.

Exercise 15.4: The Work of Ealasaid Blinco

Use the view created in the previous exercise to generate a list of all tasks assigned to worker Ealasaid Blinco. The results will include 15 records, including the following sample output:

Name
GameIt Accounts Payable
GameIt Accounts Payable
GameIt Accounts Payable

Exercise 15.5: Other Databases

Look at other databases used in other parts of this book and identify places where a view might be useful as a shortcut to creating the same complicated query over and over again.

Appendix A

Bonus Lesson on Applying SQL with Python

In this bonus lesson, you'll work with MySQL and Python. It is assumed that you already know how to program in Python, so the focus will be on learning how to manage databases, tables, and data.

Learning Objectives

By the end of this lesson, you will be able to:

- Use PyMySQL to connect a Python script to a MySQL instance
- Perform basic create, retrieve, update, and delete (CRUD) operations on a MySQL database using Python scripts, including:
  - Creating and deleting databases
  - Creating and deleting tables
  - Adding, updating, and deleting fields in a table
  - Adding, updating, retrieving, and deleting data in a table

Because it is assumed you are already familiar with Python, prior to starting this lesson, you should have the following:

- The PyMySQL package installed in Python
- A MySQL instance running in the background
- The username and password for the running MySQL instance

You may also find it useful to have an active MySQL window open (command line or GUI, such as MySQL Workbench) that you can use to confirm activities managed by Python during this lesson.

NOTE This lesson assumes a working understanding of basic CRUD operations in SQL. If you've covered the lessons in this book, then you should already be familiar with these!

DATABASE OPERATIONS

While it is possible to create databases in a MySQL interface and then connect to those databases using Python, you can use the PyMySQL package to manage all database operations directly from Python, giving you a single interface to run scripts that depend on data stored in a MySQL database.

Using PyMySQL

The PyMySQL Python package will be used in this lesson to access and manage a MySQL database using Python scripts. Before you can do anything with MySQL, though, you must connect to the server that runs the MySQL instance.

Make sure you have installed the PyMySQL Python package and that MySQL is running in the background. The code examples in this lesson assume that MySQL is using the following settings:

- host: **localhost**
- username: **root**
- password: **admin**

Depending on your MySQL setup, you may need to change the code in the examples to create successful connections with MySQL.

Getting Your Version of MySQL

As an example, the connect method from the PyMySQL package will be used to get the version of MySQL currently installed. The script in Listing A.1 performs the following actions:

1. It imports the PyMySQL Python package.
2. It connects to the MySQL instance.

3. It uses the connection to create a cursor that we can use to execute MySQL queries.
4. It runs two queries (to get the current version of MySQL and to retrieve the first row of text from the results).
5. It displays the retrieved data.

LISTING A.1

Script to Get MySQL Version

```
import pymysql

con = pymysql.connect(host='localhost', user='root', password='admin', db='mysql')
with con.cursor() as cur:
  cur.execute("SELECT VERSION()")
  version = cur.fetchone()
  print("Database version: {}".format(version[0]))
con.close()
```

Enter this script and run it. This should verify that you can connect to your local MySQL instance and retrieve the current version of MySQL.

Take a closer look at the code. In the first line, pymysql is being imported so that the connect class can be used to connect to the MySQL server. This is followed by setting up the connection using connect(). You will need to adjust the setting being passed so that they match your database.

The next line of code creates a cursor object called cur that will be used to execute the MySQL queries. You can see this is used to call execute() which in turn executes the SQL command SELECT VERSION(), which is a simple query to get the current version of MySQL. The version is then fetched from the first row of the results that the SELECT VERSION() provided. This formatted version of the database is then displayed before closing the connection. The output should be similar to the following:

```
Database version: 8.0.17
```

NOTE For Listing A.1 to work, you will need to make sure that the values provided for the password matches what you created for the root account of your MySQL database server. You can also change the user and password to any other valid account on your database as well.

Create a Database

PyMySQL can be used to create new databases in a MySQL instance. Essentially, PyMySQL acts as an interpreter between Python and MySQL, using the execute method to send standard SQL commands to MySQL.

After connecting to MySQL, you can create a new database named *recordshop* that will be used to manage data related to a record store. From previous lessons, you should already know that this can be done with the following SQL command:

```
CREATE DATABASE recordshop;
```

Note that the command ends in a semicolon. All MySQL statements must end in a semicolon to be executed, just as you previously learned. Listing A.2 provides the Python code to execute this SQL command to create the database.

LISTING A.2

Create a Database

```
import pymysql

#update connection data as required for the local MySQL setup
con = pymysql.connect(host='localhost', user='root', password='admin')
with con:
    cur = con.cursor()
    cur.execute("CREATE DATABASE recordshop;")

print ("Database created")
```

This listing is again creating the connection to the database, and then with that connection creating a cursor that is used to execute a SQL query. This time the query creates a database called *recordshop*. When you run this listing, if everything is successful, you should see the following message:

```
Database created
```

Run the listing a second time to see what happens. You will find that Python has a problem when you run the script a second time. This is because database names must be unique on a MySQL server. When you run the script a second time, you cannot create the database because a database already exists with the name you are using.

Drop a Database

As you also learned previously, the DROP command is used to delete objects in a SQL database, using the following syntax:

```
DROP DATABASE databasename;
```

This is a powerful command that will instantly delete the database and any objects or data stored in the database without warning or feedback. *It should be used with caution.* Most active MySQL installations will allow only database administrators to execute a DROP command because once it has executed, the database is gone.

You can use the DROP command to delete the database that was created in Listing A.2. The SQL statement to do this should look familiar.

```
DROP DATABASE recordshop;
```

The Python code to do this is presented in Listing A.3. Just like before, you need to make sure the values passed to open the connection match the login information for your database.

LISTING A.3

Deleting the recordshop Database

```
import pymysql

#update connection data as required for the local MySQL setup
con = pymysql.connect(host='localhost', user='root', password='admin')
with con:
    cur = con.cursor()
    cur.execute("Drop DATABASE recordshop;")

print ("Database deleted")
```

This listing should look similar to the previous one, except that you are passing the SQL DROP command via the execute function. When you run this listing after having created the recordshop database, you should get a notice that the database was deleted.

```
Database deleted
```

Connect to a Database

In the previous listings, you simply connected to the MySQL instance, which does not automatically connect to a database. Because MySQL Server can host multiple databases, when you are using MySQL, you must use a USE command to explicitly tell MySQL which database you want to use.

```
USE databasename;
```

In PyMySQL, the specific database you want to connect to is specified in the connect statement, along with the other connection details for the MySQL server. In Listing A.4, the connection information is similar to what was done in the previous listings; however, this time, the mysql database is identified as to be used immediately after connecting.

```
host='localhost', user='root', password='admin', db='mysql'
```

NOTE The mysql database is a default database maintained by MySQL, so it is always available.

LISTING A.4

Specifying the Database to Use

```
import pymysql

#update connection data as required for the local MySQL setup
con = pymysql.connect(host='localhost', user='root', password='admin', db='mysql')
print(con)
```

As you can see, nothing is being done in this listing other than connecting to the database and then printing the value stored on con. The output you see should be similar to the following, although note that the hex number is instance-specific, so what you see might differ:

```
<pymysql.connections.Connection object at 0x000001FF6BEA6E50>
```

With the database now connected, you can start to do a little bit more, as shown in Listing A.5. In this listing, you are putting together everything you've done to this point.

LISTING A.5

A More Complete Connection Process

```
import pymysql

#update connection data as required for the local MySQL setup
con = pymysql.connect(host='localhost', user='root', password='admin')
with con:
    cur = con.cursor() #create a cursor object
    cur.execute("DROP DATABASE IF EXISTS recordshop;")
    cur.execute("CREATE DATABASE recordshop;")
    cur.close() # close connection to MySQL
print ("Database created")

#update connection data as required for the local MySQL setup
con = pymysql.connect(host='localhost', user='root', password='admin',
db="recordshop")
with con:
    cur = con.cursor()
    cur.execute("SELECT DATABASE();")
    for row in cur:
        dbname = row[0]

print("Connected to " + dbname)
```

This script performs the following actions:

1. It connects to the MySQL server without specifying a database.

2. It checks for the recordshop database and drops it if it exists.

3. It creates the rescordshop database.

4. It closes the connection with MySQL.

5. It reconnects to MySQL and the recordshop database.

All these steps are needed at this point because you dropped the database in the previous step. In most cases, when the database already exists, you simply need the last step to connect to MySQL and the database you intend to use. The output from this listing should be similar to the following:

```
Database created
Connected to recordshop
```

Display All Databases

Occasionally, you might need to know what databases are currently available on the MySQL server, sometimes to verify that a database exists, but also at times to simply remember what a database is named. The SQL command that displays a list of available databases is as follows:

```
SHOW DATABASES;
```

You can use PyMySQL to generate a list of databases on the MySQL server. Running the command through PyMySQL runs the command on the server and returns a table showing the available databases, but it does not return the output to Python. This means we have to print the rows from the table separately using a Python for loop, as shown in Listing A.6.

LISTING A.6

Displaying All Databases

```
import pymysql

#update connection data as required for the local MySQL setup
con = pymysql.connect(host='localhost', user='root', password='admin')
with con:
    cur = con.cursor() #create a cursor object.
    cur.execute("SHOW DATABASES;")
    for row in cur:
        print(row[0])
```

You can see in this script that most of the code is the same. The only new elements are that the SHOW command is being executed and then the for loop is being used to print the values in each row of the data that was returned to cur. The following is the output we received running the listing on our system:

```
information_schema
mysql
performance_schema
recordshop
sakila
sys
vinylrecordshop
world
```

Your results may be different from those shown here depending on the databases available in your MySQL instance. You should, however, confirm that the recordshop database exists.

TABLE OPERATIONS

In relational databases, all data is stored in tables, which organize the data into columns (or fields) and rows (or records). You can use PyMySQL to perform CRUD operations on tables in MySQL.

Create a Table

The SQL CREATE TABLE command is used to create new tables. While it is possible to modify tables after they have been created, it is better practice to define the fields that will exist in the table at the same time the table itself is created. In Listing A.7, a CREATE TABLE statement is used to create the artist table in the recordshop database. With this listing, you should connect to the database on MySQL and run the query to create the table.

NOTE We follow standard SQL naming conventions in this lesson:

- All table and field names are named in camelCase, where the first word is lowercase and subsequent words are initial capitalized.

- Table names are singular and represent the entity whose data will be stored in the table.

- The name of a primary key field is most often the name of the table, followed by _id, unless the table includes multiple fields in the primary key.

LISTING A.7

Creating the artist Table

```
import pymysql

create_table_query = """
            CREATE TABLE artist (
                artist_id int(11) NOT NULL,
                fname varchar(40) NOT NULL,
                lname varchar(40) NOT NULL,
                isHallOfFame tinyint(1) NOT NULL
            ) ENGINE=InnoDB DEFAULT CHARSET=latin1;
        """
print(create_table_query)

show_table_query = """SHOW TABLES;"""

describe_table_query = """DESCRIBE artist;"""

#update connection data as required for the local MySQL setup
con = pymysql.connect(host='localhost', user='root', password='admin',
db='recordshop')
with con:
    cur = con.cursor() #create a cursor object used to execute MySQL queries.
    cur.execute(create_table_query)

    cur.execute(show_table_query)
    for row in cur:
        print(row[0])

        cur.execute(describe_table_query)
        for row in cur:
            print(row)
```

In this listing, you can see that the SQL queries to be executed are created and assigned to the variables. A CREATE TABLE query is assigned to the variable create_table_query, a query to show the table is assigned to show_table_query, and a query to list the artist table's fields and their properties after it has been created is assigned to describe_table_query. You can see that each of these queries is standard SQL code that you learned previously in this book. By assigning the queries to variables, it makes the execution easier when using Python. Note that each query variable can store at most one SQL query, although any given query can be as complex as necessary for the required results.

With these variables declared, the listing then follows what you've seen before in this lesson. The connection is established, a cursor object is created to use to execute the MySQL queries, and then queries are executed and the results returned from the execution are displayed. The full output from the listing should be as follows:

```
CREATE TABLE artist (
    artist_id int(11) NOT NULL,
    fname varchar(40) NOT NULL,
    lname varchar(40) NOT NULL,
    isHallOfFame tinyint(1) NOT NULL
) ENGINE=InnoDB DEFAULT CHARSET=latin1;

artist
('artist_id', 'int', 'NO', '', None, '')
('fname', 'varchar(40)', 'NO', '', None, '')
('lname', 'varchar(40)', 'NO', '', None, '')
('isHallOfFame', 'tinyint(1)', 'NO', '', None, '')
```

Alter a Table

In addition to creating a table, you can update an existing table by adding or removing fields or changing the properties of existing fields.

In Listing A.8, the artist table is altered to define `artist_id` as the primary key and to set the key to auto-increment the value as records are added to the table. Like the previous listing, the SQL statements are defined as Python objects, and then PyMySQL is used to execute the saved statements.

LISTING A.8

Altering a Table

```
import pymysql

alter_query_1  = """ALTER TABLE artist
            ADD PRIMARY KEY (artist_id);"""

alter_query_2 = """ALTER TABLE artist
            MODIFY artist_id int(11) NOT NULL AUTO_INCREMENT, AUTO_
INCREMENT=0;"""

describe_table_query = """DESCRIBE artist;"""
```

```
# update connection data as required for the local MySQL setup
con = pymysql.connect(host='localhost', user='root', password='admin',
db='recordshop')
with con:
    cur = con.cursor()  # create a cursor object.
    cur.execute(alter_query_1)

    cur.execute(alter_query_2)

    cur.execute(describe_table_query)
    for row in cur:
        print(row)
```

Once again, queries are created and the execute function is used to run them. A Python for loop prints the results of the DESCRIBE command, which should show the altered table.

```
('artist_id', 'int', 'NO', 'PRI', None, 'auto_increment')
('fname', 'varchar(40)', 'NO', '', None, '')
('lname', 'varchar(40)', 'NO', '', None, '')
('isHallOfFame', 'tinyint(1)', 'NO', '', None, '')
```

Remove a Table

You can delete entire tables using a DROP command similar to the one used to delete databases.

```
DROP TABLE tablename;
```

This is a powerful command, and it should be used with care. This will delete the entire table and all data inside the table without warning, and most active databases require database admin privileges to execute the command for this reason.

PyMySQL can be used to delete the artist table you created in the previous listing. This is done in Listing A.9.

LISTING A.9

Removing a Table

```python
import pymysql

drop_query  = """DROP TABLE artist;"""

show_table_query = """SHOW TABLES;"""

# update connection data as required for the local MySQL setup
con = pymysql.connect(host='localhost', user='root', password='admin',
db='recordshop')
with con:
    cur = con.cursor()
    cur.execute(drop_query)

    cur.execute(show_table_query)
    for row in cur:
        print(row[0])

print("Ready")
```

This listing will execute the DROP command to remove the database and then the SHOW command so that you can see all tables in the recordshop database. When the SHOW TABLES; statement is executed, you can see that there are no results:

```
Ready
```

Rebuild the Table

You've been working with the recordshop database and the artist table. Let's re-create the table in its entirety, defining all field properties required in the CREATE TABLE statement. This is shown in Listing A.10.

LISTING A.10

Rebuilding the artist Table in the recordshop Database

```python
import pymysql

drop_artist = "DROP TABLE IF EXISTS artist;"

create_artist  = """
        CREATE TABLE artist (
            artist_id int(11) NOT NULL AUTO_INCREMENT,
            fname varchar(40) NOT NULL,
            lname varchar(40) NOT NULL,
            isHallOfFame tinyint(1) NOT NULL,
            PRIMARY KEY (artist_id)
        )
        ENGINE=InnoDB DEFAULT CHARSET=latin1;
    """

show_tables = """SHOW TABLES;"""

describe_artist = """DESCRIBE artist;"""

# update connection data as required for the local MySQL setup
con = pymysql.connect(host='localhost', user='root', password='admin',
db='recordshop')
with con:
    cur = con.cursor()  # create a cursor object.
    cur.execute(drop_artist)

    cur.execute(create_artist)

    cur.execute(show_tables)
    for row in cur:
        print("Tables in database: \n" + str(row[0]))

    cur.execute(describe_artist)
    print("\nFields in table:")
    for row in cur:
        print(row)
```

Because you might want to use this script to rebuild the database, a DROP TABLE IF EXISTS statement is included that will drop an existing table with the same name before creating the new one. Overall, this listing mimics what you did in the previous listings. The output from running this should look like the following:

```
Tables in database:
artist

Fields in table:
('artist_id', 'int', 'NO', 'PRI', None, 'auto_increment')
('fname', 'varchar(40)', 'NO', '', None, '')
('lname', 'varchar(40)', 'NO', '', None, '')
('isHallOfFame', 'tinyint(1)', 'NO', '', None, '')
```

DATA OPERATIONS: CRUD

Activities related to managing databases and tables typically fall to a limited number of database administrators (DBAs) within an organization, mainly to avoid accidental but potentially catastrophic deletion of the data in a database or table. However, it is common to create applications that an authorized user can use to manage the data itself. For example, an employee in a university's registration office should be able to add new students to the database, update data like their address or phone number, and retrieve student-related data when necessary, without having to go through a DBA for everyday tasks.

The basic create, retrieve, update, and delete (CRUD) SQL functions that you learned about can be used from Python. Each of these can be seen in action in the following sections. The listings presented assume that MySQL is actively running and that it has a database named *recordshop* with a table named artist in the database. The artist table should include the fields and properties shown in Table A.1.

Table A.1 The artist Table Fields and Properties

Field name	Data Type	Required (Y/N)	Other
artist_id	int(11)	Y	Primary key, auto-increment
fname	varchar(40)	Y	
lname	varchar(40)	Y	
isHallOfFame	tinyint(1)	Y	

Create Data

Before data can be used, you must create it. MySQL uses the INSERT INTO *table* command to add data to an existing table. This command requires that you list each record individually.

In Listing A.11, data is created for the artist table within the recordshop database. This is again done using PyMySql and Python.

LISTING A.11

Creating Data in the artist Table

```python
import pymysql
insert_query = """INSERT INTO artist (artist_id, fname, lname, isHallOfFame)
                VALUES
                    (1, 'John', 'Lennon', 0),
                    (2, 'Paul', 'McCartney', 0),
                    (3, 'George', 'Harrison', 0),
                    (4, 'Ringo', 'Starr', 0),
                    (5, 'Denny', 'Zager', 0),
                    (6, 'Rick', 'Evans', 0),
                    (10, 'Van', 'Morrison', 0),
                    (11, 'Judy', 'Collins', 0),
                    (12, 'Paul', 'Simon', 0),
                    (13, 'Art', 'Garfunkel', 0),
                    (14, 'Brian', 'Wilson', 0),
                    (15, 'Dennis', 'Wilson', 0),
                    (16, 'Carl', 'Wilson', 0),
                    (17, 'Ricky', 'Fataar', 0),
                    (18, 'Blondie', 'Chaplin', 0),
                    (19, 'Jimmy', 'Page', 0),
                    (20, 'Robert', 'Plant', 0),
                    (21, 'John Paul', 'Jones', 0),
                    (22, 'John', 'Bonham', 0),
                    (23, 'Mike ', 'Love', 0),
                    (24, 'Al ', 'Jardine', 0),
                    (25, 'David', 'Marks', 0),
                    (26, 'Bruce ', 'Johnston', 0);"""

view_records = """SELECT *
                FROM artist
                LIMIT 5;
                """
# use appropriate values to connect to the local MySQL server
con = pymysql.connect(host='localhost', user='root', password='admin',
db='recordshop')
with con:
    cur = con.cursor()  # create a cursor object
    cur.execute(insert_query)  # execute insert query

    cur.execute(view_records)
    con.commit()
    for row in cur:
        print(row)
```

In this query, a series of artists is added to the artist table, and then the first five records are selected and printed. This is done by creating two queries. The first contains a SQL INSERT INTO statement that specifies the field order and the values for each record, which are presented in the same order. The second query contains a SQL SELECT statement that grabs the first five records from the artist table. The rest of the listing is similar to previous listings in this lesson. You connect to the database, create a cursor, and then execute the queries. The listing ends by displaying the records that were obtained from the SELECT statement, which should match the following:

```
(1, 'John', 'Lennon', 0)
(2, 'Paul', 'McCartney', 0)
(3, 'George', 'Harrison', 0)
(4, 'Ringo', 'Starr', 0)
(5, 'Denny', 'Zager', 0)
```

Retrieve Data

The *R* in CRUD stands for *retrieve* or *read*. Essentially, it means that existing data can be viewed without making changes to it. The basic retrieve statement in MySQL uses the following syntax:

```
SELECT field1, field2, field3, ..., fieldN
FROM table;
```

This statement retrieves the data in the named fields from the named table, sorted in ascending order by the values in the primary key field.

You can also perform more elaborate retrievals using optional clauses.

```
SELECT field1, field2, field3, ..., fieldN
FROM table
WHERE criterion
ORDER BY field1, field2, ..., fieldN ASC/DESC;
```

The WHERE clause allows a Boolean criterion to be defined that limits the number of records retrieved. For example, a query with the following clause:

```
WHERE fname = "john"
```

would retrieve only records where the values in the fname field are John, while the clause:

```
WHERE price > 1000
```

would retrieve only records where the values in the price field are greater than 1000.

The ORDER BY field allows a sort order to be defined for the query results. By default, SQL will display the records sorted on the primary key values, but you could use the following:

```
ORDER BY lname ASC
```

to sort the results alphabetically by the values in the lname field, or to sort the results with the price field from largest to smallest, you could use the following:

```
ORDER BY price DESC
```

While you can name each field in the table, if you want to retrieve the data in all fields, then you could also use the * operator. The * operator corresponds to "all fields." In Listing A.12, all fields are retrieved and displayed for all records from the artist table using a SQL statement and Python.

LISTING A.12

Retrieve Data from the artist Table

```
import pymysql
retrieve_query = """SELECT *
                FROM artist;"""

# use appropriate values to connect to the local MySQL server
con = pymysql.connect(host='localhost', user='root', password='admin',
db='recordshop')
with con:
    cur = con.cursor()            # create a cursor object
    cur.execute(retrieve_query)  # execute retrieve query
    for row in cur:
        print(row)
```

This listing is similar to previous listings, but with the retrieve_query being set to use a SELECT command. The output should match the following:

```
(1, 'John', 'Lennon', 0)
(2, 'Paul', 'McCartney', 0)
(3, 'George', 'Harrison', 0)
(4, 'Ringo', 'Starr', 0)
(5, 'Denny', 'Zager', 0)
```

```
(6, 'Rick', 'Evans', 0)
(10, 'Van', 'Morrison', 0)
(11, 'Judy', 'Collins', 0)
(12, 'Paul', 'Simon', 0)
(13, 'Art', 'Garfunkel', 0)
(14, 'Brian', 'Wilson', 0)
(15, 'Dennis', 'Wilson', 0)
(16, 'Carl', 'Wilson', 0)
(17, 'Ricky', 'Fataar', 0)
(18, 'Blondie', 'Chaplin', 0)
(19, 'Jimmy', 'Page', 0)
(20, 'Robert', 'Plant', 0)
(21, 'John Paul', 'Jones', 0)
(22, 'John', 'Bonham', 0)
(23, 'Mike ', 'Love', 0)
(24, 'Al ', 'Jardine', 0)
(25, 'David', 'Marks', 0)
(26, 'Bruce ', 'Johnston', 0)
```

Update Data

Updating data means changing data that already exists, including activities such as changing someone's address or phone number, adding data that was originally missing when a record was created, or removing specific values in a record without deleting the entire record. MySQL uses the following syntax to change a value in an existing record:

```
UPDATE table
SET fieldname = value
WHERE fieldname = value;
```

Each part of this statement is critical.

- UPDATE table specifies the table where the existing data resides.
- SET fieldname = value specifies what field in the table should be changed and what the new value should be.
- WHERE fieldname = value limits the records that the change applies to.

UPDATE statements should be used with care because they change existing data without any warning or notification as soon as you run the query. The WHERE statement is technically optional but functionally critical. If you leave it out, the query will run, and *all* records in the named table will be changed.

As a general rule of thumb, if you want to change exactly one record, the WHERE clause should use the record's primary key value, to be 100 percent sure that only that record will change. However, because the primary key value is typically meaningless, it is common to use other fields in smaller datasets.

It is also a good idea to run a corresponding SELECT query using the same WHERE statement to verify which records will be changed before you run the UPDATE query.

CAUTION There is no "undo" command if you change data by accident!

In Listing A.13 the UPDATE clause is used within a Python script to change the value in the isHallOfFame field in the artist table for John Lennon. Note that the following clause is used to identify which record should be changed in the table:

```
WHERE lname='Lennon'
```

In this case, you know that there is only one record with the last name Lennon, so the query works as expected. In a larger database, be aware that this will change the isHallOfFame field for *every* artist with the last name Lennon (like his son, Julian Lennon).

LISTING A.13

Updating Data in the artist Table

```
import pymysql

select_query = """SELECT *
                  FROM artist
                  WHERE lname = 'Lennon';"""

update_query = """UPDATE artist
                  SET isHallOfFame = 1
                  WHERE lname='Lennon';"""

# use appropriate values to connect to the local MySQL server
con = pymysql.connect(host='localhost', user='root', password='admin',
db='recordshop')
with con:
    cur = con.cursor()        # create a cursor object
    cur.execute(select_query) # view the record before changing the data
    for row in cur:
        print(row)
```

```
cur.execute(update_query) # execute the update query

con.commit()

cur.execute(select_query) # view the record after changing the data
for row in cur:
    print(row)
```

This listing is again similar to previous listings in how it creates the queries that will be used and then runs them. In this case, two queries are created, including one for selecting data (select_query) and one for updating the artist (update_query). Note that select_query is run both before and after the update so that you can see the values before and after. The results of the listing should be as follows:

```
(1, 'John', 'Lennon', 0)
(1, 'John', 'Lennon', 1)
```

Delete Data

The final part of CRUD is deleting. Use the DELETE command with extreme care, because it deletes the entire record of the selected rows, not just the value in the fields used to select the rows. The MySQL syntax for a DELETE statement is as follows:

```
DELETE FROM table
WHERE fieldname = value;
```

As with the UPDATE query, the WHERE clause is functionally required if syntactically optional. If you simply use the following:

```
DELETE FROM table;
```

then *all* records in the named table will be deleted immediately when you run the query, without warning.

Additionally, just like with the UPDATE query, you should run a SELECT query with the same WHERE clause before running the DELETE query, to be sure that you know exactly which records the query will delete.

CAUTION There is no "undo" command if you delete data by accident!

The query in Listing A.14 deletes all records from the artist table where the artist's last name is Fataar.

LISTING A.14

Delete Data from the artist Table

```
import pymysql
select_query = """SELECT *
                  FROM artist
                  WHERE lname = 'Fataar';"""

update_query = """DELETE FROM artist
                  WHERE lname='Fataar';"""

# use appropriate values to connect to the local MySQL server
con = pymysql.connect(host='localhost', user='root', password='admin',
db='recordshop')
with con:
    cur = con.cursor() #create a cursor object
    cur.execute(select_query) # view the record before changing the data
    for row in cur:
        print(row)

        cur.execute(update_query) #execute update query

        con.commit()

        cur.execute(select_query) # view the record after changing the data
        for row in cur:
            print(row)
```

When you execute this listing, you should see the following output:

```
(17, 'Ricky', 'Fataar', 0)
```

Note that even though the SELECT statement is executed twice, the results appear only one time. Because the record was deleted by the DELETE query, the second SELECT query has zero records in the results.

SUMMARY

In this lesson, you learned how to use PyMySQL to execute SQL queries from your Python applications. The lesson covered all of the basic operations including creating databases, creating tables, and doing CRUD operations.

EXERCISES

The following exercises are provided to allow you to experiment with concepts presented in this bonus lesson:

Exercise A.1: Creating an Employee Database

Exercise A.2: Removing a Database

Exercise A.3: Creating a Table of Employees

Exercise A.4: Adding Employees

Exercise A.5: Retrieving Employees

Exercise A.6: Updating Employees

Exercise A.7: Deleting Employees

Exercise A.8: Nobel Laureates

Exercise A.9: Restaurants

Exercise A.1: Creating an Employee Database

Just as you did in Listing A.2 of this lesson, create a database. Call this database *employeedb*. What happens if you run this command more than once?

Exercise A.2: Removing a Database

Write the Python code necessary to delete the employeedb database you created in Exercise A.1. What happens if you try to delete a database you have already deleted?

Exercise A.3: Creating a Table of Employees

Write a script that will drop and build (or rebuild) an employee table in a database called *employeedb*. The table should be created with all attributes shown here:

Table name: employee

Table fields:

Field name	Data type	Required (Y/N)	Other
employee_id	int(10)	Y	Primary key, auto-increment
empLastName	varchar(50)	Y	
empFirstName	varchar(35)	Y	
empMidInit	char(1)	N	

You should verify that the table exists and that all field properties are correct. You should be able to run the script multiple times in a row without errors.

Exercise A.4: Adding Employees

Create a script that adds at least 10 valid records to the employee table of the *employeedb* that was created in Exercise A.3. After you have a script that works as expected, test the following questions:

- What happens if you run the same script more than once?
- Do you have to include values for the employee_id field? What happens if you don't?

You may need to drop and rebuild the table multiple times to answer these questions.

Exercise A.5: Retrieving Employees

Write scripts that perform the following tasks on the data in the employeedb.employee table from the previous exercises:

- Retrieve all records from all fields and display the results.
- Retrieve and display only the first and last name values, sorted by last name and then by first name.
- Retrieve and display all name fields only for records where a middle initial is present in the data.

Can you think of any other questions you could ask about the data?

Exercise A.6: Updating Employees

Use PyMySQL to update multiple records in the employeedb database. Perform each of the following tasks:

- Change one employee's last name.
- Change the first and last names of one employee using the same UPDATE statement.
- Attempt to run an UPDATE statement without the WHERE clause to see what happens.
- Can you change any of the employeeid values?

Like the previous exercise, you might need to drop and rebuild the database a few times as you experiment.

Exercise A.7: Deleting Employees

Use a DELETE statement to delete a record in the employee table.

- What happens if you attempt to delete a record that does not exist?
- Can you delete multiple records at the same time with the same criteria?
- What does the query DELETE FROM tablename do?

You will likely have to drop and rebuild the database multiple times to answer all of these questions.

Exercise A.8: Nobel Laureates

Use Python and PyMySQL to answer questions about the Nobel Laureates dataset, which includes all Nobel Prize recipients through 2018. You can find the dataset called laureate.json included in the book files that can be downloaded from www.wiley.com/go/jobreadysql.

1. Transform the JSON data into a suitable format to save the data in MySQL.

2. Implement the necessary code to save the data to MySQL.

3. Use the dataset to answer the following questions:

   a. Identify the Laureate with the most Nobel Prizes.
   b. What country has the most Laureates?
   c. What city has the most Laureates?

Exercise A.9: Restaurants

For this exercise, use the dataset called restaurants.json that can be found in the book files that can be downloaded from www.wiley.com/go/jobreadysql. This dataset includes records of restaurants in New York City, including where they are located, what kind of cuisine each restaurant serves, and customer ratings. Here is a sample record:

```
{"address": {"building": "1007", "coord": [-73.856077, 40.848447], "street":
"Morris Park Ave", "zipcode": "10462"}, "borough": "Bronx", "cuisine":
"Bakery", "grades": [{"date": {"$date": 1393804800000}, "grade": "A",
"score": 2}, {"date": {"$date": 1378857600000}, "grade": "A", "score": 6},
{"date": {"$date": 1358985600000}, "grade": "A", "score": 10}, {"date":
{"$date": 1322006400000}, "grade": "A", "score": 9}, {"date": {"$date":
1299715200000}, "grade": "B", "score": 14}], "name": "Morris Park Bake
Shop", "restaurant_id": "30075445"}
```

Write the Python code that will import the restaurant data to MySQL.

- Create the necessary tables in MySQL to store the data in the most efficient way.
- Create the necessary code in Python to read the data from the JSON file and import it into the MySQL tables.

After moving the data to MySQL, use Python and MySQL to find the following information:

- Compute the average score for each restaurant.
- Compute the minimum score for each restaurant.
- Compute the maximum score for each restaurant.
- Compute the average score for each type of cuisine in each borough.
- Compute the minimum score for each type of cuisine in each borough.
- Compute the maximum score for each type of cuisine in each borough.

Appendix B
SQL Quick Reference

This appendix is a quick reference containing much of the basic syntax for accomplishing standard tasks with SQL. The following areas are covered:

- Working with databases
- Defining tables, columns, and rows
- Performing table queries
  - Filtering and grouping selection results
  - Queries using multiple tables
- Basic SQL data types

WORKING WITH DATABASES

Creating a new database:

```
CREATE DATABASE databaseName;
```

Using an existing database:

```
USE databaseName;
```

Deleting a database:

```
DROP DATABASE databaseName;
```

DEFINING TABLES, COLUMNS, AND ROWS

Creating a new table:

```
CREATE TABLE tableName
(
    columnName1 dataType,
    columnName2 dataType,
...
);
```

Removing a table:

Option 1:

```
DROP TABLE tableName;
```

Option 2:

```
DELETE FROM tableName
WHERE columnName = value;
```

Option 3:

```
DELETE * FROM tableName;
```

Option 4:

```
DELETE FROM tableName;
```

Renaming a table:

Option 1:

```
ALTER TABLE originalTableName RENAME TO newTableName;
```

Option 2:

```
RENAME TABLE originalTableName TO newTableName;
```

Adding a new column to a table:

```
ALTER TABLE tableName
ADD [COLUMN] columnName datatype;
```

Removing a column from a table:

```
ALTER TABLE tableName
DROP [COLUMN] columnName;
```

Adding a column to a table:

```
ALTER TABLE tableName
ADD newColumnName datatype [columnConstraint(s)] [AFTER existingColumn];
```

Altering a column in a table:

```
ALTER TABLE tableName
MODIFY columnName [columnDefinition] [columnConstraint(s)];
```

Adding a row of data into a table:

```
INSERT INTO tableName [(columnName1, columnName2, ...)]
  VALUES (value1, value2, ...);
```

Inserting multiple rows of data into a table:

```
INSERT INTO tableName [(columnName1, columnName2, ... ;)]
  VALUES (row1Value1, row1Value2, ...),
        (row2Value1, row2Value2, ...),
        ... ;
```

Updating a value in a table:

```
UPDATE tableName
SET columnName = value [, columnName2 = value2]
WHERE condition;
```

Creating a view:

```
CREATE VIEW viewName AS
  SELECT columnName(s)
  FROM tableName
  WHERE condition;
```

Creating an index:

```
CREATE [UNIQUE] INDEX indexName
ON tableName (columnName);
```

Deleting an index (MySQL):

```
DROP INDEX indexName;
```

PERFORMING TABLE QUERIES

Selecting all columns from a table:

```
SELECT *
FROM tableName;
```

Selecting specific columns from a table:

```
SELECT columnName1, columnName2, columnNameX
FROM tableName;
```

Sorting columns in ascending (ASC) or descending (DESC) order:

```
SELECT *
FROM tableName
ORDER BY column1 [ASC | DESC];
```

Filtering and Grouping Selection Results

Filtering with the comparison operator:

```
SELECT *
FROM tableName
WHERE BooleanCondition [AND BooleanCondition2][OR BooleanCondition3];
```

Filtering with the LIKE operator:

```
SELECT *
FROM tableName
WHERE columnName LIKE pattern;
```

Filtering based on ID:

Option 1:

```
SELECT *
FROM tableName
WHERE keyField_Id IS value;
```

Option 2

```
SELECT *
FROM tableName
WHERE keyField_Id IN (value1, value2, ...);
```

Filtering based on having a value:

```
SELECT *
FROM tableName
WHERE columnName IS NOT NULL;
```

Filter based on a range:

```
SELECT *
FROM tableName
WHERE columnName BETWEEN value1 AND value2;
```

Filtering with aggregates:

```
SELECT *
FROM tableName
[WHERE columnName operator value]
[GROUP BY columnName]
HAVING aggregateFunction (columnName) operator value;
```

Basic grouping:

```
SELECT *
FROM tableName
[WHERE columnName operator value]
GROUP BY columnName [, columnName2];
```

Performing Queries Using Multiple Tables

Using INNER JOIN (also basic JOIN)

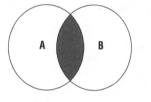

```
SELECT *
FROM tableName1
[INNER] JOIN tableName2
  ON tableName1.columnName = tableName2.columnName;
```

Using LEFT JOIN

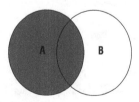

```
SELECT *
FROM tableName1
LEFT JOIN tableName2
  ON tableName1.columnName = tableName2.columnName;
```

Using RIGHT JOIN

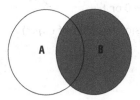

```
SELECT *
FROM tableName1
RIGHT JOIN tableName2
  ON tableName1.columnName = tableName2.columnName;
```

Using FULL JOIN

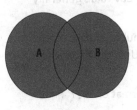

```
SELECT *
FROM tableName1
FULL JOIN tableName2
  ON tableName1.columnName = tableName2.columnName;
```

Using CROSS JOIN

```
SELECT *
FROM tableName1
CROSS JOIN tableName2;
```

BASIC SQL DATA TYPES

The following are the core data types you can use in standard SQL:

- CHARACTER or CHAR: Holds a single character.

- CHARACTER(n) or CHAR(n): Holds up to n characters.

- VARCHAR(n) or CHARACTER VARYING(n): Holds up to n characters.

- BIT(n) or BIT VARYING (n): Holds up to n bits. A bit can be 0 or 1.

- DECIMAL(p, s): Holds a numeric value where p is the precision (number of digits) and s is the scale (number of digits after decimal point).

- INT or INTEGER: Holds an integer value.

- SMALLINT: Holds a smaller integer value.

- BIGINT: Holds a larger integer value.

- FLOAT(p,s): Holds a floating-point value where p is the precision (number of digits) and s is the scale (number of digits after decimal point). FLOAT stores an approximate numeric value.

- REAL(s): Holds an approximate floating-point number. REAL is the same as FLOAT(24).

- DATE: Holds a value representing a date in year, month, and day value generally from 0001-01-01 to 9999-12-31.

- TIME: Holds a value representing a time of day in hours, minutes, and seconds format, and can also store an optional nanoseconds value. Uses the format of 'HH:MM:SS.nnnn'.

- TIMESTAMP: Holds a combined date and time value in the format of 'YYY-MM-DD HH:MM:SS'.

Index